THE PRESENT MOMENT

in Psychotherapy and Everyday Life

BOOKS BY DANIEL N. STERN

The First Relationship: Infant and Mother

*The Interpersonal World of the Infant:
A View from Psychoanalysis and
Developmental Psychology*

Diary of a Baby

The Motherhood Constellation

The Birth of a Mother

The
PRESENT MOMENT
In Psychotherapy
and Everyday Life

Daniel N. Stern, M.D.

W. W. NORTON & COMPANY
New York • London

For information about permission to reproduce selections
from this book, write to Permissions, W. W. Norton & Company, Inc.
500 Fifth Avenue, New York, NY 10110

Production Manager: Leeann Graham
Manufacturing by Haddon Craftsmen, Inc.

Library of Congress Cataloging-in-Publication Data
Stern, Daniel N.
The present moment in psychotherapy and everyday life / Daniel N.
Stern.
p.   cm. — (Norton series on interpersonal neurobiology)
Includes bibliographical references and index.
ISBN 0-393-70429-7
1. Psychotherapy.   2. Stern, Daniel N.   I. Title.   II. Series.
RC480.5.S683 2004
616.89'14—dc22   2003060984

W. W. Norton & Company, Inc.
500 Fifth Avenue, New York, N.Y. 10110
www.wwnorton.com

W. W. Norton & Company Ltd.
Castle House, 75/76 Wells St., London W1T 3QT

7   9   0   8

In Memory of Jerry

To see a World in a Grain of Sand
and a Heaven in a Wild Flower
Hold Infinity in the palm of your hand
And Eternity in an hour.

WILLIAM BLAKE

CONTENTS

Preface

MANY OF THE IDEAS for this book have followed me doggedly for decades, some since the beginning of my career and others since I can first remember.

Perhaps the most pervasive idea running through the book is a focus on the small momentary events that make up our worlds of experience. What interests me most is when these moments enter one's awareness and are shared between two people. These lived experiences make up the key moments of change in psychotherapy and the nodal points in our everyday intimate relationships. These are the *present moments* of the title.

Note that this book is not about meaning in the usual clinical sense of explaining the present in terms of the past and establishing associative linkages that are interpretable. It is about experience as it is lived. It is essential to hold this in mind.

My appreciation of the present moment first came about in the 1960s and 1970s when I began to use film and video to study mother-infant interaction. These tools gave me a sort of microscope to see an interaction unfold. A fascinating world opened up. I grew to realize how much occurs in a moment that lasts only seconds. I began to think of these moments as the basic building blocks of experience. Once I got the hang of these techniques (e.g., freeze frame, slow motion, segment repeats) I could even use them, unsystematically, in real time, for very short stretches, to see my psychotherapy patients differently. I was just beginning as a therapist.

Certain moments in therapy began to reveal aspects of the therapeutic process different from those I was trained to see. My notes from a meeting with a patient in 1969 illustrate this: "She enters my office and sits in the chair. She drops into it from high up. The chair cushion deflates rapidly, then takes another five seconds to stop accommodating itself. She clearly waits for that, but just before the cushion lets out its last sigh, she crosses her legs and shifts to the other haunch. The cushion deflates again and reequilibrates. We wait for it to get done. Rather, she does, she is listening to it, feeling it. I've been ready since she came in, but now I'm waiting, too. It's hard to know when the cushion has given up all its air. But everything waits. Does she sense she is waiting, or holding time? Everything waits for her readiness. I feel restrained from moving until it's done. Almost as if I should hold my breath to hasten it along, to better judge when the still point is reached and the session can 'start.' When I finally think that her body and the cushion have reached their readiness, that the sound and feel of settling has stopped, I begin to shift in my chair, in anticipation, breathing more freely. But she is still hearing the sound recede and is not quite ready. My shift is arrested in midflow by her still waiting. I feel like I have been caught in a game of 'statue.' It is ridiculous. And I can sense an annoyance building in me to have my rhythms so disrupted and controlled. Should I let it go on? Should I bring it up? She wouldn't dream that we had already played out the main themes of the session, and an important theme in her life."

Before my experience with the micro-momentary world of implicit happenings, all of this would never have jumped to the foreground. I would have passed it over, waiting for her to speak.

Such experiences eventually led me to construct the *micro-analytic interview* as a way of getting closer to lived subjective experience at the micro-momentary level. Granted, one can not get to the lived subjective experience and stay there while talking about it. But that does not stop me from thinking about it and approaching as close as I can.

This book is about subjective experience—especially experiences that lead to change. How do experiences do that? What are such experiences made of? When do they take place? The nature of experience is a vast topic. I will be interested in only a small quadrant, namely, experiences that bring about change in psychotherapy and in personal relationships in everyday life.

The basic assumption is that change is based on lived experience. In and of itself, verbally understanding, explaining, or narrating something is not sufficient to bring about change. There must also be an actual experience, a subjectively lived happening. An event must be *lived*, with feelings and actions taking place in real time, in the real world, with real people, in a moment of presentness. Two simple examples of such a lived experience are: looking at someone in the eyes who is looking at you and taking a deep breath while talking to someone. Both of these are actions with a feeling.

The idea of *presentness* is key. The present moment that I am after is the moment of subjective experience as it is occurring—not as it is later reshaped by words. The present moment is the process unit for the experiences that will most interest us. A first step towards understanding experience is to explore and understand the present moment. This book recounts that exploration. The aim of the journey is to alter your vision of what is happening in a psychotherapy session, and thereby change how you approach it and what you might do in it.

A tracing of the changes I made to the working title of the book as I wrote it may help prepare you for that exploration. Working titles capture the central idea that is the focus of concern for a given period and phase of the work. Taken together, the series of working titles for this book reveals the ideas behind it. Although the book is in part a summary of some ideas that I have worked with for years, plus many new ones, it is above all a new integration. As this integration evolved, one working title would displace the one before it.

In considering the micro-world of the present moment, I first thought of the working title *A World in a Grain of Sand* from William Blake. Besides being poetic, it captured the size of the small world revealed by micro-analysis and at the same time drew attention to the fact that one can often see the larger panorama of someone's past and current life in the small behaviors and mental acts making up this micro-world. Also, and vitally important, seeing the world at this scale of reality changes what can be seen, and thus changes our basic conceptions accordingly.

The experienced micro-world always enters awareness but only sometimes enters consciousness (verbalizable awareness). It is largely about implicit knowing rather than explicit, verbalized knowledge. As the importance of the implicit world became more apparent to me, I toyed with the working title *The Obscure Side of the Moon*, to refer to the nature of implicit knowing.

The temporal aspect of the present moment (as a world in a grain of sand) had to be addressed. What would the temporal architecture of such moments tell us? And how could the phenomenal experience of presentness be discussed? After all, the presentness of lived experience is central. This question sent me on an extended learning journey into the realm of phenomenological philosophy, which was a new and strange land for me at first. It was there that the hidden but obvious fact that we are psychologically and consciously alive only now became apparent. What intrigued me most was the question: Why did clinical psychology not take directly lived experience in the present as its starting point? (Therapists have been doing this more recently.) This is, of course, a radical departure from the path historically taken by most psychologies that put the central emphasis on the past and its influence. It also implies that consciousness, rather than the unconscious, is the key mystery, another radical departure (made possible by the enormous amount of work already done on the workings of the unconscious).

In light of this, the next working title became *A Phenomenological View of Psychotherapeutic Experience*. However, phenomenology was only a necessary and useful perspective. It was not the subject of the book.

Another feature of the present moment that intrigued me was that it has psychological work to do. It has to chunk and make some sense of the moment as it is passing, not afterwards. It has to lean toward a next action. With this in mind, the next working title became *kairos*, the Greek word for the propitious moment or the moment of something coming into being. *Kairos* is both a subjective and a psychological unit of time. Clearly the present moment has to have aspects of *kairos* because it must make sense of what has happened in the past, what is happening now, and how to act upon it. It demands a full grasping of events as they unfold. This reinforced the need for an examination of the temporal architecture of the present moment and the realization that it composes a short emotional "lived story." *Kairos* was also attractive as a title because it implies the meeting of unrelated and independent elements at a point in time causing the emergence of special moments. And this is exactly what the Boston Change Process Study Group (BCPSG) was finding in the clinical process as we looked for moments leading to therapeutic change. The problem with *kairos* as a title was that it is usually conceived in the framework of a one-person psychology. And I was finding in our Boston Group work that clinical material is largely coconstructed—that we are dealing with a two-person psychology.

This led to the next working title, *The Moment of Meeting*. In our clinical work together the importance of intersubjectivity (i.e., mind reading another's thoughts, feelings or intentions) seemed to grow and grow. Intersubjective motives so well accounted for the flow of small moves and moments that the partners made during a session. Also, *Moments of Meeting* described the nature of cocreativity and the enlargement of the intersubjective field that served as the main context for other changes in treatment. As I pursued the pervasive importance of intersubjectivity in therapy and in all intimate and well-coordinated group experience, it became apparent that intersubjectivity was not only a useful intermental process, but also that it constituted in itself a major motivational system essential for human survival—akin to attachment or sex. The implications of raising intersubjectivity to such a status could not be followed through to their end without writing a different book.

Reflections on intersubjectivity as the matrix of a two-person psychology also led to the concept of a possible new form of consciousness: "intersubjective consciousness," a form of reflectivity arising when we become conscious of our contents of mind by virtue of their being simultaneously reflected back to us from the mind of another.

The Moment of Meeting had another great advantage as a title. It brought together the present moment, the notion of *kairos*, intersubjectivity, and cocreation in the therapeutic process. Also, because it is an event that unfolds in the present, it became clear that something affective had to happen and be shared in that moment to alter the implicitly felt intersubjective field. What is shared in a moment of meeting is an emotional lived story. It is physically, emotionally, and implicitly shared not just explicated. The notions of "vitality affects" and "shared feeling voyages," which are presented later in the book, were needed to give substance to the idea of a shared lived story. Also I needed such moments to reach a kind of consciousness that was therapeutically useable. Here the inter-subjective consciousness that accompanies a shared feeling vovage came about.

But in the last analysis, the moment of meeting is only a special kind of present moment. So I arrived at the title *The Present Moment in Psychotherapy and Everyday Life*. This was the title that kept reappearing when other provisional titles were dropped. It is the most inclusive title, encompassing all the others, and best keeps the focus on the integration of these various ideas and on the role of time and presentness. It also accurately reflects that the point of view taken in the book is micro-analytic as well as phenomenological. This small-grain view is perhaps the most unique feature of the descriptions given. The phenomenal reality of the present moment captures that.

All of the steps in the evolution of these ideas are realized in the plan of the book. Each chapter attempts to put into place another essential aspect of the present moment as the process unit of experiences that may lead to change.

Here is the plan:

Part I of the book is an exploration of the present moment. The first chapter deals with the problem of "now." After all, that is when a present moment happens. Chapter 2 deals with the nature of the present moment. Chapter 3 examines the temporal architecture of the present moment. And Chapter 4 discusses its organization.

Part II contextualizes the present moment by bringing in some of the major notions needed to situate it in the thera-peutic process. The three main notions I explore are intersub-jectivity, implicit knowledge, and consciousness.

Two minds (or more) can interpenetrate and share roughly the same experiences. They are capable of intersubjectivity (especially between patient and therapist). The present moments of most interest are those when two minds meet. Chapter 5 describes the pervasive intersubjectivity in which treatments are conducted and social life is lived. Chapter 6 suggests the adaptive importance of intersubjectivity for evolution as well as for psychotherapy.

Much of what is grasped in the present moment falls into the domain of implicit knowledge. Accordingly, a close look at this form of knowledge is required. This is the subject of Chapter 7.

Finally, the position of the present moment along the dimension of consciousness is essential if one is to consider how experiences occurring "now" can be remembered, reflected upon, verbalized, and narrated. This is discussed in Chapter 8.

Part III comprises a view of the present moment as it operates in the clinical situation. Chapter 9 introduces the operation the present moment in clinical settings. Chapter 10 explores what happens in a session moment by moment. It discusses the unpredictability and "sloppiness" of the therapeutic process and its two most important resulting emergent properties, the *now moment*, and the *moment of meeting*. This involves a close description of what happens at the local, micro level of the present moment. This is the nuts and bolts of the flow of a session. Chapter 11 deals with interweaving the implicit and explicit. Much of what happens in psychotherapy is explicated in language, including interpretations. The mutual influences between the implicit and explicit are explored. Chapter 12 discusses the past and the present moment. It elaborates on how the present moment is influenced by the past, and it discuss the necessity of being able to hold a past as well as a present, without which there is no basis for psychodynamic thinking. It examines ways this can be accomplished. Finally, Chapter 13 summaries the role of the present moment in psychotherapeutic change and offers clinical implications.

I shall begin, then, with the problem of *now*, as a first step in exploring the present moment, our microscope for viewing how change comes about.

Acknowledgments

MY FIRST INTRODUCTION to the presursor of the *present moment* was when I began learning about the micromomentary world of naturally occuring mother-infant interaction. At the time, several decades ago, I knew a handful of other researchers and clinicians who were exploring this small world with film and TV techniques. Among them were Lou Sander, Colwyn Trevarthen, Berry Brazelton, Ed Tronick, and Beatrice Beebe. This small band of dispersed researchers kept in contact, and shared a common enthusiasm. Otherwise it was lonely work. I wish to thank them for encouraging one another and helping to form a critical mass who explored the micro-world.

Almost simultaneously, I met a group of choreographers in New York. At that time they were experimenting with similar techniques in dance: short-sequence repeats, still frames, running events backwards, and so on. They would come uptown to my lab at Columbia, N.Y.S. Psychiatric Institute, to watch some of my mother-baby film analyses, and I would go downtown to watch their work with dancers. At first glance, they seemed an unlikely group of colleagues for me to learn from and be inspired by. But not at second glance. In this context I was fortunate to form lasting friendships with the choreographer Jerome Robbins and the theater artist Robert Wilson. Our friendship has permitted me to watch dances and theater pieces take form from conception, through rehearsals, to premiere. An exchange lasting decades followed. It was an unbelievable opportunity for me to learn about the nonverbal realms. I wish to acknowledge all they have taught me.

Then, nine years ago, a group of us began a rich collaboration. The fields of psychotherapy, psychoanalysis, developmental psychology, and pediatrics were represented. We called ourselves the Boston Change Process Study Group. The members of that group during the time of formulating and writing the book were: Nadia Bruschweiler-Stern, Alexandra Harrison, Karlen Lyons-Ruth, Alexander Morgan, Jeremy Nahum, Louis Sander, and Edward Tronick. Many of the important ideas for this book emerged from our collaboration.

It became apparent that when we worked as a group, which we did intensively, a powerful process of cocreation took over. The group would rework an idea that originated from one of us, transforming it into a different or more elaborated idea, or linking it to an idea that came from someone else to make a new notion altogether. It was then impossible to disentangle its history. It is for this reason we decided to publish as a collective after our first two publications. We were examining the process of cocreation in psychotherapy, so perhaps it was not surprising to find the same process in our work together. Or maybe it was the other way around?

The clinical material is the most directly derived from our work together, particularly Chapters 10 and 11, which borrow heavily from our collective publications. However, I have given this material a rather different slant, and many of the concepts or emphases are not necessarily in accord with those the group might have developed. Also, individual members may disagree with where I have taken things. To respect the contributions of the group and its individual members I have tried to reference as carefully as possible the publications both of the group and of its individual members, as they relate to the subject at hand. I wish to thank these colleagues deeply and express the pleasure I have had in working with them. This book would have been a different book without the Boston Change Process Study Group.

Two very knowledgable people read the book in preliminary stages: Elizabeth Fivaz-Depeursinge in Lausanne and Daniel Siegel in Los Angeles. Their encouragement, criticisms, and suggestions have been invaluable.

I want to give special thanks to my editor, Deborah Malmud. After she read the first submitted draft she wrote me a seven-page, single-spaced letter. It was full of suggestions, queries, requests for clarification, and ideas for a major reordering of sections. But it still managed to be encouraging. At first, I was taken aback and not happy. After many readings I began to appreciate it, but not exactly like it. As I got back to work, dealing with what she wrote, I grew to rely more and more on her advice. I came not only to like the letter, but also to consider it a brilliant job of editing. The book is leaner and clearer thanks to her.

Finally, I wish to thank my family for their encouragement, particularly my wife, Nadia, who read parts with great sensibility and a surpurb ear for tone as well as content.

THE PRESENT MOMENT
in Psychotherapy and Everyday Life

Part I

EXPLORING THE
PRESENT MOMENT

Chapter 1

THE PROBLEM OF "NOW"

THE IDEA OF A PRESENT MOMENT is put forward to deal with the problem of "now." It is remarkable how little we know about experience that is happening right now. This relative ignorance is especially strange in light of the following:

First, we are subjectively alive and conscious only *now*. *Now* is when we directly live our lives. Everything else is once or twice removed. The only time of raw subjective reality, of phenomenal experience, is the present moment.

Second, most psychotherapies agree that therapeutic work in the "here and now" has the greatest power in bringing about change. That is where and when mutually aware contact between the minds of the therapist and patient takes place. Also, in everyday relationships, the nodal events that change one's course of life usually occur in a moment that is experienced as key, not only after it has happened, but also while it is happening. In spite of this we must still ask the question, what is *now*?

Third, psychodynamic theories of therapeutic change are based on the idea that the past plays a huge role in determining the present. In a sense the past holds center stage. Accordingly, we know a great deal about how past events influence present experience. But we have not paid the same attention to the nature of present experience as it is being influenced and is happening. How would psychotherapy and therapeutic change look if the present moment held center stage?

This book places the present moment at center stage and holds it there. This makes the process of psychotherapy look different and alters our conceptions of how therapeutic change comes about. How we conduct psychotherapy will shift because our view of what is happening will be different. We may also find that our vision of daily experience is enriched. These are the goals of the book.

Before jumping toward these larger goals, we must explore the nature of present experience and then apply it to the clinical situation. This exploration begins with some important questions about the present moment or *nowness*. When is now? What is now? Does now exist and if so, how long is it? How is now structured? What does it do? How is it related to consciousness, to the past? How does it lead to meanings? Why does it occupy such a special place in psychotherapy? And related to these questions, how is now experienced when it is cocreated and shared with someone? Finally, what role does now play in change? In short, how do we conceive of a present moment?

There is another aspect of the subjective now that is both startling and obvious. The present moment does not whiz by and become observable only after it is gone. Rather, it crosses the mental stage more slowly, taking several seconds to unfold. And during this crossing, the present moment plays out a lived emotional drama. As the drama unfolds it traces a temporal shape like a passing musical phrase. As we shall see, this is of great importance because it puts time back into experience.

"Putting time back into experience" is a curious phrase. Here is what lies behind it: It is easy to put linear, clock time (*chronos*) into our stories about ourselves—the before, after, and meanwhile of our narratives. But it is less clear how to put subjective time (whatever that may prove to be) into experiences that are happening now. And without this subjective time we could never link the many sequential happenings that occur during a present moment into a whole coherent experience. Life would be discontinuous and chaotic even in the small-time scale of the present.

There is a longer history to this issue of now. In fact, it is only a piece of the larger history of time. I will not enter this huge subject except to make certain points that bear on the problem of the subjective now. First, we see time as arising from our human sensibilities. It is an invention of our minds. We know nothing about the time of *things*, if one could even imagine that. In the natural sciences and in managing the daily schedules of life, we use the ancient Greek view of *chronos*. *Chronos* is the objective view of time used not only in science but also in most of our psychologies. In the world of *chronos*, the present instant is a moving point in time headed only toward a future. It does not matter whether its course is viewed as a straight line or a circle or a spiral, the present instant is always moving. As it moves, it eats up the future and leaves the past in its wake. But the present instant itself is very short. It is an almost infinitessimally thin slice of time during which very little could take place without immediately becoming the past. Effectively, there is no present.

There are other human constructions of time. In narrative time, the temporal ordering of events is created by the teller of a story, regardless of chronological sequence (Ricoeur, 1984–1988). Freud's complex psychic time disregards linear succession, shifts speed of passage, and doubles back and folds forward on itself—a time that Green (2002) called fragmented time. There are various forms of heterochronicity with several parallel times. And there are meditative states where time does not move but passes out of existence into a homogeneous, continuous "now."

But when one considers psychotherapy and life as normally lived, there are problems with these views. The problem with *chronos* is that if there is no now long enough that something can unfold in it, there can be no direct experience. That is not intuitively acceptable. Also, life-as-lived is not experienced as an inexorably continuous flow. Rather, it is felt to be discontinuous, made up of incidents and events separated in time but also somehow connected.

There are also problems with the narrative view of time, for our purposes at least. Narratives select episodes of life and mark them in time: before, after, again, and so on. These episodes are then rearranged, not necessarily in historical order, but to tell the most coherent story about what life felt like. The narrative aims at life verisimilitude, not historical truth. In this way, narratives give us back the feeling of continuity in life. They tame *chronos*, make the passage of time seem familiar and tolerable, and make us feel coherent along this infinite dimension (Bruner, 1990, 2002b; Ricoeur, 1984–1988). They do not, however, tame the present moment. In spite of the great achievement of narrative-making, now has no place in a narrative account except as a point of reference. In a narrative, the now that is being talked about has already happened. It puts past and future nows into relation. It is not a direct experience. Only the telling is happening now.

In Freud's fragmented psychic time, as with narrative time, little attention is paid to the temporal structure of now. It is not seen to be temporally dynamic, within itself—i.e. to trace a temporal profile of small changes as it unfolds. In psychic time, the major interest in now lies in its relation to other pieces of time, not in its own nature.

So, what is to be done with the *now* while life is actually being experienced—while the present is still unfolding? The Greek's subjective conception of time, *kairos*, may be of use here. *Kairos* is the passing moment in which something happens as the time unfolds. It is the coming into being of a new state of things, and it happens in a moment of awareness. It has its own boundaries and escapes or transcends the passage of linear time. Yet it also contains a past. It is a subjective parenthesis set off from chronos. *Kairos* is a moment of opportunity, when events demand action or are propitious for action. Events have come together in this moment and the meeting enters awareness such that action must be taken, now, to alter one's destiny—be it for the next minute or a lifetime. If no action is taken, one's destiny will be changed anyway, but differently, because one did not act. It is a small window of becoming and opportunity. One of the origins of the word comes from shepherds watching the stars. As the night progresses and the stars turn in the sky, they appear to rise and then fall against the horizon. The moment when a star has reached its apogee and appears to change direction from ascending to descending is its kairos (Kathryne Andrews, personal communication, November 23, 2000).

In both everyday life and the clinical situation a present moment could be called a moment of micro-*kairos*, because only minor life-course decisions and short destiny paths are in play. This book attempts to show why all present moments are also moments of *kairos*, regardless of magnitude.

Narrative provides us with a psychological way of fitting our lives into the reality of chronos. In this book we will explore the present moment as a psychological approach to understanding the experience of *kairos*.

THE STARTING POINT

Given the unique and fundamental position of subjective "nowness" in everyone's experience, we propose to begin an exploration of clinical theory and practice, as well as everyday subjective life, by placing the phenomenal "now" at the center—as our starting point. Existential and some Gestalt theories have certainly done just this, but with large brushstrokes. We are proposing to do it at the micro level of the passing present moment. At first glance, begining such an inquiry with the present moment as the magnifying glass to view psychotherapy and everyday experience seems difficult and unlikely. But the present moment is our primary subjective reality, so why not start there? Where better? It may have interesting implications not only for clinical psychologies but also for the neurosciences.

This conception of the present moment relies heavily on a phenomenologic perspective. Phenomenology is the study of things as they appear to consciousness, as they seem when they are in mind. This includes: perceptions, sensations, feelings, memories, dreams, phantasies, expectations, ideas—whatever occupies the mental stage. Phenomenology is not concerned with how these things were formed by or popped into the mind. It also avoids any attempt to explore the external reality that may correspond to what is in mind. It concerns only the appearance of things as they present or show themselves to our experience. It is about the mental landscape we see and are in at any given moment. That is phenomenal reality (see Moran [2000] for a comprehensive introduction). This book, then, is about the small but meaningful affective happenings that unfold in the seconds that make up now.

There is, however, a large question. The present moment, while lived, can not be seized by language which (re?)constitutes it after the fact. How different is the linguistic version from the originally lived one? At this point, even the neurosciences can make only limited suggestions. In spite of this, the book is largely about the unreachable present moment. Such a lived experience must exist. It is the experiential referent that language builds upon. It is the ungraspable happening of our reality. So it must be explored, as best we can, to better think about it and devise therapeutic approaches.

The interview discussed below is just such an approach.

About fifteen years ago I began to do a special kind of interview that helps to identify present moments and the affective happenings that occur during them. Now called the micro-analytic interview, it was initially referred to as the "breakfast interview." (An extended explanation of how to conduct a micro-analytic interview is included in the Appendix.) Here is how it goes: I ask individuals, "What did you experience this morning at breakfast?" (I ask several hours after breakfast is over.) They usually answer, "Well, nothing, really." I pursue it until they recall something. I am looking for any happening that has a clear beginning and end (good boundaries). This is an example of what they might recall: "Well, I remember picking up the teapot to pour my tea. Actually, I don't remember picking it up, but I must have done that. Anyway, while I was pouring, I had a memory of something that happened last night. Just then, the telephone rang and I became conscious of pouring the tea because I wondered if, I should finishing pouring to the top of the cup or put the teapot down and get the phone. I put the pot down, got up, and answered the phone." (All this took about five seconds.)

I then conduct an interview about what was experienced in that five seconds. The interview lasts about an hour and a half. I ask what they did, thought, felt, saw, heard, what position their body was in, when it shifted, whether they positioned themselves as an actor or an observer to the action, or somewhere in between. I ask them to make a movie of their experience as if we could make a montage of what was on their mental stage. They are the director and I am the cameraman. They have to tell me what to do with the camera. Is this shot a closeup or distance shot? How am I to cut from one scene to the next? Where is the camera and its angle relative to the action? In other words, I ask about anything I can think of to capture their subjective experience most fully.

The interview unfolds in a special way. The subjects and I try to draw or graph the experience along a timeline, where time stretches out on the horizontal axis and the intensity, effort, and fullness of the event / feeling / sensation / thought / affect / action is delineated on the vertical axis. This results in several curves, each a temporal contour of the distribution of intensity of whatever was experienced over time (see Figure 1.1). I take the subjects on many passes through the experience. For instance, I ask them if any memories were evoked during the experience. If so, they are added to the graph. I ask them what affective experiences they had. These are drawn by the subjects with a contour over time that represents the shifts in the intensity of the affect as it occurred. These affect contours are then also added to the graph. At each pass, the entire drawing can be revised if needed. It usually is. After many passes, we end up with a record that looks much like a symphonic musical score with many things going on simultaneously.

Continuities and discontinuities are carefully recorded and broken into the following units: *Episodes of consciousness* are continuous periods of consciousness separated by holes in the flow of consciousness, *non-CS holes*. These episodes are made up of one or more *present moments* that are demarcated by a change in the scene (place, time, characters, action) or a shift in the narrative stance. The identification of separate present moments and the boundaries between them are chosen by the subjects.

It must be noted that the present moments in the graph are not *original* present moments. Rather, they are the told recollections of moments that were, earlier in the morning, actually lived present moments. Obviously, we cannot get a verbal account of experience as it is happening without interupting the experience. The goal is to draw a picture of what a present moment is probably like.

One more note: In retelling there are actually the two present moments involved, the original unnarrated lived present moment during breakfast, and the present moment of telling me about it later. At this point we are interested only in the originally lived present moment. I will address the present moment of telling later.

As the interview continues, I strongly insist that the subject distinguish what must have happened from what was actually consciously experienced that morning (only the later is graphed). The interview ends when the subject feels that the graphed record has adequate verisimilitude with what he or she recalls as having been experienced.

This process may sound tedious, but it actually generates great interest and curiosity in both the subject and me, despite the apparent banality of the events. Although the present moments are ordinary, they are triggered by novelty, the unexpected, or a potential problem or trouble. They are the stuff of low-level everyday drama. We go after the uncovering with a sort of growing excited complicity. And we become increasingly amazed at all that is recalled as happening in such short stretches of ordinary life moments and how the microdramas are resolved.

Following are four examples of present moments. These examples actually only sneak up on the phenomenon of the present moment for reasons that will become evident later. Nonetheless, they clarify some of the key issues. The first two examples are from situations in which I was conducting micro-analytic interviews. The third is a clinical example, and the fourth is from ordinary life.

EXAMPLE 1*

Present Moment 1

(The subject entered the kitchen, turned on the radio, and walked over to the refrigerator. She opened the refrigerator door, looking for butter to put on her bread. She did all of this automatically without being specifically conscious of doing it. Her first moment of consciousness then began.) *I was aware that Chancellor Kohl of Germany was being interviewed on the radio, I heard his voice, then tuned it out of my mind. Looking in the refrigerator, I did not find any butter. I thought to myself, "There is no butter." As I was not finding the butter, there was a growing mild frustration and some kind of negative feeling, somewhere between disappointment and annoyance. These feelings increased.* (This lasted an estimated three seconds. Then there was a transition to the next moment without a break in the continuity of consciousness.)

Present Moment 2

I then thought, "Oh, that's all right, it's good for my diet." As I thought this, the frustration and annoyance faded and I experienced a surge of relief that continued to grow a bit. (This lasted an estimated three seconds. She then entered a period of acting outside of consciousness. After a short while, a third recalled moment of consciousness begins.)

---

* Italics are used to indicate everything that the subject reported to have been her conscious experience. Everything relevent that must have happened but never entered into the subject's consciousness, probably because it was too routine and automatic, has been put in parentheses. Refer to Figure 1.1 as the dialogue unfolds.

Present Moment 3

I thought to myself, "I could take some honey." (The honey was in place of the butter. Normally she ate honey only on Sundays. It was a family tradition. Honey was special and not for other days. This was a Tuesday.) *I asked myself, "Do I dare take the honey?" At first when I thought this, I felt a burst of surprise at this unexpected thought. Then, a sense of feeling good at solving the no-butter problem took over and began to grow. As this was happening, I saw in my mind's eye the jar of honey in its usual place in the cabinet behind my back* (and out of view). *I saw in my mind's eye the honey jar and its exact position on the shelf.* (Still without turning around.) *I then decided to act and get the honey.* (She turned, opened the cabinet door, and took the honey jar, but without being conscious of these routine acts.) *Then with the honey in my hand I began to feel a mounting guilt and feeling of avarice that I would actually eat the honey on a Tuesday.* (This moment took an estimated five seconds. There was then a gap in the consciousness of her experience. She then became conscious again.)

Present Moment 4

I am holding a slice of bread, not yet spread with honey. But it is a different kind of bread than I normally buy. It feels strange and I am surprised by it. I think, "What do I do with this bread?" A mild negative feeling arises. (This moment took about three seconds. She then spreads honey on the bread without paying conscious attention to the act. A new moment begins adjacent to the previous one.)

Present Moment 5

I am then aware of biting into the honeyed bread. I like the texture and think, "It's not so bad." And with that a sense of feeling better builds up. I then become conscious of the radio interview again. (This moment took an estimated three to four seconds.)

This small example, banal as it is, illustrates some of the issues about experience that must be addressed. Granted, this account is (re)constructed after the event and is a narrative of remembered experiences put together in an unusual manner. It is not a spontaneous narrative. Nor has it ever been rehearsed. It has been taken apart and rebuilt piece by piece in successive passes. It is a deconstructed then progressively co-constructed narrative that has been reformed in progressive layers. Despite these problems and with appropriate caution, the following points can be made about lived present moments as they are unfolding, not as they are remembered and narrated.

- Present moments are unbelievably rich. Much happens, even though they last only a short time.
- Present moments occupy the subjective now. The present moment is viewed as whatever is in mind, now, whether the object of mental concern is real or virtual. (Her imagined view of the location of the honey behind her back was a virtual experience.)
- The moment is a whole happening, a gestalt. The psychological subject matter is the whole, not the smaller units that make it up.
- When she experienced these events it occurred in a now that she could identify and put boundaries around.
- The present moment is short. In this case, the five present moments each lasted between three and five seconds, as estimated by the subject.
- Consciousness is the main criterion used to identify episodes containing present moments. In this case, they probably

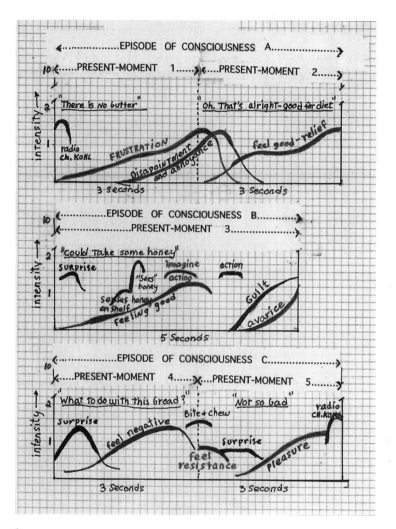

Figure 1.1. A schematic representation of episodes of consciousness and present moments as recalled and coconstructed using a micro-analytic interview. The ordinate is the subjective intensity of the experience on a scale from 1 to 10. The abscissa is the estimated time as recalled by the subject. The beginning and ending of each episode of consciousness and present moment are determined by the subject. Where the curves become thick, the subject is relatively certain that he or she became conscious of the event. Often the subject will say, "I know I was feeling such and such before (or after) but about here it entered consciousness (line thickens), or left consciousness (line thins.)

triggered consciousness because they were violations of the expected. They were novel and there was a problem.

- The feelings experienced (e.g., frustration and pleasure) trace a time-shape (a temporal profile) of analogic risings and fallings. In other words, they are carried on vitality affects (dynamic time-shapes) that contour the experience temporally.
- A lived story unfolds within each present moment. It is made of many small experiences that are put together in the subjective present. The storyline, even if minimal, rides on the temporal feeling shape of the contoured affects. The unfolding micro-story resolves the novelty or problem.
- Such moments are not cut off from the rest of life, isolated and unconnected. Rather, they capture a sense of the subject's style, personality, preoccupations, or conflict—in other words, their experience of the past. Each such moment is psychodynamically relevent.

This last point merits further discussion. Take the "no butter" example. The subject seemed to fashion together affective / moral couplets:

- No butter. That's bad. / Oh, yeah, I'm on a diet, so it's good.
- Could use honey. That would taste good. / Oh, but it would be sinful.
- What's this weird bread? / Oh, it's not so bad after all.

She is constantly balancing good / bad, moral / immoral, pleasureable / unpleasurable. Is keeping this kind of balance sheet a characteristic way she is with herself in the world? We don't know, but she gave that impression outside the experiment. (Data external to present experience is not needed to establish a present moment. It is needed, however, to establish the relationship of the present moment to the past or to continuing psychological events.)

EXAMPLE 2

This example better demonstrates how the present moment is an instance of past and future patterns. This is important if the present moment is to play a role in a comprehensive psychodynamic view. During a "breakfast interview," G.S., a young graduate student, told of two present moments that stood out during the morning. This is a partial transcript.

G.S.: *Well, I opened the refrigerator door, like this.* (He made a gesture of how he opened the door.)

D.S.: (I was intrigued that he made a gesture to show how he opened the door. Normally the opening of a refrigerator door does not need such gestural explaining.) *Why did you show me how you opened the door? Is there something special about it?*

G.S.: *Yes, in fact, there is. The door is sort of broken. If I pull it open too gently, it will swing shut by itself. And if I pull it open with too much force, it will not stop swinging and will hit the cabinet alongside of it. So I have to pull it just right, not too weak, not too strong, so it stays open, resting at a point of equilibrium. I am conscious of doing it because it is like a game requiring attention. [Pause] Then I guess I got the container of orange juice out. I don't remember this but it is automatic. I must have walked with it over to the table, getting a glass on the way.*

D.S.: *Yeah.*

G.S.: *The next thing I was conscious of was pouring the juice into the glass.*

D.S.: *Oh. And how is that?*

G.S.: *What I usually do is pour as much juice into the glass as I can, but not to the very top. Just high enough that it is full, but not so high that I will spill it when I bring it to my mouth. That requires that I act consciously.*

17

D.S.: *Oh.*
G.S.: *It's sort of a game.*

What is interesting about these two moments is that they are instantiations of the same theme, namely, finding the exact balance between going too far or not far enough. Interestingly, G.S. spontaneously picked up on this and mentioned that the night before this breakfast he was trying to finish the discussion section of his doctoral thesis. What made the writing difficult was that he could not decide how far he dare push his findings and conclusions. This had been on his mind all night. He said, "It's like the refrigerator door and the glass of juice."

It is worth adding what I know about this young man who was a subject and former student, not a patient. He had a strong, healthy tendency to push the limits in most things, to dare and see how far it could go. It was an asset but also had the potential for making trouble.

So the two moments of consciousness (door and juice), his preoccupation from the night before, and his general makeup (and perhaps conflicts) all said the same thing. "I test and play with the boundary between too much and too little. I push limits. There is something intriguing and important for me there." Is not a world being reflected in a grain of sand?

I was prepared to see present behavior as an instantiation of larger behavioral and psychological patterns. That is the essense of the psychodynamic hypothesis. However, I was surprised to see larger psychodynamic patterns reflected in units as small as present moments. This realization opened up the way to consider the present moment, like a dream, as a phenomenon worthy of deeper exploration for therapeutic purposes. Such a view adds another path to follow clinically. I will take up this point again in the chapters on clinical applications.

This book is largely about certain moments that can change the course of psychotherapy as well as regular life. Looking closely at such moments provides a different view on the process of psychotherapy. This different vision will be explored for its theoretical and clinical implications.

EXAMPLE 3

As a regular practice, a therapist I knew shook hands with his patients when they entered the consulting room. It was a way of saying hello before they started to work. And at the end of each session as the patient started to leave, they shook hands again as a goodbye. One day the patient recounted a very moving series of events that affected him (and the therapist) deeply. The patient was sad and almost overwhelmed. At the end of the session, during the "goodbye" handshake, the therapist brought his left hand up and laid it on the patients right hand, which he was already holding, in a two-handed handshake. They looked at each other. Nothing was said. The whole thing lasted several seconds. It was not talked about in subsequent sessions either. Yet, the relationship had shifted on its axis. Something vital was added to whatever had been said in the session—something so vital that the whole session was altered. The moment entered consciousness and was memorable. In fact, that handshake may stand out as one of the most memorable moments in the entire therapy. Often when someone is asked five or ten years after concluding a succesful therapy, "What were the most important or nodal moments in your therapy that changed things?" they may well reply, "A certain handshake we shared one day as I left."

I want to draw several points from this anecdote that add to what was described for the breakfast interviews:

• Whatever happened in this moment was understood implicitly by both of them and never had to be talked about to have its effect. It created implicit knowledge about their relationship.

19

- Each of them sensed the experience of the other, and both sensed the mutual participating in the other's experience. There was, in this sense, an interpenetration of minds—a new state of intersubjectivity was created between them.
- While the moment was prepared for by multiple events in the preceding minutes and probably weeks and months, the exact instant of its appearance was not planned or predictable. It emerged spontaneously. Life changes in leaps.
- During the moment, a story unfolded, albeit a very short, minimal, and tightly packed one. The story was directly experienced, not written nor told. The moment created a "world in a grain of sand" that came into being as the moment was lived, not afterwards.
- The moment was engraved in each of their minds. Even without being verbalized, it entered into memory, could be recalled, and become conscious.

EXAMPLE 4

This example is far less charged; it is quite banal, in fact. It happened after a crowd of strangers and I witnessed an amusing exchange between a talented street mime and a passerby. I was sitting on the steps of a museum overlooking a sidewalk. On the sidewalk, the mime was walking behind different passersby for ten or twenty yards (several seconds), imitating the individuals' walks, posture, and apparent moods—quickly "capturing" something about them. The passersby usually did not realize they were being imitated and made fun of. They just kept walking. Then the mime would stop, turn around, and follow the next passerby going back in the opposite direction. And so on, back and forth. The crowd on the steps was greatly amused. He then began to follow a woman. But she quickly realized what was happening. She stopped, turned around, faced the mime, and started to upbraid him. The mime then began to imitate her scolding. Then she began to imitate his imitation of her. He went the next step until the two of them began to laugh. They shook hands and parted. Everyone clapped. (This is not the example—though it could be, because a moment was shared between the street mime, the woman and the crowd. It is only the prologue.) At that point I stood up to go and so did a couple sitting a little to the left of me, whom I did not know. We looked at each other, smiling, raised our eyebrows, tilted our heads in a funny way, made some kind of indescribable facial expression, and opened our hands, palms up to the sky—all as if to say, "It's a crazy, amusing world." They went their way, I mine.

The important thing about the present moment I shared with this couple was that a particularly human contact had been made—a contact that reaffirmed my belonging to other members of my society, mentally, affectively, and physically. I was not alone on earth, I was part of some kind of psychological, intersubjective human matrix. The effect was short-lived. But it was a good temporary fit.

This book is about such moments, particularly how they operate in psychotherapy to bring about change.

Several features of the approach taken here are relatively unique. First, the book explores the archipeligo of islands of consciousness, the present moments, that make up our subjective experience, rather than the unconscious underwater mountain range (be it psychodynamic or neural circuitry) that occasionally pierces the surface to make the islands. These islands are the psychological foreground, the primary reality of experience. The present and consciousness are the centers of gravity, not the past and the unconscious.

The book's exploration of the therapeutic process is microanalytic and adjusted to the size of the present moment. It goes from small event to small event in the scale of seconds. That is where the present moment is revealed and where we will find a different view of things.

Finally, I am most interested in present moments that arise in the context of two or more people interacting. After all, our major interest is the psychotherapeutic process involving two people. The breakfast interview examples were about someone alone. But even when someone is alone, that person is addressing his or her conscious mental activity for someone else. It may be to a phantasied audience, to someone specific, or to one of his or her context-dependent selves.

The central idea about moments of change is this: During these moments a "real experience" emerges, somewhat unexpectedly. This experience happens between two (or more) people. It is about their relationship. It occurs in a very short period of time that is experienced as *now*. That *now* is a present moment with a duration in which a micro-drama, an emotional story, about their relationship unfolds. This jointly lived experience is mentally shared, in the sense that each person intuitively partakes in the experience of the other. This intersubjective sharing of a mutual experience is grasped without having to be verbalized, and becomes part of the implicit knowledge of their relationship. The sharing creates a new intersubjective field between the participants that alters their relationship and permits them to take different directions together. The moment enters a special form of consciousness and is encoded in memory. And importantly, it rewrites the past. Changes in psychotherapy (or any relationship) occur by way of these nonlinear leaps in the ways-of-being-with-another.

The overall idea is to draw a picture of lived experience that is somewhat different than what is usually found in the psychotherapeutic process. I anticipate that this new view, through the looking glass of the present moment, will change many aspects of how we think about and do therapy.

Chapter 2

THE NATURE OF THE PRESENT MOMENT

THE PRESENTNESS OF SUBJECTIVE LIFE seems evident. How could it be otherwise? Still, the notion remains troublesome. The idea of living subjectively only in the present strikes one as counter-intuitive. For instance, when having a memory about a past event, we may be slightly surprised to realize that the entire experience of remembering is happening now. We may be reliving something, but the reliving is going on now. We intuitively feel that we are not back in that time. Even the telling about something that just happened is actually happening now. Telling is a now experience, even though it refers to a present moment that occurred in the past. We also have anticipations about the future, but these too are being experienced now. The same holds for fantasies, dreams, and revisions after the fact. This tight locking of experience into the present is a basic aspect of any phenomenological approach.

The sense of presentness poses a challenge to the neurosciences. How do we know that something took place in the past and when? How do we recognize the present now? How is the future marked? How is the time marker inserted into the memory trace and where in the brain does that take place? These are old problems raised in various forms by many for over a century (Bergson, 1896 / 1988; Husserl, 1964; James, 1890 / 1972; Merleau-Ponty, 1945 / 1962).

Recently Dalla Barba (2001), among others, has proposed that consciousness is not a unitary dimension, but a set of distinct modes to address the object of consciousness. Dalla Barba suggested two modes: knowing consciousness and temporal consciousness. Knowing consciousness addresses the object in order to know it. Temporal consciousness addresses the object in order to temporalize it, in terms of past, present, and future. Others have made similar suggestions (e.g., Chalmers, 1995; Damasio, 2002). Pathological memory disorders presumably result from a dissociation of these two modes.

These are promising beginnings but probably the most difficult time-marking task will be knowing that we are in the present. There are many questions about the phenomenology of presentness for which a neural basis would prove interesting.

Presentness is something like an existential affect. The neurosciences must come to grips with it. This is of great clinical import because pathological states of dissociation can influence the sense of presentness. The enactment of traumatic memories is a case in point. There seems to be a loss of the existential sense of being in a felt present or past.

The feeling of presentness seems also to require a sense of self. And what is that neurophysiologically? (I will return to this question momentarily.)

It often happens that one feels only partially in the present moment. But then where else are you? For instance, you can be attending to something, here and now, but at the same time be preoccupied by someting that happened yesterday or is happening now in the next room. At such times you feel only weakly in the present moment, as if part of you were elsewhere in some other temporal space. But there is no other such subjective time space. You are still in the present moment, only there are two experiences (at least) going on in parallel, like a duet. One experience may impinge on the foreground experience and push it into the background, but you have not escaped the present. Phenomenologically, there is no escape. Rather, experiences in the present can be polyphonic or polytemporal.

The present moment is a subjective, psychological, process unit of which one is aware. The way it begins and ends may at times be difficult to define. Merleau-Ponty (1945 / 1962) described the arrival of a present moment before us as the upsurge of a fresh present—the all-of-a-suddenness of a memory or a new thought or perception. We are unaware of how it got there because we composed it unconsciously, intuitively. This upsurge can also crash upon us like a wave, or appear almost without notice and then slip away like a sea swell.

THE DURATION OF NOW

How can now have a duration long enough for something to happen in it? Or: Can we pour time back into the present moment so that it is an event lived analogically in real time? The duration of now depends on how we conceive of the passage of time. Here we must return to the distinction between *chronos* and *kairos*. Both psychology and psychoanalysis have mostly been able to live with the view of the present described by *chronos*. However, common experience—our subjective sense of life as lived at the second-by-second local level—does not sit well with the idea that the present has no temporal thickness. The experience of listening to music, watching dance, or interacting with someone require a present with a duration (as we shall see), so does life at the local level.

Psychological present moments must have both a duration in which things happen and at the same time take place during a single, subjective now. An example from music makes this apparent contradiction clear: A short musical phrase is the basic process unit of the experience of hearing music. A phrase is the musical analog of a present moment in ordinary life. A musical phrase is intuitively grasped as a global unit with boundaries. It has a duration that is sensed (usually in the range between two and eight seconds). And most interestingly, the musical phrase, as heard, is felt to occur during a moment that is not instantaneous, but also not parcelled out in time into sequential bits like the written notes. Rather, it is a continuous, analogic, flowing whole occurring during a now. Usually we are not aware of the passage of time during a now, still, the time flow is being registered somehow out of consciousness.

The phrase stands as a global entity that cannot be divided up without losing its gestalt. You cannot take the equivalent of a photograph of a heard musical phrase as it passes. It is not a summary of the notes that make it up. The mind imposes a form on the phrase as it unfolds. In fact, its possible endings are intuited before the phrase is completed, while it is still passing by. That is to say, the future is implied at each instant of the phrase's journey through the present moment.

The same applies to phraselike groupings in verbal and non-verbal behavior seen in ordinary life and psychotherapy.

But let us return to the problem of finding enough time within the moving present for a present moment to endure and unfold. How can we pry open *chronos* to create a present long enough to accomodate *kairos*?

This question has preoccupied a line of philosophers for centuries, including Saint Augustine (1991), Husserl (1964), Heidegger (1927 / 1996), Merleau-Ponty (1945 / 1962), Ricoeur (1984–1988), and Varela (1999). Husserl (1913 / 1930 / 1980, 1930 / 1989, 1931 / 1960, 1962, 1964) provided the key conception of how this problem could be tackled. He proposed a present moment that has a duration and consists of three parts: a present-of-the-present-moment (not so different from the present instant of *chronos*, the passing point of moving time) a past-of-the-present-moment, and a future-of-the-present-moment. Husserl called past-of-the-present-moment "retention." This is an immediate past that is still echoing at the present instant. Husserl described it as the tail of a comet. It is important to note that this retained past is still within the felt present. It has not been separated from the present instant by being forgotten or put out of mind. In this way, it is not like working memory, which can be out of mind for a short period of time but readily recalled. No recall is needed for the past-of-the-present-moment because it is still in the present moment. The future-of-the-present-moment was called "protention." This is the immediate future, which is anticipated or is implied in what has already occured during the past- and present-of-the-present-moments. This future-of-the-present-moment is part of the experience of the felt present moment because its foreshadow, even if vague, is acting at the present instant to give directionality and, at times, a sense of what is about to unfold.

Perhaps the most essential point about this three-part present moment is that all of its parts stand together, subjectively, as a single, unified, coherent, global experience occurring in a subjective now. (See also Varela [1999] for a recent discussion of this three-part present.)

PROTECTING THE PRESENT MOMENT FROM THE PAST AND FUTURE, AND FINDING A PLACE FOR IT

The present moment can be held hostage by either the past or the future. The past can eclipse the present by casting so strong a shadow on it that the present can only confirm what was already known and can add little more. It is essentially effaced. The psychodynamic past runs into this danger. It is one of the reasons that psychoanalysis has been able to downplay the present. It is viewed as only another instantiation of past patterns. The past comes in many influential forms including not only the patient's past history but also the long-range treatment goals of the therapist and the patient's expectations of treatment.

The future can also annihilate the present by reorganizing it so much and so fast that the present becomes ephemeral and almost passes out of existence. Those who propose an overly determining role for verbal / narrative reconstruction after the fact face this danger because they act as if the only clinically relevent psychological reality is conferred when experience is rendered verbally.

The challenge is to imagine the present moment in some kind of dialogic equilibrium with the past and future. If the present moment is not well anchored in a past and future it floats off as a meaningless speck. If it is too well anchored it becomes diminished. Also the present must be able to influence, perhaps to the same extent, the past and future, just as they influence the present. Again, the example of a musical phrase can help us begin to address some of these problems. Suppose the phrase is heard in the absence of any past musical experience; in other words, it is culture-free. Of course, this is impossible. However, we *are* biologically programmed to be able to formulate an idea of what the end of the passage could be like (while the phrase is still unfolding) with minimal prior experience. Principles of perceptual organization (probably universal), such as proximity, good continuation, common fate, and similarity, have been identified by Gestalt psychology. These would permit the formation of possible futures, any one of which could be realized, as the phrase unfolds. The phrase then could take some kind of form without prior experience. Other perceptual constraints and tendencies are less or not at all culture-free (see Deutsch, 1999a, 1999b).

Although there are no culture-free musical audiences, an interesting experiment bears on the question. Schellenberg (1996) has shown that partway through a novel musical phrase, we have the ability to predict the likely possible endings. We create and impose form as it is happening, while listening, and we do it without thinking. As the phrase is passing, but not completed, we naturally construct in our minds various immediately future implications of what we are now still hearing. These notions are based on the implication-realization model of Narmour (1990).

Specifically, if several people are separately asked to listen to only part of a phrase and are then asked to predict how it might end, they will have good agreement about the several possible endings. In fact, Westerners unfamiliar with Chinese music, which has a different tonal scale, can complete an unfinished phrase of traditional Chinese music, imagining roughly the same possible phrase endings as Chinese listeners (who have never heard the phrase before either). When the experiment is done in reverse, the Chinese listener does roughly as well as the Westerner in predicting possible endings of a novel phrase of traditional Western music. (Trained musicians do better.)

In this sense, a musical phrase contains an immediate past and future. The form of the musical phrase is revealed and captured by the listener as the crest of the immediate present instant passes from the still resonating horizon of the past (of the present moment) toward the anticipated horizon of the future (of the same present moment) (Darbellay, 1994). Much of the charm of listening to music lies in the surprises that the composer provides by inventing final paths that surprise us but do not overly violate the implications we sensed.

29

Some contemporary music is constructed exactly to play with, violate, or paralyse our implication making tendency.

This putting the phrase into form while it is happening is of great interest because it sheds light on the nature of now, particularly on the problem of the influence of the future on the present, in other words, the relationship of happenings to (re)constructions of happenings. In music, the form of a phrase does not wait for the subsequent phrases to come into being. Some thinkers have suggested that the form of the musical phrase is only evident after the phrase has passed and is taken up again by the mind. If that were true we would never hear anything. We would only "think" music. Yet, that is the radical position of some psychoanalytic thinkers in considering the therapeutic dialogue. They maintain that there is no happening (*coup*) until it is rendered symbolically afterwards. There is only a (re)construction (*après coup*). It is only then that the experience takes on its subjective form for the first time.

In music, at least, the phrase takes on a unitary, coherent form in the mind while it is happening. And this will prove to be the case with many other aspects of experience. It is also true that (re)construction occurs pervasively in music as well as in other life experiences.

Much of the richness of music lies in the fact that each subsequent phrase recontextualizes the previous one, and vise versa, ad infinitum. Variations and larger thematic structures contextualize and recontextualize all phrases, over and over. All recontextualizations change the phenomena, but they do not create them. And that is the essential point. A coherent experience was grasped during the present moment, even though that experience may have multiple fates.

But what about the action of the past in determining the form of the present moment, in both music and life? Take as an example the graduate student from the breakfast interview.

The pouring of the orange juice was greatly determined by his preoccupations of the night before and his long-established character traits. The past assumes many forms: e.g., schemas, representations, models, preconceptions, expectations, original phantasies. These structures from the past encounter the unfolding events in the present. A dynamic dialogue is set in motion. (The present is always somewhat novel; it has its own unique local conditions. Even if the present were only an exact repeat of something that happened before, it has the difference of occurring for the second time, which in itself makes it unique.) The present comes under much control of the past, and the past may be realized or altered or even surprised by the present. Equally, the present determines which pieces of the past will be chosen to be reanimated and assembled. Past and present are always operating on each other. Narmour (1990, 1999) makes this case forcefully for music in the moving present.

In short, the present moment is never totally eclipsed by the past nor fully erased by the future. It retains a form of its own while being influenced by what went before and what comes after. Also it determines the shape of the past that is brought forward into the present and the outlines of the imagined future. This trialogue between past, present, and future occurs almost continuously from moment to moment in art, life, and psychotherapy.

CHARACTERISTICS OF THE PRESENT MOMENT

The present moment has been relatively but not wholly ignored by psychology. Some of the most important work on the subject, essential to the writing of this book, has been done during the past century. In its recent investigations of consciousness, psychology has rediscovered the phenomenological perspective. But the present moment as a psychological entity has existed well before that going by several names: the "specious present" (James, 1890 / 1972); the "personal present" (W. Stern, 1930), the "actual present" (Koffka, 1935), and the "perceived present" or "psychological present" (Fraisse, 1964). It is a crucial entity in the phenomenology of perception (Merleau-Ponty, 1945 / 1962), and in the current views of consciousness. They all capture slightly different aspects of this subjective experience. Some of these process units are more meaning-oriented, others more perception-oriented, and some focus mainly on the nature of consciousness. But in any event, they try to identify a process unit I am calling the present moment.

Some of the phenomenological features of the subjective world, described almost a century ago by Husserl, are fairly straightforward; others continue to surprise, even astound, me. At the same time, they are so obvious that they usually go unnoticed. They are hidden in full view.

A minimal list of the features of a clinically relevent present moment follows.

1. *Awareness or consciousness is a necessary condition for a present moment.* The present moment unfolds during a stretch of awareness or some kind of consciousness. However, the present moment and consciousness are not the same thing. The present moment is the felt experience of what happens during a short stretch of consciousness.

2. *The present moment is not the verbal account of an experience.* It is the experience as originally lived. It provides the raw material for a possible later verbal recounting.

3. *The felt experience of the present moment is whatever is in awareness now, during the moment being lived.* On this point we must return to the phenomenological perspective. The content of a present moment is simple—it is what is on the mental stage now. Subjective experience does not pas-

sively "reach" or pop into awareness fully formed. It is actively constructed by our minds and bodies working together (Clark, 1997; Damasio, 1994, 1999; Sheets-Johnstone, 1999; Varela, Thompson, & Rosch, 1993). But subjectively, the current contents of mind contained in a present moment seem to slide unnoticed or sometimes jump into awareness without cognizance of its being composed. We accept that as totally natural.

The present moment is often hard to grasp because we so often quickly jump out of the present ongoing experience to take the objective, third-person viewpoint. We try to seize what we have just experienced by putting it into words or images in the moment after. These attempts at introspection (immediate retrospection) appear to objectify the experience. And from that more distant position, we can ask, "Can it not be explained by such and such?" or "What really happened was. . . ." What we usually overlook is that when we jump out of one present moment we simply jump into another (the next) present moment—in this case, the new present experience of wondering about the last present experience. But we act as if the second experience is from an objective perspective compared to the first. Actually it is still a first-person experience about trying to take a third-person stance relative to something that just happened.

This natural problem is why Husserl insisted that to capture phenomenal experience and examine it for itself, we have to put a bracket (Husserl's *époché*) around it to protect it from being "explained away" at another level. It is this that makes subjective experience so hard to grasp. It is too evident, like oxygen in the air we breathe.

4. *Present moments are of short duration.* The present moment has a duration of roughly several seconds. (Count four seconds out loud. It is surprisingly long.) Dictionary defi-

nitions of "experience" refer to "living through" or "personally undergoing," each of which implies duration.

There are many very short events lasting well under a second that we also experience, like the immediate recognition of a familiar face. But we are not usually conscious of these experiences as they happen, only if they endure in mind for some reason over several seconds. Accordingly they do not qualify as present moments. I will pursue this issue further in the following chapter on the temporal aspects of the present moment.

The present moment not only has a duration but we somehow sense that what is happening now is happening in the time slot of immediate presentness.

5. *The present moment has a psychological function.* A subjective experience must be sufficiently novel or problematic to enter consciousness and become a present moment. Present moments form around events that break through ordinariness or violate expected smooth functioning. Thus, they require mental (and perhaps physical) action. Because something must or could be done to deal with the breakthrough into consciousness, these moments carry a sense of consequence and engagement with the world. Again, think of *kairos*. Stated another way, the present moment carries an implicit intention to assimilate or accommodate the novelty or resolve the problem. This can be experienced as a sense of moving or leaning forward toward some unrevealed but progressively implied goal as the present moment is traversed. All of this can happen with very small magnitudes of novelty or problem. For instance, in the first breakfast interview from Chapter 1, the first present moment begins with an implied problem that is not exactly novel but is unexpected. "There is no butter." Hardly a severe violation of expectancy, but its a violation all the same.

So far we have referred only to the psychological meaning of intention, namely to commit an action (mental or physical) with a goal in mind, and to adjust the means to the ends. The philosophical meaning of intentionality refers to the purely mental action of the mind "reaching" for or "stretching" toward some content of mind—a memory, an image, and so on. For example, what happens when someone says, "Think about the moon." Your mind will "reach" for an image. There is an end state involved. The present moment is concerned with this form of intentionality as well (Brentano, 1874 / 1973).

The present moment, thus, has psychological work to do. Its work is the very mobile task of constantly dealing with or preparing to deal with what is happening in an almost constantly changing world. It takes the sequences of small, split-second events that the world throws at us and pulls them together into coherent units that are more useable for adaptation.

6. *Present moments are holistic happenings.* The present moment is a gestalt. It organizes sequences or groupings of smaller perceivable units (like notes or phonemes) that pass below focused consciousness into higher order units (like a meaningful phrase). Consider the experience of saying "hello" to someone you dislike. This experience can be broken apart by stepping outside yourself, so to speak, and observing yourself in the third-person. From that removed perspective you can divide it up into separate components: affects, cognitions, and a sequence of actions, perceptions, as well as sensations. Each can be looked at separately. But first-person experience is not broken up like that; it is felt as a whole.

7. *Present moments are temporally dynamic.* Much of our thinking about psychological phenomena has been either time-blind or ignored the temporal dynamics of lived expe-

rience (Sheets-Johnstone, 1999). The present moment, in contrast, has a marked time dynamic, as does a musical phrase. As noted earlier, these dynamic time-shapes are called *vitality affects* (discussed in Chapter 4; see also Stern, 1985; Stern, Hofer, Haft, & Dore, 1984).

Consider two quite different examples: watching fireworks rise in the sky, explode, and fan out; or someone saying to you, "I don't think you're telling the truth," followed by a few seconds of silence. As these present moments unfold, there are split-second micro-shifts in the intensity or quality of our feelings. In the fireworks example, there is a rising arousal and expectation as the rocket ascends, a sudden surge of feeling as it explodes, then a fading in excitation, and with it, a growing wonder and pleasure as the light display fans out and falls. At the same time there is a changing feedback of our movements (e.g. modulations in tonicity or tension, position), and fluctuations in interest, intentional force, and so on. These constant shifts trace a temporal profile, like a musical phrase. Vitality affects emerge as the moment unfolds. This is captured in terms such as *accelerating, fading, exploding, unstable, tentative, forceful,* and so on. These temporally contoured feelings could be associated with affects, movements, streams of thought, sensations, and any and all activity, mental or physical. Several time-shapes could be progressing simultaneously. Rather than view these different time-shapes as unrelated to each other, we see them as polyphonic and polyrhythmic. This feature is crucial because vitality affects play a strong role in providing a time contour that helps the chunking process essential to composing a present moment. It does this by enveloping the chunk and thus marking it and holding it together as a unit.

A temporally dynamic perspective is critical to many of the ideas presented in later chapters of this book, especially: "now moments," "moments of meeting," "temporal feeling shapes," and "shared feeling voyages." The notion of vitality affects has been around in various forms for a while, but to my knowledge it has not yet been seriously picked up by the clinical, behavioral, or neurosciences, even though such notions go far in helping us understand phenomenal experience as it unfolds, as it is remembered, and as it is networked.

Thanks to advances in brain imaging and neurophysiological recording techniques, the neurosciences are now in a position to shed light on these issues. Two kinds of data are needed. First, accurate timing of brain activity correlated with phenomenal experiences. Second, the timing of the analogic shifts in intensity or magnitude of neural firing during the same phenomenal experiences. With just that much, one could propose a scientific correlate to the subjective experience of vitality affects. More important, a typology of time-shapes of neural activity related to various experiences would emerge. Such a typology could be invaluable in further exploring the workings of memory, network linking, and associative pattern formation, both neuroscientifically and mentally. For instance, are the temporally dynamic qualia of "crescendoing" or "fading away" linked or linkable across modalities, across time, across contexts? If so, many problems of memory and association have another handle, a handle that clearly works at the clinical level.

A typology of temporally dynamic qualia has another appeal. This typology concerns mainly affective and feeling experiences. Up to now, affects and feelings have lacked many of the features or markers of physical objects that permit associations, such as form, size, color, texture, and so on. Temporally dynamic qualia, by contrast, provide affects with markers that are far more highly marked may permit associative activity. Just where more features for a basis of association are needed. In short, temporal dynamics is an insufficiently studied phenomenon.

In addition, using the timing capacities and vitality affect typing capacities of neuroscience, aspects of intersubjectivity could be explored. To what extent may two minds share the same experience, at least as measured by the temporal shape of vitality affects seen at the level of neural activity? This opens up explorations into mental contagion, resonance, identification, empathy, sympathy, and so on.

A related question concerns how the temporal aspects of polyphonic and polyrhythmic experience are handled at the neural level and coordinated at the phenomenal level. Recall that much of our subjective mental activity is polyphonic and polyrhythmic even when we are alone, let alone interacting with someone. For instance, metaphor, and what I will later call *multi-temporal presentations*, flipping foreground and background, and *relational progressions* all depend on keeping two or more simultaneously processed inputs straight while they are being compared. A further dialogue between the phenomenal / descriptive and the neuroscientific levels on these points could be important.

8. *The present moment is partially unpredictable as it unfurls.* You cannot know exactly how the present moment will turn out because you are riding its crest and the ride isn't over yet. Each small world of a present moment is unique. It is determined by the local conditions of time, space, past experience, and the particularities of constantly shifting

conditions in which it takes its form. Thus it is not knowable in advance.

9. *The present moment involves some sense of self.* During the lived present moment you are the sole experiencer of your own subjective experiences. You know that it is you who is experiencing. It does not simply belong to you, it *is* you. Our mental subjective experiences are so deeply embodied in our actions and movements and in the physiological shifts that permit, create and accompany experience, that it is not strange that we know that we are experiencing (Clark, 1997; Damasio, 1999; Sheets-Johnstone, 1984, 1999). Although this is self-evident, its neuroscientific underpinning remains to be clarified. (Certain intersubjective experiences are potential exceptions we will address later.) There is another related problem. Subjectivity, itself, is thought to be constructed from experience. In contrast, there is also an essentialist position that holds that subjectivity is a human given, and that constructivism must build on something (Zahavi, 2002). I believe that both views are true.

10. *The experiencing self takes a stance relative to the present moment.* A "stance" refers to the distance from or closeness to the experience, the degree of involvement in it, the participation, the interest, the emotional investment, and the evaluation of what is happening. Again, it is unclear how we feel and register our position relative to the actions we live, but nonetheless we do it without effort and without thinking. Here, too, the neuroscientific underpinnings remain to be elucidated, as they involve aspects of the subjective self and the experiencing self.

11. *Different present moments have different importance.* There is a broad spectrum of present moments, from the rare and momentous (*kairos* with a capital *K*), where the broad

sweep of a life can change, to the almost inconsequential. Depending on the local context and what is at stake, these various moments go by many names: "a moment in time," "a moment out of time," "the decisive moment" (in taking a photograph, Cartier-Bresson, 1952), "a defining moment" (as in capturing the essence of a situation), "a moment of truth" (as in bullfighting), a "weird fucking moment" (as in police lingo where a life or a relationship hangs in the balance of a momentary decision, à la novelist Scott Turow [1987]), and a "now moment" (in therapy, Stern, Sander, Nahum, and colleagues [1998]).

There are also extremely banal present moments (micro-*kairos*) that alter the course of a life, moment by moment, in small but traceable ways: "There is no butter." They are the stuff, the pieces, of our ongoing experience and, importantly, they are what brings about change at the local level in psychotherapy.

Chapter 3

THE TEMPORAL ARCHITECTURE OF THE PRESENT MOMENT

Some process unit with a duration is needed to understand human interactions that unfold in real time, as almost all of them do. It takes time to parse what is happening when observing someone doing or saying something. It takes time to put together the units of your own behavior. And it takes time of exposure for events caused by humans to arise to consciousness. The present moment is this process unit. Knowing its temporal parameters is crucial.

The present moment lasts between 1 and 10 seconds, with an average duration of around three to four seconds. There are three main reasons for this time span. It is the time needed to make meaningful groupings of most perceptual stimuli emanating from people, to compose functional units of our behavioral performances, and to permit consciousness to arise.

GROUPINGS OF PERCEPTUAL STIMULI

Humans can perceive separate events in a sequence that last only between 20 and 150 milliseconds. These are the basic units of perception. But in themselves they do not make life meaningful. We are bombarded with almost constant sequences of such small units. If we considered each such perceptual unit as a potentially important and meaningful event requiring attention and awareness, it would be like continually being under the fire of a machine gun. These sequences must get chunked into larger units more suited to adaptation.

Even though present moments are largely nonverbal experiences, speech provides the most studied example of the chunking of smaller perceptual units into larger meaningful wholes. Phonemes are the basic perceptual units of speech. They last between 40 and 150 milliseconds on average. There are also units (such as a word) in an intermediary range, 150–1000 milliseconds. (But words have limited meaning outside the context of a phrase.) Several words are chunked to make a single psychological aggregate, the phrase, which is a highly meaningful grouping that lasts several seconds. The duration of a present moment is the duration of a phrase. This temporal hierarchy is a general phenomena (see Trevarthen, 1999/2000; Varela, 1999). A major task for the mind is to make sense of the almost uninterrupted flow of stimulation. The phrase is the smallest chunk that gives us the maximum meaning to get by in the world of language. We can find the same time parameters in music, poetry, dance, gesture, kinetics, and discourse. Each discipline that deals with the flow of serial events in time has had to deal with this problem on its own terms.

Why is the present moment not longer than ten seconds? Actually, it can be under special conditions. Longer continuous present moments are sought in meditative states achieved through various techniques practiced in traditions such as Vedanta, Buddhism, Taoism, and Zuanzang (see Kern, 1988; Lancaster, 1997; Shear & Jevning, 1999; Wallace, 1999) or when one enters what has been called the "flow" of optimal experience (Csikszentmihalyi, 1990). Similarly, some of the moments that Virginia Woolf (1977) has called "moments of being" can last much longer.

Such mental states, however, are different from what we are calling present moments. In the meditative or flow states, the idea is to lose the sense of self and for consciousness to maintain a concentrated focus, relatively impervious to other stimulation. In contrast, during the present moments that concern us, attention and consciousness tend to flit about and focus on a single happening for shorter periods of time while remaining open to any and all other stimulation potentially interesting or distracting. As William James put it, "Like a bird's life, [the stream of consciousness] seems to be made [up] of an alternation of flights and perchings" (amended by Bailey, 1999 [quoting James, 1890 / 1972], p. 243). The present moments are the perchings. The flights are the spaces between moments of consciousness that are part of the present moment. These "flights" are inaccessible and ungraspable. Consciousness is thus left free to switch focus from one present moment to the next, and the sense of the self as experiencer is never felt to be interrupted, even though the perchings are discontinuous. These present moments are the stuff of subjectivity during ordinary mental states.

The ten-second time limit of present moments does not mean that there are not larger time units made up of several present moments chunked together. This is clearly the case in music and elsewhere. Trevarthen (1999 / 2000) has argued that there is a larger unit of about 30 seconds tied to cycles of autonomic system arousal. It is my sense that these larger units are usually made up of variations of several present moments in sequence that deepen or extend the experience. (This idea will be brought up again in the chapters on clinical applications when I discuss "relational progressions.") But the present moment remains the fundamental unit.

In short, the flow of perceptual stimulation must be chunked into meaningful units best sized to make us most adaptive, rapidly and efficiently. Chunking is the work of the present moment. It is the basic building block of psychologically meaningful subjective experiences that extend in time.

FUNCTIONAL UNITS OF BEHAVIORAL PERFORMANCE

The second reason that present moments last no longer than ten seconds is because meaningful human behavior (communicative, expressive, etc.) seems to be naturally produced / performed / packaged in units of one to ten seconds. Following are examples from different domains.

The Duration of the Present Moment in Language

Linguistics has quite successfully struggled with the problem of hierarchizing events of different duration: the phoneme, to the word, to the phrase (clause), to the sentence, to the paragraph, and so on. Although the two high frequency levels (the phoneme, 20–150 milliseconds, and word, 150–1000 milliseconds) are heard, it is the phrase that is the unit for parsing the sense of what is being said. One hears past the phonemes and words, so to speak, to get to the phrase, which is the basic gestalt in speech as heard. It is the unit in which the syntax is revealed and the functional meaning grasped. Of course the exact phonemes and words are registered and can be recalled with fairly good fidelity for a short time afterward. The meaning of the phrase, however, lasts much longer.

Although linguistics has focused on these units from the point of view of their contribution to meaning, there is also a temporal dimension. In this light, it is instructive to survey briefly the duration of some parsing units for meaning in speech, as well as the duration of groupings that regulate verbal discourse in dyadic situations (Jaffe & Feldstein, 1970; Trevarthen, 1999 / 2000). In general:

- Most spoken phrases last in the range of three seconds. Longer spoken sentences rarely last more than 4 to 5 seconds (Trevarthen, 1999 / 2000).
- When listening to recorded normal speech, a subject will interrupt the flow to report what was just heard roughly every three seconds—in other words, at phrase boundaries. The phrase acts as a processing chunk. (Wingfield & Nolan, 1980).
- It takes an average of 3 seconds and a maximum of 5 seconds to recite a line of poetry out loud (Turner & Pöppel, 1988).
- It takes 2 to 3 seconds, on average, for two speakers to take a speaking turn (i.e., a vocalization by one speaker, plus the switching pause after the first speaker has stopped and before the second speaker starts) (Jaffe & Feldstein, 1970).
- A breath cycle (one inspiration and one expiration) takes about 3 seconds (occurring about fifteen times a minute).

It appears that the physiological unit for producing a sound grouping (the breath cycle), the mental unit for parsing speech (the phrase), and the discourse units governing conversation (the turn) are of similar duration. It is likely that the temporal units for speech production, meaning parsing, and dialoguing all evolved together. Any other arrangement would be most unwieldy.

The Duration of the Present Moment in Music

Music has had to resolve the same general problems of grouping, but here the dimension of time is in the forefront. Instead of phonemes and words we have notes, beats, and measures, which must be grouped into phrases (or motifs), be they dominated by a melodic line or a rhythmic pattern. And here, too, as with language and vocalization, the 3–4 second range seems to be the most common. Here are some revealing examples:

- The *perceptual present* in music is thought to be a stretch of time during which the contents of the present are active and directly available without any mediation of memory (Husserl's three-part present). A musical phrase perceived as a gestalt would fill such a perceptual present. Whether or not the perceptual present can be viewed in terms of working memory is discussed later (Clarke, 1999; Michon, 1978).

- Fraisse (1978) suggested that the perceptual present in music lasts no longer than 5 seconds.

- Clarke (1999), in reviewing several authors, placed this perceptual present in music somewhere between 2 and 8 seconds.

- The subjective sensation of *forward movement* in music is felt only if two tonal events occur within a 3-second span. After a 3-second silence, the forward motion is felt to stop (Whittman & Poppel, 1999 / 2000). Some modern music violates these time limits by separating tonal events by more than 3 seconds, thus creating effects such as shifting tonal surfaces and textures rather than forward movement. (A similar effect is true in speech; after a 3-second pause, the turn or the topic is likely to change.)

The Duration of the Present Moment in Actions

The same grouping problem has to be solved for activities such as movement, ritual, and dance. This is especially true for modern dance, which is less often locked to a musical beat than, say, ballet. With movement, several different time units may be in play to compose units of meaning: the breath cycle (3 seconds); the cycle of contraction–relaxation, (in modern dance variable, but usually from 1 to 10 seconds), and the temporal limitations imposed by the size, speed, extension, abduction / adduction, and strength of body parts.

Many movements, be they a gesture, step, facial expression, or otherwise, have a frequency in the intermediary range of 150–1000 milliseconds. For instance, at a fast walk, a step takes 300–700 milliseconds, at an easy pace, 700–1500 milliseconds (Trevarthen, 1999 / 2000). Interestingly, we tend to create groupings of a series of steps. For examples, often, when one becomes conscious of walking, the steps become synchronized with the breath cycle. We tend to take two steps per inspiration and two or three steps per expiration. That results in four or five steps per grouping. And if the steps occur at intervals of 700 milliseconds, there will be 2.8 to 3.5 seconds for each grouping. We arrive again at the average phrase duration of a present moment. (These fractions change with speed and effort.)

Another grouping example is readily seen in the military. To synchronize the marchers, someone calls out the beat. There are four counts per grouping—in other words, four steps per phrase, with the left foot on the accented sound (e.g., SOUND off, ONE two, SOUND off, THREE four). We end up with a grouping of 2 to 3 seconds. (Actually, the four counts do not have to be unevenly stressed; gestalt psychology demonstrates that when two equal beats are heard, the first is subjectively felt to be stressed.)

Dance and ritual can use sound (music), breath cycles, contraction–relaxation cycles, natural groupings, or any combination thereof to create its phrases. Again the phraseology conforms to the temporal range of 1 to 10 seconds. For example: A full greeting ritual of two approaching friends consists of roughly simultaneous smiles, eyebrow raises, head raises, vocalizations, and some shared hand gesture or embrace (Kendon, 1990). This physical and mental process takes several seconds and establishes a new local meaning context for what happens next. "What's the matter?" or "You look happy today."

In partially ritualized, culturally shaped interactions among dyads there is a hierarchy of movements from small to large (from eyes, to head, to torso, to pelvis or the weight bearing parts). The larger slower movements frame the smaller ones (Fivaz-Depeursinge, 1991; Frey, Hirsbrunner, Florin, Daw, & Crawford, 1983; Frey, Jorns, & Daw, 1980). For example, during a seated conversation, when one partner shifts at the level of the pelvis, uncrossing one leg, shifting the weight to the other haunch, crossing the other leg, and readjusting the torso and head, a meaningful shift in the interactive state is signaled. The entire posture is repositioned. It is analogous to closing out one paragraph and beginning another. A new or altered interpersonal topic or attitude is being ushered in. A fresh present moment has entered. Shifts at this level take about 2 to 5 seconds.

Imitation is a complex perceptual-motor-proprioceptive act of communication and belonging. It can be of actions or vocalizations (which are also actions). Kugiumutzakis (1998, 1999) reported that episodes of imitation between adults and babies in their early weeks and months lasts about 2 to 7 seconds. Nadel (1986) and Nadel and Peze (1993) found bursts of imitation among older children lasting around 4 seconds. Imitation is particularly interesting in this light because it requires the assembly of perception of the other with proprioceptively guided movement from the self.

The mind has both innate and cultural strategies for grouping these lumps and discontinuities into larger meaningful units—into coherent wholes. A recent study by Zacks and colleagues (2001) showed that both can operate together. They showed subjects television recordings of daily activities such as ironing a shirt or other less obvious actions and recorded neural activity in specialized brain regions using functional magnetic resonance imaging (fMRI). When subjects were asked to segment the activity into units there was an increase in neural activity around boundaries of functional movements, suggesting that their knowledge of the activity was driving the parsing during this active viewing. However, when the same subjects were asked to watch the television with no directions and no task in mind (i.e., passive viewing), they showed increased neural activity at the same boundaries. This suggests that there are many cues that an innate process could pick up on, such as change in density, direction, or speed of movement, even when the subject is neither familiar with nor paying attention to the function of the activity.

The Duration of the Present Moment in Nonverbal Mother-Infant Interaction

From the beginning of life, infants are exposed to various forms of human phraseology in the range of 3 seconds:

- Vocalizing turns between mothers and nonverbal infants (made up of reciprocal babytalk and babbling) take about 2 to 3 seconds (Beebe, Jaffe, Feldstein, Mays, & Alson, 1985; Jaffe, Beebe, Feldstein, Crown, & Jasnow, 2001; Malloch, 1999 / 2000; Stern, 1977).
- Short phrases in mothers' songs to babies are in the same range (Malloch, 1999 / 2000; Trevarthen, 1999 / 2000).
- During face-to-face play with young infants, mothers perform short runs of exaggerated facial expressions or strings of gestures or touching sequences. These packages of maternal movement (and sound) provide the stimulus spectacle that parents and infants use to mutually regulate the baby's state of arousal and activation from moment to moment. These packages last about 2 to 5 seconds (Beebe et al., 1985; Beebe, Stern, & Jaffe, 1979; Stern, 1974, 1977; Stern et al., 1985; Weinberg & Tronick, 1994).

- Fivaz (personal communication, January 12, 2002) found that the episodes of activity in the triad (mother, father, baby) last 3.5 seconds on average, with a range between 2 and 10 seconds.
- Infants learn rapidly, but the learning situation must respect the duration of the present moment. By three months of age babies acquire a repetoire of instrumental behaviors (to get a response) such as social smiling and vocalizing. These behaviors are easily reinforced by the parents in a natural setting. However, for this kind of conditioning to work, the parents' reinforcer (a return smile or vocalization) must be delivered within three seconds of the infant's behavior. If the lapse between the desired behavior and the reinforcer is greater, no learning will occur (Watson, 1979). In other words, the behavior and its reinforcer must occur in the same present moment for the infant to associate the two. It is as if the forward movement of the music stopped for the baby.

The Duration of the Present Moment in General Mental Operations

Many have suggested that the psychological present (i.e., the present moment) is essentially the same as working memory. Working memory is the short-term storage that holds a small amount of information in active storage for a limited time. While in active storage, information can be retrieved and used as needed (Baddeley, 1986, 1989). The duration of this active storage (without rehearsal) is roughly the same as that of the present moment. Again, the memory delay time depends on a multiplicity of variables, as does the duration of the present moment.

There are several reasons, however, not to equate the present moment with working memory. First, the present moment is a subjective process unit. Working memory is objective. Also, a basic notion of working memory is that it contains at least two components: the material that is currently under the focus of active attention, and the material that is out of attentional focus, but remains activated and can be retrieved, or brought back into the focus of attention, during the limited time period (Cowan, 1988). The present moment, on the contrary, has no element that is outside of the focus of attention. If something can be pulled back into attention, where was it phenomenologically before it was retrieved? It could not have been in the present moment.

Working memory decays rapidly over the first 2 seconds, then more slowly for another 15 to 30 seconds or so (Baddeley, 1984, 1989; Cowan, 1984, 1988). It can, however, be maintained longer with repeated rehearsal. It is for this reason that most experiments on working memory use interference paradigms, where information is presented and then unrelated (interfering) information is presented to prevent rehearsal before recall of the original information is tested.

Such a procedure is contrary to the central idea of a present moment, namely, that one coherent continuous event fills the entire duration of a present moment. The present moment is a single whole. It concerns analogic events. Working memory, on the other hand, is usually concerned with a series of unrelated bits of information (i.e., digital events), some of which can be brought back into attentional focus after the mind has been distracted.

There are several well-known designs that can be seen in two quite different ways. One is of a vase or two people: Viewed one way the image appears to be a vase in the center of the picture; viewed another way, it appears to the profile of two people facing each other. We can see only one of the two images at a time. But we can switch from seeing the vase to seeing the two profiles. It usually takes around 1 to 3 seconds to effect the switch (if one is not practiced). This suggests that certain mental manipulations also require a one-to-several-second period to create a new whole (Kelso, Holroyd, Hovarth, Raczaszek, Tuller, & Ding, 1994; Rubin, 2001).

THE ARISING OF CONSCIOUSNESS

It takes a certain amount of time for incoming stimulation to reach consciousness. As I discuss in Chapter 8, consciousness is thought to arise, in neural terms, through the process of reentry (e.g., Edelman, 1990). Stated very simply, when a group of neurons is activated by an incoming stimulus, they may send a signal to another group of neurons. The second group then reactivates (reports back to) the first group and a reentry or recursive loop is created. This could then spread to a third group that would report back to the first and second groups. This combination of an experience plus a second or third experience about the original experience is what opens the door to the phenomenon of consciousness.

The first go around the reentry loop is rapid and the activation of the loop is likely to be very short. Its duration is around a quarter of a second. This is the time it takes to have unconscious intuitive likes or dislikes. If, however, there are several trips around the reentry loop, its activation can be stabilized for a long enough time for the phenomenal experience of consciousness to arise. If there were four or more trips around the loop, we would be in the time range of a present moment.

The continued stabilizing activation of the reentry loop that takes one or more seconds serves the function of protecting the mind from becoming conscious of happenings every split second. Events must, so to speak, earn consciousness by being sufficiently salient (value-laden) to momentarily stabilize a reentry loop. The present moment is the time it takes for such a loop to be sufficiently stabilized to give rise to consciousness.

It is appealing to think that the time it takes to chunk groupings of perceptual stimuli, to perform functional units of behavior, and to become conscious of an event should all have roughly the same duration: 3 to 4 seconds. If they did not, it would be much harder to make our experience coherent. Humans appear to be constructed so that they mind-size events into basic units of present moments: the fundamental units for understanding temporally dynamic experiences that occur between people.

Depending on what exactly is being grouped together, we can expect variability in the duration, within limits. It is a flexible rather than a rigidly fixed psychobiological unit. Factors such as modality, the number or frequency of events to be grouped, complexity, whether the time (or space) is empty or filled, familiarity, and so on may all influence the actual duration of the grouping process. For this reason it is wiser to think in terms of a range of approximately 1 to 10 seconds for the present moment.

Present moments are strung together in highly variable ways, and the time between two present moments can be difficult to determine. Sometimes holes in consciousness separate them (like the flights of William James's bird of consciousness en route to the next perching). Other times they are tightly packed in sequences of adjacent moments, with short transitions like a sharp cut to a new scene in a movie montage. Our awareness of these transitions is vague at best and usually is nonexistent. But the sequence may trace a theme, directional progression, or some other pattern.

Additionally, the time between present moments varies widely depending on what is going on. In some situations of focused concentration or high-affective charge, present moments seem to follow one another at close intervals. At other times a present moment seems to elongate well past ten seconds. On closer scrutiny, however, there appears to be a renewing of the "same" present moment every several seconds. For instance, when watching something fascinating, but relatively unchanging, like an eclipse of the sun, one can appear to get lost in the same present moment scene for long periods—30 seconds or more. But within that 30-second stretch, every few seconds there is a slight shift in thoughts, feelings, actions, stance, and so on, which rapidly renews or reengages the mind. The basic unit of the present moment is preserved; it is only reapplied for a number of times.

Now that we have an idea of what we mean by *now*, how long a present moment is, and what it achieves in that time, we can ask, in the next chapter, how present moments are organized.

Chapter 4

THE PRESENT MOMENT AS A LIVED STORY: *Its Organization*

A PRESENT MOMENT CONTAINS the essential elements to compose a *lived story*. This is a special kind of story because it is lived as it happens, not as it is put into words afterwards. It is nonverbal and need not be put into words, even though it could be with difficulty. It is of very short duration compared to most stories. It is made up mostly of feelings that unfold, a sort of untold emotional narrative.

Certain terms need to be clarified. The *narrative format* is a structure for mentally organizing (without language) our experience with motivated human behavior. *Lived stories* are experiences that are narratively formated in the mind but not verbalized or told. A told story—i.e., a narrative—is the telling to someone about the lived story.

A look at child development may help clarify these distinctions. First, the child must be able to parse and format his or her experience into the narrative format—into a lived story. This occurs very early, before language, well before 18 months of life. The central idea is that infants, early in preverbal life, tend to parse and experience the human world in terms of intentions, as do adults. This is a natural tendency of mind. The narrative format is designed to build meanings around intentions (there are emotional as well as cognitive *meanings*). This is largely what Bruner (1990) meant when he argued for the primacy of "acts of meaning" in our parsing of human social interactions. Second, the child must become verbal with a fair use of tense (i.e., past, present, future). This happens during the second year of life. Finally, the child must acquire the ability to render into language the lived story in the form of a told story. Beginning around three or four years of age, children start to tell autobiographical narratives. Their told stories remain fairly primitive until about six years of age (Favez, 2003; Nelson, 1989; Peterson & McCabe, 1983). This developmental sequence of lived stories, then language, then told stories is well known in development where comprehension appears much earlier than production.

The lived story and the told story (as well as the narrative format) have essential elements in common. In the present moment some of these elements may appear in incomplete form. These elements are as follows:

First, there must be a reason to create the story or become aware of a story being lived. Something must happen to bring it to psychological life. The trigger can be novelty, the unexpected, a problem, a conflict, or some kind of trouble or upset that wants resolution. It cannot be simply a list of happenings. This is why stories captivate us. A story depends upon an implicit assumption about how the world works and what can be normally expected (Bruner, 2002a, 2002b). When the normal expectation is not confirmed or is upset by events, an attempt is made to get the situation back to normal. And, finally, a coda is needed to adjust the original expectation, taking into account what just happened (Bruner, 2002). (It is like the need for assimilation and accommodation conceived by Piaget.) Bruner provided an example of what is meant by *upsetting*. "I was walking down the street when a man came up to me and said, 'would you like to buy a personal myth?' " The question violates normal expectations that personal myths are not sold (Bruner, 2002b). The coda could be something as simple as thinking, "The world is weird sometimes."

So what triggered the present moments identified in the breakfast interviews from Chapter 1? They seem utterly banal. And they are, but each is triggered by a trouble, however insignificant, in the everyday world. "Where is the butter?" and the accompanying negative feelings reflect the violation of an ordinary daily expectation. "Okay, that's all right—good for the diet" and the flood of good feelings resolves it. "What to do with this bread?" is a response to novelty, and so on. The structure of the situation is roughly the same even if the magnitude of the consequence varies widely.

Second, stories are structured around a plot. They contain a who, why, what, when, where, and how that make all the elements of the story cohere. In schools of journalism one learns to position the narrative elements to quickly capture human interest by answering the questions of who? what? where? when? why? and how? in the first sentence or two. The details are filled in later. These questions provide the information that grabs people's attention. They are the backbone of the narrative format used to understand and talk about motivated behavior (Burke, 1945). They are the stuff of gossip, that quintessential form of comprehending and relating certain human affairs, as well as the stuff of novels, myths, legal criminal cases (Bruner, 2002), and clinical life narratives (Schafer, 1981; Spence, 1976).

Finally, a story must have a line of dramatic tension that acts to carry and push the story forward from the buildup, through the crisis, to the resolution (Labov, 1972). This ties the story together temporally.

It should not be surprising that so much can be packed into a present moment; after all, the narrative format is our fundamental way of perceiving and organizing (as well as telling about) motivated human behavior. This is apparently the case at the smallest coherent units of experience as well as the larger ones, and for emotional experiences as well as cognitive ones.

The present moment as a lived story can also be shared. When that happens intersubjectivity starts to take on flesh. The moment when someone can participate in another's lived story, or can create a mutually lived story with them, a different kind of human contact is created. More than just an exchange of information has occured. That is the secret of the *here and now*. We will return to this later.

The present moment carries within its brief existence a lived story, a sort of "world in a grain of sand." Usually, the size or duration of a told narrative structure is larger and longer. This is especially so in the clinical domain, where we talk of life narratives or even transgenerational narratives. Yet, larger narrative structures are made of smaller ones that are embedded in them. The size of the smaller nested life stories is not usually explored in detail. This leads to the question: Are there minimal lived stories from which all larger narrative structures are built? I am going to answer yes, and propose that present moments are the basic building blocks.

The initial idea of a present moment that contains a lived story has been presented in a preliminary form under the name of a "proto-narrative envelope" (Stern, 1994). The word *proto* was used because it was presumed to be more primitive than and prior to language. Here, I, however, view this phenomenon not as primitive at all, but rather as a fully developed, normal and pervasive aspect of children's and adults' lives. Also, I see it as an emotional narrative that is felt rather than as a cognitively constructed story that is verbalized. For these reasons I have shifted the name from *proto-narrative envelope* to *lived story*.

Following is an exploration of each of the elements required for a lived story that follows the narrative format and the form they take within the short confines of a present moment.

THE ELEMENTS OF PLOT

Who?

Somehow, during the present moment, we have the background awareness that it is we who are living the experience. (Damasio's [1999] "background feelings" from the body—its position, tonus, arousal, and so on—would be essential to any existential sense of self.) This awareness is also concordant with current ideas of the self as a product of the embodied mind (Clark, 1997; Schore, 1994; Sheets-Johnstone, 1999; Varela, Thompson, & Roach, 1993). The early differentiation of a self who does the experiencing has been argued to occur perhaps from birth (Stern, 1985). The sense of an experiencing self survives the many experiences that partially obliterate the mental boundaries between people, such as emotional contagion, empathy, identification, projective identification, imitation, intersubjective sharing, sexual orgasm, and so on.

Regardless of, or perhaps alongside, these highly plausible explanations, the phenomenal reality remains that we are aware of our status as the experiencer. This is especially so during a present moment when James's bird of consciousness is perching and a fresh present landscape opens up. It is also true, but less so, when James's bird of consciousness is in flight, because there is so little formed experience to hold on to, only the process.

The *who* is us, as the owner of experience. Depending on the nature of the experience, the self is felt to be the subject, or agent, or patient. This awareness of experiencing hangs in the background or foreground during the entire present moment.

When?

I argued that the present moment is felt to occur during an extended now, with an immediate past, present, and future. But I did not address the phenomenal reality that we "know" or sense that the experience we are living is happening now, regardless of whether it refers to a past or future happening. Husserl and others have amply described this. I do not intend to take this point any further except to point out that the present moment is clearly situated in time phenomenologically. It has a *when*, even if that when is complex (e.g., "Yesterday I remembered that next week I will meet her at the station."). The lived present is both the reference point and the moment of experience—in other words, it is when the remembering of yesterday's memory about the future is occurring.

Why?

The question "Why?" asks about intentions. Intentions are key to both narratives and the present moment as a lived story. Intentions provide the thrust. Let us examine this more closely.

A feeling-flow of intentionality runs through the present moment. Once a fresh present is before us, its intentionality starts to unfold during its seconds on stage. Whatever is experienced during the new present moment is temporally dynamic. It flows in analogic time. There is no sequencing of separate, discrete entities; there is only a time-contoured whole—as in a musical phrase. This unfolding has a feeling of forward movement, of directionality oriented toward some goal that gets more specified en route. The present moment is going somewhere. It may reach that destination, or stop abruptly and never get there. It may be of so little interest that we do not stay with it for the ride. Regardless of the outcome, it has a momentum.

In other words, the present moment has the feeling of intentionality in movement (even if the intention is to do nothing, say nothing, think nothing, and hold still). I will call this sense of movement the "intentional-feeling-flow." But even in the philosophical sense of intention or *aboutness* there is a directionality, a "reaching out" or "stretching" of the mind toward something. The mind has been put in mental motion, so to speak.

The literature on child development, in particular, has been concerned with defining the necessary criteria for a "true" (psychological) intention, so they can reasonably ask when intentions arise developmentally. There is a general agreement that true intentions must be purposeful, and goal-directed, with means adjusted to the ends, and have some mental existence prior to action. All these criteria are met around 18 months of life (see Zelazo, 1999).

The issue of true intentions versus proto-intentions or partial intentions is worth following a little further, not only because infants appear to have many intentionlike behaviors well before 18 months, but also because unthought, unverbalized, implicit intentions and intentions that are not true (in which not all the criteria are present), also exist in adults. In fact, there are probably far more of these intentions than true intentions, given the ad hoc, ad-libbed nature of most of life.

Regardless of which criteria are used to define a true intention, psychology views the criterial elements as discrete, separate entities making up the pieces of a sequence. In contrast, from the phenomenological perspective, the intentional-feeling-flow is the analogic time-shape of the experience. It runs as a whole phrase underneath the specific contents of the intention. It is, in part, what makes the intention feel like it is leaning forward. It adds what is called a line of dramatic tension as the action closes in on an endpoint. It is part of the temporal dynamics of the experience.

In short, we can speak about the place of intentions—the *why*—as a major element of the present moment.

What, How, and Where?

These elements of the narrative structure fall into place by virtue of the specifics of the exact context of the local level in which the present moment occurs and the possibilities it presents.

In short, the essential elements of plot can be discerned in a present moment.

THE LINE OF DRAMATIC TENSION: VITALITY AFFECTS

Temporal contours and vitality affects are at the heart of micro-temporal dynamics, and the sense of dramatic tension that is crucial to lived stories. They are a large part of what makes direct experience analogic.

Vitality affects were first introduced to explain the mother's affective attunement to her infant, as an early form of inter-subjectivity (Stern et al., 1984; Stern, 1985). But the idea has a much wider application. There are two complementary notions involved. The first concerns stimulation that impinges on the nervous system from within or without. Most stimulation is contoured in real time. It has a temporal shape or contour that consists of analogic shifts (split second by split second) in the intensity, rhythm, or form of the stimulus. (Recall the firework example given earlier.) This was referred to earlier as a time-shape. I will reserve the term *temporal contour* for the objectifiable time-shape of a stimulus.

For instance, a smile seen on another's face has a distinct temporal contour that takes time to form. It grows (one might say *crescendos*) in perhaps a second or so; reaches its high point of fullness of display, which is held for a moment with small modulations; and then decomposes over, say, a second. This decomposition can be rapid, like a shutdown, or slow, like a fade-out, or anywhere in between. The whole performance flows together as one uninterrupted, several-second stimulus package. There is an anologic unfolding, not a sequence of discrete states or events. It is a behavioral phrase that is captured in a single present moment.

There are, of course, a million smiles. And the difference between them lies, in part, in their temporal contours. These differences are not trivial because much of the signal value resides in the orchestration of the temporal contouring of the performance, not in the simple fact that it is a smile with a conventional meaning. Imagine that someone you know greets you on the street with a smile. The crescendo time of the smile (is it explosive or does it sneak up?) may indicate spontaneous pleasure or guilty surprise at seeing you. The duration of holding the high point may reflect the level of pleasure. The speed of decomposition may speak to the authenticity of the display, and so on. The conventional form of a smile is only a skeleton on which the truely important part of the communication is fleshed out in the form of its temporal contour: How happy are they really to see you? Are they surprised to see you at all, or in that place, at that time? Do they want something from you that you had not anticipated? Has your relationship with them been altered in some way since you last met? The same is true for gestures and most human behavior.

Words are only partial exceptions. The symbolic reference is captured so rapidly that it is impossible to speak of the temporal contour of the transmission of the symbol. But the word as spoken, as a sound, is very rich in temporal contours, because of the presence of paralinguistics. This is evident in everyday life and in psychotherapy (Crystal, 1975; Knoblauch, 2000). Without contours, words would sound as if they were spoken by a robot. As is often said, It's not what you say; it's how you say it.

Everything we do, see, feel, and hear from people has a temporal contour. We also attribute contours to many events in nature. We are immersed in a "music" of the world at the local level—a complex polyphonic, polyrhythmic surround where different temporal contours are moving back and forth between the psychological foreground and background.

These temporal contours of stimulations play upon and within our nervous system and are transposed into contours of feelings in us. It is these contoured feelings that I am calling *vitality affects*. They are the complement to temporal contours. In other words, by *temporal contour*, I mean the objective changes (even small) over time (even short) of intensity or quality of the stimulation (internal or external). By *vitality affect*, I mean the subjectively experienced shifts in internal feeling states that accompany the temporal contour of the stimulus.

The feeling quality of vitality affects is best captured by kinetic terms such as, *surging, fading away, fleeting, explosive, tentative, effortful, accelerating, decelerating, climaxing, bursting, drawn out, reaching, hesitating, leaning forward, leaning backward,* and so on. From the moment of birth, we have continuous daily exposure to these experiences in the form of breathing, sucking, moving, defecating, swallowing, having cramps, and so on. Each has its own temporal contour and vitality affect.

Vitality affects are intrinsic to all experiences in all modalities, domains, and types of situations. They occur both in the presence and absence of Darwinian categorical affects. For example, a rush of anger or joy, a sudden flooding of light, an accelerating sequence of thoughts, a wave of feeling evoked by music, a surge of pain, and a shot of narcotics can all feel like "rushes." They share a similar distribution of excitation / activation over time, a similar feeling-flow pattern—in other words, a similar vitality affect. And because of our capacities for cross-modal translation, a vitality affect evoked from one modality can be associated to a vitality affect from any other modality, or from any other time or situation. Vitality affects lend themselves to the formation of associative networks, as do symbols. These vitality affects reflect the manner in which an act is performed and the feeling behind the act that gives it its final form.

Exactly how the nervous system executes this transformation from the temporal contours of stimulation to the vitality affects of our subjective feelings is not yet fully understood. Tomkins (1962), suggested that the temporal contour of stimulation evokes a corresponding temporal contour of the density of neural firing in the nervous system. Furthermore, he linked specific patterns of neural firing to specific discrete Darwinian emotions, suggesting, for example, that regardless of the modality of the stimulation, a rapid rise in stimulus intensity (e.g., an unseen motorcycle revving up at close range causes fear, a slower rise causes interest, and so on. A sort of temporal isomorphism exists between the contour of the stimulus and the contour of neural activity. Clynes (1978) proposed a similar model but associates the temporal shape of stimulation to a different palette of feelings.

The transposition of temporal contours observed in another's behavior into the vitality affects evoked in the observer is becoming more explicable in light of research on mirror neurons, adaptive oscillators, and internal timing mechanisms (e.g., tau theory).

The basic notion behind vitality affects has been around for a long time. Philosopher Langer (1967) spoke in terms of "forms of feeling" in the experience of music. In movement, music, and dance, the notion of "effort/shape" described by Lamb (1979) and the methods of Dalcroze (Bachman, 1994; Boepple, 1910) are essentially based on the intuition of vitality affects. Kestenberg (1965a, 1965b, 1967) has developed a system of movement analysis for children with various disorders, using the work of the aforementioned authors and particularly that of Laban (1967).

Vitality affects are also a pervasive feature of modern dance, under various guises and styles (Jowitt, 1988). Tustin (1990) described the "feeling shapes" experienced by autistic children during their stereotypic motor behaviors. My notion of vitality affects is less specific than that of Tompkins or Clynes, more situationally general than that of Langer or Tustin, and more focused on feelings than on movements. I assume that vitality affects result from any and all experiences, and the type of feeling evoked is not innately or tightly tied to the nature of the temporal contour of the stimulation. The "background feelings" identified by Damasio (1999) appear to overlap with vitality affects. However, he is less concerned with the diachronic, analogic aspects and he focuses mainly but not only on feelings emanating from the body.

Vitality affects also underlie the appreciation of most abstract art forms that are formally devoid of "content," such as most music and much dance. (see Jowitt, 1988; Langer, 1967; Stern, 1985). Anyone involved in the arts takes all this for granted. Still, it may be instructive to look at the micro-momentary local level in the performing arts.

Given that the phrase is the process unit at the local level in music, it is fascinating to listen to a conductor shape the performance of his orchestra. Many radio programs broadcast rehearsals or master classes. The conductor says things like "No, attack those first notes more fiercely, *da da daaa.* . . . Yes, good. Now, more pianissimo right after, and for the next phrase, too. . . . Now, here, build up more slowly, s-l-o-w-l-y. . . . No, it can't just stop, it fades away, like this. . . ."

Choreographers do the same type of shaping and refining. And again it is at the level of the gesture and the phrase.

"When you turn your head there, don't just turn it fast. It's got to snap to the other side like you've been slapped. . . . Here, wait just a moment, behind the beat, before you rush together, then explode, *wham*. . . . Stop like you're surprised. . . . No, that position is too solid; make it like you're leaning over a cliff and could fall forward. . . ."

These fine tunings of the written notes or dance steps involve the adjustment of the vitality affects embodied in the phrases. This is what makes an interpretation, and what distinguishes an artistic performance from a technical one. The difference is one of elastic rhythms versus formal rhythms. The magic of elastic rhythms is in the precise shaping of the vitality affects to express the exact feelings that are behind the acts transmitted to the audience. And the magic in a therapy session or in intimate relations, beyond or underneath the explicit meanings, also lies there. This is where authenticity resides.*

All of this is highly relevant because one of our major questions is: How do we transmit to others what we feel and what it feels like to be us?

Many visual arts like painting and photography appear to

---

* The distinction between technical performances and artistic interpretations has always been marked as important, even essential. It has an interesting technical history in the evolution of "recorded" music. By the end of the nineteenth century, pianos driven by folded strips of paper with indendations was well advanced. It produced that characteristic mechanical timing. To capture the temporally dynamic sound of an interpretation, a "welte-mignon" was designed in 1904. It was a piano containing a machine that rolled out paper, and whenever a note was struck it drew a line on the paper. Known artists were invited to play their renditions of musical classics on this machine and their temporal style was faithfully recorded in this fashion. Afterwards, the lines that the notes made while the artist was playing were cut out, leaving an indented paper that could be played back on a specially adapted player piano and produce a replica of the actual interpretation, with all the vitality affects characteristic of the performer (Benhôte, 1972). The phonograph soon made the welte-mignon obsolete. But the efforts taken say much.

have no temporal contour because they freeze an image in time. It becomes timeless. Although that is true for the work, it is not true for the physical and mental acts of viewing. Physically, there are scanning eye movements, head adjustments, and sometimes position changes needed to "see" the work (Clark, 1997; Sheets-Johnstone, 1984; Varela, Thompson, & Rosch, 1993). These take time to execute and usually the artist has constructed the work so that the eye follows certain scanning paths with their own time-shapes based on color complements or contrasts, lines of force, movements between background and foreground, and so on. These scanning paths are visual-motor-affective-cognitive phrases producing temporally filled vitality affects. The impressionist painter Bonnard is reported to have said, "A picture is a succession of blobs that link up and eventually give its form to the object, allowing the eye to travel over its detail without a hitch" (Melikian, 2002, p. 9).

Painter David Hockney has consciously explored this reality by creating collages of photographs of the "same" subject from several slightly different angles and distances. His idea is that the activity of seeing, especially up close (e.g., seeing the face of the person in bed with you), involves many different views of the same object over a short time period, so that reality is more like a cubist painting than not (Hockney, 1986). And the more one looks, the more the scanning patterns shift.

Besides the physical act of viewing, which has a temporal contour, there are two different mental acts that occur when one is faced with a static image. Both have a temporal dimension. The first is the interplay between immediate perception and immediate memory. The viewing of one section of a painting during one instant occurs with the immediate memory of another section that was just viewed, and so on. The path of scanning has a memorial-perceptual unfolding. This is not so different from the situation with music.

The second mental act involves imagining a temporal narrative line. This is most evident in photography, which captures an action or "story" in midstream, or as Cartier-Bresson (1952) called it, the "decisive moment." What is fascinating about the decisive moment is that the viewer provides, in imagination, the action leading up to the decisive moment, and the resolving action. An imaginary temporal contour is added while one watches a static image. It becomes a small emotional narrative—again, "a world in a grain of sand."

The way a static image is framed and centered can also evoke a temporal experience. For example, a hanging Japanese scroll of fish in a stream, created by Maruyama Okyo (1733–1795)*, led to three different senses of felt movement: the rapid flow of the water, the circling of the fish with and against the current, and, most extraordinary, the desire of the viewer to move his head and eyes. The picture is framed so that only a very small part of the stream is seen, as if you were on the bank of the stream, leaning down toward it and tilting your head. You feel that in the next second you will have to pull back and raise your head to look up-or downstream to situate the scene. But of course, you are held there by the frame. A muscular dynamic is put in motion with its own vitality affect.

Temporal contours and vitality affects are part of all our experiences, banal and aesthetic. They make up not only the style or manner of doing things, but provide the feeling behind our experience. They put dynamic time back into experience. The style in which performances, everyday or otherwise, are done requires much more attention from the field of psychology. It involves temporal dynamics (see Sheets-Johnstone 1999). Vitality affects are part of what has been missing in our

---

* "Sweetfish in Summer and Autumn," exhibited in *Exhibition of Japanese Art from the Mary Griggs Burke Collection*, Metropolitan Museum of Art, New York, March 22–June 1, 2000.

psychologies. We have been surprisingly blind to temporal dynamics, especially micro-temporal dynamics, even though we live them every moment and even though we cannot begin to explain the specialness of an interpretative performance without them.

We can now return to the feeling of moving or leaning forward that runs through the present moment. Recall the forward movement of a musical phrase toward some resolution. Vitality affects, like musical phrases, carry the feeling of leaning forward across the present moment.

In sum, vitality affects acting with the intentional-feeling-flow provide a line of dramatic tension that gives a feeling-coherence to the unfolding of the present moment. The vitality affects act like a temporal backbone on which the plot is hung. They also help the chunking process by containing the phrase within one envelope. They give the present moment the dramatic feel of a lived story.

UPSETTING EXPECTATIONS OR "TROUBLE"

One cannot speak of upsetting the expected or trouble in the narrative unless the elements of the narrative structure are clear, their balance intuitively measured and their noncanonicality sensed. However, phenomenologically, while one is in the middle of a present moment as it evolves, its exact outcome is unpredictable and open to all sorts of troublelike eventualities and upsets. In this sense there is an inherent incertitude as to what may happen. This is a kind of nonspecific, potential trouble. There are also specific upsets from unexpected or unwanted affects that arise as the moment unfolds.

In summary, the present moment is subjectively experienced as a lived story. And it can be objectively described as an experience that has a narrative format, structurally and temporally. As we shall later see, this makes it more usable as a clinical phenomenon.

Now a context must be provided for the present moment so its relevance in clinical situations becomes more apparent.

Part II
CONTEXTUALIZING
THE PRESENT MOMENT

Chapter 5

THE INTERSUBJECTIVE MATRIX

THE PRESENT MOMENTS that interest us most are those that arise when two people make a special kind of mental contact—namely, an intersubjective contact. This involves the mutual interpenetration of minds that permits us to say, "I know that you know that I know" or "I feel that you feel that I feel." There is a reading of the contents of the other's mind. Such readings can be mutual. Two people see and feel roughly the same mental landscape for a moment at least. These meetings are what psychotherapy is largely about. They also provide the happenings that change our lives and become the memories that compose the story of our intimate relationships. Accordingly, the moments of intersubjective contact between people become a most relevant context for us to examine.

Moments of intersubjective creation are special present moments. I return to a question posed in the beginning of the book. How is *now*, or the present moment, experienced when it is cocreated and shared with someone in a moment of intersubjective contact?

We are capable of "reading" other people's intentions and feeling within our bodies what they are feeling. Not in any mystical way, but from watching their face, movements, and posture, hearing the tone of their voice, and noticing the immediate context for their behavior. We are quite good at this "mind reading," even though our intuitions need verifying and fine-tuning (Whiten, 1991).

Nature has designed our brain and mind so that we can directly intuit others' possible intentions by watching their goal-directed actions (even without knowing the goal). As they raise their hand to the side of their head we immediately assume that they will scratch their head, adjust their glasses, probe their ear, or smooth their hair. As their hand gets closer and starts to position itself for the chosen goal, we guess it. Similarly, by seeing their facial expression, posture, and movements, we can directly feel something very like what they are feeling. And, while we are talking to them and they are silently listening, we can feel their shifting responses to what we are saying by watching the small movements of their facial features, their head and gaze direction, and the tone of the background sounds of their voice. Affective expressions tell about what we are thinking as well as what we are feeling. And when they move, we can feel what it must be like to move that way. We feel it in our body and sense it in our mind, together. You can also grasp what a group is experiencing.

Our nervous systems are constructed to be captured by the nervous systems of others, so that we can experience others *as if* from within their skin, as well as from within our own. A sort of direct feeling route into the other person is potentially open and we resonate with and participate in their experiences, and they in ours. (I will give the evidence that supports this view shortly.)

Other people are not just other objects but are immediately recognized as special kinds of objects, objects like us, available for sharing inner states. In fact, our minds naturally work to seek out the experiences in others that we can resonate with. We naturally parse others' behavior in terms of the inner states that we can grasp, feel, participate in, and thus share.

This must be seen in the light of our being highly social animals who probably spend the majority of our lives in the presence of others, real or imagined. Sometimes our imagined companions are vivid presences; at other times, they are vague background figures or audiences or witnesses that float in and out of our awareness. But they are there nonetheless.

When we put all this together, a certain intersubjective world emerges. We no longer see our minds as so independent, separate, and isolated. We are no longer the sole owners, masters, and guardians of our subjectivity. The boundaries between self and others remain clear but more permeable. In fact, a differentiated self is a condition of intersubjectivity. Without it there would be only fusion (Rochat & Morgan, 1995; Stern, 1985). We live surrounded by others' intentions, feelings, and thoughts that interact with our own, so that what is ours and what belongs to others starts to break down. Our intentions are modified or born in a shifting dialogue with the felt intentions of others. Our feelings are shaped by the intentions, thoughts, and feelings of others. And our thoughts are cocreated in dialogue, even when it is only with ourselves.

In short, our mental life is cocreated. This continuous cocreative dialogue with other minds is what I am calling the intersubjective matrix.

The idea of a one-person psychology or of purely intrapsychic phenomena are no longer tenable in this light. Current thinking in psychoanalysis has moved a great distance in the recent past from a one-person to a two-person psychology (Renik, 1993). I am suggesting here that we move even further. We used to think of intersubjectivity as a sort of epiphenomenon that arises occasionally when two separate and independent minds interact. Now we view the intersubjective

77

matrix (which is a special subset of the culture and of psycho-therapy) as the overriding crucible in which interacting minds take on their current form.

Two minds create intersubjectivity. But equally, intersubjectivity shapes the two minds. The center of gravity has shifted from the intrapsychic to the intersubjective.

Similarly, intersubjectivity in the clinical situation can no longer be considered only as a useful tool or one of many ways of being with another that comes and goes as needed. Rather, the therapeutic process will be viewed as occurring in an ongoing intersubjective matrix. All physical and mental acts will be viewed as having an important intersubjective determinant because they are embedded in this intersubjective tissue. Of course, some material comes from the repertoire (past and present) of one individual, but even then, its moment of appearance on the scene, the exact final form it takes, and the coloration of its meaning are fashioned in the intersubjective matrix.

EVIDENCE FOR THE INTERSUBJECTIVE MATRIX

What, then, is the evidence for such an intersubjective matrix? The following discussion attempts to answer this question. It is not meant to be exhaustive, but rather to simply lend support for the idea.

Neuroscientific Evidence

The discovery of *mirror neurons* has been crucial. Mirror neurons provide possible neurobiological mechanisms for understanding the following phenomena: reading other people's states of mind, especially intentions; resonating with another's emotion; experiencing what someone else is experiencing; and capturing an observed action so that one can imitate it—in short, empathizing with another and establishing intersubjective contact (Gallese & Goldman, 1998; Rizzolatti & Arbib, 1998; Rizzolatti, Fadiga, Fogassi, & Gallese, 1996; Rizzolatti, Fogassi, & Gallese, 2001).

Mirror neurons sit adjacent to motor neurons. They fire in an observer who is doing nothing but watching another person behave (e.g., reaching for a glass). And the pattern of firing in the observer mimics the exact pattern that the observer would use if he were reaching for the glass himself. In brief, the visual information we receive when we watch another act gets mapped onto the equivalent motor representation in our own brain by the activity of these mirror neurons. It permits us to directly participate in another's actions without having to imitate them. We experience the other *as if* we were executing the same action, feeling the same emotion, making the same vocalization, or being touched as they are being touched. These *as if* mechanisms have been described by Damasio (1999) and Gallese (2001). This "participation" in another's mental life creates a sense of feeling / sharing with / understanding the person, in particular, the person's intentions and feelings. (I am purposely using the term *feelings* instead of *affects* so as to include sentiments, sensory sensations, and motor sensations, along with classical Darwinian affects.)

Clearly, the mirror neuron system may take us far into understanding (at the neural level) contagion, resonance, empathy, sympathy, identification, and intersubjectivity. At this point, the evidence for such a resonance system is solid for hand, mouth, face, vocal and foot actions. Some have stressed a potential role for mirror neurons in language acquisition. I believe that will prove a less interesting path than its importance for intersubjectivity in general.

There is another feature of this system: It is particularly sensitive to goal-directed actions (i.e., movements with a readily inferrable intention). Further, the perception of an attributable intention seems to have its own brain localization—a sort of intention-detecting center (Blakemore & Decety, 2001). For example, the intention-detector brain center is activated if the action, in its context, seems to have an intention. If the exact same movement is seen, in a different context where no intention can be attributed, the brain center will not activate.

The long-standing idea of a human tendency of mind to perceive and interpret the human world in terms of intentions is strengthened by such findings. And the reading of others' intentions is cardinal to intersubjectivity.

There is another finding that may serve as a neural correlate for intersubjectivity. To resonate with someone, you may have to be unconsciously in synch with that person. You could move in synchrony, as lovers may do when they sit across a coffee table and trace a dance as they simultaneously approach and withdraw their faces from one another or move their hands together at the same instant. Or you could coordinate the speed and rate of change of your movements to jointly create some kind of everyday practical pas de deux—for example, you wash the dishes and the other person dries them. You hand the wet washed dish to the dryer in one smooth joint motion with no pause in between. And you regard each other only with a peripheral gaze.

Some mechanisms must be available for this dyadic coordination. The discovery of adaptive oscillators may provide a clue. These oscillators act like clocks within our body. They can be reset over and over and their rate of firing can be adjusted to match the rate of an incoming stimulation. These inner clocks use the real-time properties of incoming signals (e.g., from someone handing you a dish) to "set" your adaptive oscillators, so that they immediately bring their own rate of neural firing into synch with the periodicity of the incoming signal (Port & van Gelder, 1995; Torras, 1985). The result is that the outreaching arm of the person drying the dishes is perfectly coordinated in time with the outreaching hand of the person handing over the dish. Lee (1998) has devised elegant models (tau theory) to describe how this kind of dyadic coordination and synchrony could occur.

The need for such a mechanism is evident when one thinks about the extraordinary temporal coordination human beings and animals are capable of. Think how easy it is for us to kick a moving soccer ball while we are running or catch a fly ball on the run. In interpersonal interactions the problems of temporal coordination may be even more complex because we alter trajectories more rapidly and unpredictably than moving balls do. Even so, when two people move their heads together for a kiss, even for a first-time, sudden, passionate kiss, they rarely end up breaking their front teeth. There is usually a soft landing.

Other recent work on phase synchronization and large scale integration in the brain promises to throw more light on these phenomena at fundamental levels (Varela, Lachaux, Rodriguez, & Martinerie, 2001).

The essential point is that when people move synchronously or in temporal coordination, they are participating in an aspect of the other's experience. They are partially living from the other's center.

So far, all of this evidence is applicable to one-way intersubjectivity ("I know what you are feeling."). But what about two-way, or full, intersubjectivity? An apparent redundancy? ("I know that you know that I know what you are feeling, and vice versa.") This requires another step. Could the mechanisms previously described be sufficient? At least two "readings" of the other are required for two-way intersubjectivity. The first is to know what the other is experiencing. The second is to know how the other is experiencing your experience of him or her. There is a recursive or reiterative reading going on. The role of context is crucial here. The presence of one-way intersubjectivity is the determining context in which the second reading of the other must be interpreted to arrive at full inter-subjectivity. Still something more than a resonant mechanism, even reiterated, may be needed. We will address this shortly as a developmental issue.

There is a problem. If these mechanisms work so well that we live completely in an intersubjective matrix, why are we not constantly captured by the nervous systems of others and permeated by their experience? Now that we know that clear mechanisms exist to permit intersubjectivity, the question becomes not how do we *do* it, but how do we *stop*? Clearly the system needs brakes. In fact, there are three sets of brakes. The first is selection. There must be a gating of attention so that the other is sufficiently taken in and engaged by the mind, or is excluded from the process. Another set is needed to make sure the activation of mirror neurons does not spill over to trigger corresponding motor neurons with the result of automatic or reflexive imitation as seen in demented patients with echo-praxia, or "imitative behavior" (cited in Gallese, 2001). A third set is needed to inhibit, or, more accurately, to dose the degree of resonance with the other. This is an area of great potential, both neuroscientifically and clinically. Recall that many psy-chiatric disorders are characterized in part by a lack of empathy and an inability to adopt the others' point of view. I am not thinking of the extreme case of autism, but of narcissistic, bor-derline, and antisocial personalities, where this lack can be striking and causes patients the problems that bring them to psychotherapy.

Even within the normal range, people differ greatly in the manifestation of certain forms of intersubjectivity. Are their basic mechanisms for resonance compromised? Or are their systems of braking and inhibiting their intersubjective immer-sion overworking? What is the role of experience during devel-opment in setting these parameters? Much research is needed here.

Developmental Evidence

Beginning right after birth, early forms of intersubjectivity can be seen in infants. This argues for the fundamental nature of the intersubjective matrix in which we develop. Several researchers have described intersubjective behaviors in preverbal, presymbolic infants. This very early manifestation of intersubjectivity speaks to the issue of innateness. Beebe, Knoblauch, Rustin, and Sorter (2002) provided an excellent review and comparison of three parallel approaches to early intersubjectivity.

Trevarthen (1974, 1979, 1980, 1988, 1993, 1999 / 2000; Trevarthen & Hubley, 1978) found primary intersubjectivity in very young infants by observing the tight mutual coordination of infant and mother behavior in free play: the timing of their movements, the onset of their facial expressions, and their anticipation of the intentions of the other. For instance, in one experiment, the mother and infant interact via a television setup, so that they are actually in separate rooms but see and hear each other on a monitor as if sitting face-to-face. If a split-second delay in the sound or sight of the behaving mother is experimentally introduced, the infant quickly notices and the interaction breaks up. Correspondence is already expected in interhuman contact. Correspondence is the key word that leads Trevarthen to speak of "primary intersubjectivity."

Early imitation has been another major route to proposing early forms of intersubjectivity (Kugiumutzakis, 1998, 1999, 2002; Maratos, 1973; Meltzoff, 1981, 1995; Meltzoff & Gopnik, 1993; Meltzoff & Moore, 1977, 1999). Meltzoff and colleagues began by focusing on neonates imitating actions seen on an experimenter's face (e.g., sticking the tongue out). How could one explain such behaviors when the infant did not know he had a face or tongue—when he only saw a visual image of the experimenter's act—yet responded with a motor act guided by his own proprioceptive (not visual) feedback? And when there had been no previous learning trials to establish such an (invisible) imitation? The answer lay in an early form of intersubjectivity based on cross-modal transfer of form and timing. Other such examples of early imitation were found. Meltzoff and colleagues concluded that infants take in something of the other in the act of imitation, which solidifies the sense that the other is "like me" and "I am like them." He further speculates that for an infant to learn about (make internal representations of) inanimate objects she must manipulate or mouth them, but to learn about (and represent) people she must imitate them. The infant's mind uses different channels for people.

My collegues and I have taken a third route (Stern, 1977, 1985, 2000; Stern et al., 1984). I have been more interested in how the dyad lets each other know about their inner feeling states. For instance, if an infant emitted an affective behavior after an event, how could the mother let the infant know that she grasped not simply what the infant did but also the feeling the infant experienced that lay behind what he did? The emphasis has shifted from the overt behavior to the subjective experience underlying it. I proposed *affect attunement*, a form of selective and cross-modal imitation, as the path to sharing inner feeling states, in contrast to faithful imitation as the path to sharing overt behavior.

Jaffe and colleagues (2001) added another piece of suggestive evidence. They showed how preverbal infants (4 and 12 months) and mothers precisely time the starting, stopping, and pausing of their vocalizations to create a rhythmic coupling and bidirectional coordination of their vocal dialogues. This implies that they have "captured" not only their own timing but that of the other as well.

The issue of coordinated timing is obviously central for synchronicity and the access to another's experience. Watson

(1994) and Gergely and Watson (1999) have found a fascinating way that the infant becomes sensitive to the behavior and timing of others. They propose that we, and infants, have "innate contingency detection analyzers." Such modules measure the extent to which someone's behavior is exactly synchronous or responsive with your own. They find that before 3 months, infants are most interested in events that are perfectly contingent with their behavior. This would make babies most sensitive to themselves. Between 4 and 6 months there is a shift. Infants become most interested in events that are highly but imperfectly contingent with their own behavior. That is exactly what an interacting other person does. They now become most interested in the behavioral timing of others, using themselves as the standard.

The work of many others also bears significantly on these issues (e.g., Emde & Sorce, 1983; Klinnert, Campos, Sorce, Emde, & Svejda, 1983; Sander, 1975, 1977, 1995b; Stern, 1971, Stern & Gibbon, 1978; Tronick, 1989; Tronick, Als, & Adamson, 1979; Tronick, Als, & Brazelton, 1977). Most significant, all of these authors agreed that infants are born with minds that are especially attuned to other minds as manifested through their behavior. This is based in large part on the detection of correspondences in timing, intensity, and form that are intermodally transposable. The result is that from birth on, one can speak of a psychology of mutually sensitive minds.

Further, these researchers agree that during preverbal infancy, the baby is especially sensitive to the behavior of other humans; they use different perceptual and expectational capacities in interpersonal interactions, compared to interactions with themselves or inanimate objects. They treat and expect others to be similar to them but not identical. They form presymbolic representations of others or of being-with-others. They can participate in another's mind state. In short, an early form of intersubjectivity is present.

No studies of mirror neurons or adaptive oscillators have been attempted in infants of this age. Yet, such oscillators, or something very like them, must be present.

After roughly 7 to 9 months, the scene changes somewhat. The infant becomes capable of a more elaborate form of inter-subjectivity—what Trevarthen and Hubley (1978) have called "secondary intersubjectivity" (see also Stern, 2000). These forms of intersubjectivity are also being put in place well before the infant is verbal or symbolic. The sharable mental states start to include goal-directed intentions, focus of attention, affects and hedonic evaluations, and, as before, the experience of action. Each is a partially separate domain of intersubjectivity. The participating in the other's feelings is only one such domain. There is far more work going on concerning the sharing of the focus of attention in order to triangulate an object, where the infant "passes through the other" to reach the object. This is a more cognitive aspect of intersubjectivity necessary for symbolization and language (e.g., Hobson, 2002).

Our interests are more in the feeling / experiencing domain of intersubjectivity. In this domain, the reading of intentions deserves a special mention, because intentions are central to the forms of intersubjectivity that will interest us most clinically. The argument, to summarize in advance, is that the ability to read intentions appears very early to the infant.

In all perspectives on motivated human activity, intention is central. Some psychological element is needed to push, pull, activate, or somehow put events in motion. Intentions go under many guises and variations. In folk psychology, using the examples of journalism and gossip, it is the motive—the why?—that propels the tale. In psychoanalysis it is the wish or desire. In ethology it is the activated motivation. In cybernetics it is the goal and its value. In narrative theories it can be the desire, belief, goal, motive, or trouble. Intentions, in one form or another, and in one state of completeness or another, are always there, acting as the engine driving foward the action, story, or mind.

We see the human world in terms of intentions. And we act in terms of our own. You cannot function with other humans without reading or inferring their motives or intentions. This reading or attributing of intentions is our primary guide to responding and initiating action. Inferring intentions in human behavior appears to be universal. It is a mental primitive. It is how we parse and interpret our human surroundings. If one is unable to infer the intentions of others, or profoundly uninterested in doing so, they will act outside of the human pale. Autistic people have been assumed to be in this position. So have some schizophrenics. (For a discussion of autism in schizophrenia from a phenomenological perspective, see Parnas, Bovet, & Zahavi [2002].) Recognizing and deciphering intentionality is a reasonable starting point for adaptation and survival.

There is another reason to place such weight on parsing behavior into intentions as a kind of mental primitive: The perceiving / inferring of intentions in human actions begins so early in life. Meltzoff (1995; Meltzoff & Moore, 1999) has described two situations in which preverbal infants grasp the intention of someone acting, even when they have never seen the intention fully enacted, in other words, as having reached its intended goal. In such a situation, grasping the intention requires an inference.

In one experiment, the preverbal infant watched an experimenter pick up an object and "try" to put it into a container. But the experimenter dropped the object en route, so the intended goal was not reached. Later, when the infant was brought back to the scene and given the same material, he picked up the object and directly put it into the container. In other words, he enacted the action that he assumed was intended, not the one he saw. The infant had chosen to privilege the unseen, assumed intention over the seen, actual action.

In another such experiment a preverbal infant watched an experimenter act as if he wished to pull a knob off of a dumbell-like object, but he failed. Later, when the infant was given the object, he immediately tried to pull the knob off. He succeeded and seemed pleased. If, however, the "experimenter" was a robot that performed the same failed actions, the infant, did not try to pull the knob off. Infants seem to assume that only people, not robots, have intentions that are worth inferring and imitating.

Gergely, Nadsasdy, Csibra, and Biro (1995) and Gergely and Csibra (1997) have performed a related experiment with younger infants using animated televised cartoons. Here, too, the infants watching the animation interpret the scene in terms of the intentions they infer rather than the actions they see. (The fact that the objects are animated—i.e., act like people would—is certainly crucial.) Rochat have shown the same primacy of inferred intention over seen action in infants of 9 months (Rochat, 1995, 1999; Rochat & Morgan, 1995).

In any event, the reading of intentions (at whatever developmental level) is possible and necessary from very early in life. Again, a neuroanatomical question can be asked. Is there not an already-developed center in the infant's brain, as there is in adults, that is activated in the presence of behavior to which a goal-directed intention can be attributed? There would have to be.

Braten (1998a, 1998b) has pulled together the above developmental evidence in the presymbolic infant by coining the term *altero-centered participation*. By this he meant that intersubjectivity is available in infancy by virtue of the innate ability to enter into the other's experience and participate in it. He suggested that the human mind is constructed to encounter "virtual others" and, of course, real others. His conclusions fit very well with the presence of underlying mechanisms of mirror neurons and adaptive oscillators. The notion of *virtual others* serves here as a prelude to the phenomenological perspective discussed at the end of the chapter.

At 12 months "social referencing" is seen (Emde & Sorce, 1983; Klinnert, Campos, Sorce, Emde, & Svejda, 1983). A common example is when an infant just learning to walk falls and is surprised but not really hurt. She will look to her mother's face to "know" what to feel. If the mother expresses fear and concern, the infant will cry. If she smiles, the baby will probably laugh. In other words, in situations of uncertainty or ambivalence, the affect state shown in others is pertinent to how the baby will feel.

After 18 months, when the child becomes verbal, new forms of intersubjectivity are quickly added (Astington, 1993). As soon as the infant can herself do, feel, or think something, she can probably participate in its being done, felt, or thought by others. The breadth of the child's intersubjectivity only awaits her own development. (There is an interesting unanswered question here. Could an infant participate in another's experience even before she could do it herself? This is a legitimate question, because, as a rule in development, receptive capacities appear before productive ones.)

Cognitive psychology assumes that children around the age of 5 years acquire a more general "theory of mind," developing a more formal capacity to represent mental states in others. Several versions of theory of mind in children are currently debated (e.g., Baron-Cohen, 1995; Fodor, 1992; Goldman, 1992; Gopnik & Meltzoff, 1998; Harris, 1989; Hobson, 2002; Hobson & Lee, 1999; Leslie, 1987). A major point of contention is whether (and to what extent) the ability to represent other minds is a formal cognitive process or relies on resonance or simulation that permits some kind of direct feeling access to the other's experience. Certainly, each could reinforce the other as development proceeds. But I cannot imagine any fundamental base for intersubjectivity without resonance, or sympathy by whatever mechanism. In the last analysis, it is about feeling, not cognition (see also Widlocher, 1996).

There are two other points worth mentioning. Dyadic intersubjectivity requires some kind of recursive participation in or representation of the other's mind. Theory of mind may be helpful in such considerations, at least after infancy. For instance, one-way intersubjectivity—("I know / feel that you . . .")—does not require a theory of mind. However, the intersubjective reiteration necessary for two-way intersubjectivity—"I (or we) know / feel that you know that I (we) know . . ."—may not need a theory of mind either, but would be greatly enhanced by it when it develops. (The sharp distinction I have drawn between one-way and dyadic intersubjectivity is excessive, especially in practice. In most situations it is more fruitful to think in terms of degrees of symmetry and asymmetry, where these represent the poles of a spectrum.)

I believe that many theory of mind theorists set too strict criteria of when a true theory of mind can be assumed, often using the ability to represent false beliefs in others as the sole and ultimate criterion (around five years). Yet the work of Dunn (1999) and Reddy and colleagues (Reddy, 1991; Reddy, Williams, & Vaughn, 2002) on younger children's joking, teasing, tricking, lying, and being mean suggests that even earlier forms of theory of mind are frequently seen in natural settings.

In brief, the developmental evidence suggests that beginning at birth the infant enters into an intersubjective matrix. This is assured because basic forms of intersubjectivity are manifest right away. As new capacities are developed and new experiences become available the infant will be swept into the intersubjective matrix, which has its own ontogenesis. The breadth and complexity of this matrix expands rapidly, even during the first year of life when the infant is still presymbolic and preverbal. Then, as the infant reaches the second year and is capable of new experiences, such as, for example, the "moral" emotions of shame, guilt, and embarassment, these emotions are drawn into the intersubjective matrix as something he can now experience within himself and in others. Intersubjective richness expands again with the advent of more developed cognitive capacities during childhood. And again, at each phase of life course development, the intersubjective matrix grows deeper and richer.

The work of Hofer (1994) provided a sort of neurobiological analogue for the intersubjective matrix. He found in the mother-pup relationship among rats that the mother's behaviors (e.g., licking, touching, vocalizing) play a crucial role in regulating the infant's physiology (e.g., heart rate, body temperature, digestion, hormone levels). What is most surprising is the specificity of which maternal behavior regulates which physiological mechanisms. These findings are analogous in the sense that the rat pups developing physiological homeostasis might appear under the control of their own regulatory mechanisms—a one-rat biopsychology. Instead, they are also under the control of the mothers overt behaviors—a two-rat biopsychology. In a similar fashion for intersubjectivity, the intentions and feelings that are laid down in the developing human baby are strongly regulated and subject to the influence of the mother's expressed experience.

Suggestive Clinical Evidence

The world experienced by autistic people continues to amaze. What makes autistic people so strange and yet so fascinating is that they look so completely human, but violate so much of what we expect of humans. They appear to live outside of our familar intersubjective matrix. There are several moving accounts of this condition. Some, such as Temple Grandin's (1995) autobiographical picture—with an introduction by Oliver Sacks—concern adults with Asperger's syndrome, a higher functioning subcategory of the autistic spectrum. These accounts are perhaps the most telling, because with Asperger's syndrome the clinical picture is less cluttered with the incapacities and other pathological forms seen in many other forms of autism when some degree of pervasive developmental disorder is present.

Other accounts focus more on children with various forms of autism (e.g. Baron-Cohen, 1995; Happé, 1998; Hobson, 1993; Maestro, Muratori, Cavallaro et al., 2002; Nadel & Butterworth, 1999; Nadel & Peze, 1993; Sigman & Capps, 1997). But there, too, these children's avoidance of eye contact (the window into the other's soul and mind), relative unresponsiveness to human contact (physical and psychological), and disinterest or inablility to communicate verbally or nonverbally (except in instrumental ways) are invariably commented on. Concerning this last point, an example serves. When infants toward the end of the first year of life start to point, two kinds of pointing are distinguished: pointing to get something and pointing to show something that is interesting or novel. Only the second kind of pointing is intersubjective in the sense that the intention is to share the same experience. Some autistic children point, but only to get something they want, very rarely to share experience.

What strikes one most about autistic people, is that they are not immersed in an intersubjective matrix. There appears to be a failure of "mindreading." Even more, one receives the impression that there is no interest in reading another's behavior or mind, as if it had no special attraction or possibilities, no more than an inanimate object. Others, like Tustin (1990), have claimed that this "disinterest" and nonattention to things human is defensive, to protect them from painfully low thresholds for human stimulation. Even if this explanation is correct, in whole for some cases or in part for others, the result is the same. The human world is not treated as special, and "like them."

There is a massive failure of intersubjectivity. They appear to be "mind blind." It is this that make autists often appear odd, or from "another world," as Sacks put it when he describes Grandin as "an anthropologist from Mars" who struggles to understand the other humans that surround her. There is no intellectual impairement here, she is a Ph.D. and world-renowned in her speciality. Yet she has to remember to ask if someone is hungry or thirsty because it does not come to her directly, empathically, but rather as a logical probability given the circumstances. One of the human events that most mystifies her is watching children play. She doesn't understand what makes them suddenly laugh or fight. She does not engage in intimate social friendships. They are too complicated and incomprehensible.

Indeed, many of the educational efforts with high-functioning autistic people are directed at social interchanges of the most instrumental kind, such as when to say "thank you," "you're welcome," "would you like to sit down," and so on. Normally, such responses flow directly from participating in another's experience.

Braten (1998b) provided an illuminating clinical anecdote on this point. When a mother puts up her hands, palms forward, her normal infant is likely to also put up his hands so that their palms touch (preliminary to pat-a-cake games). Is that an imitation? Yes, in the sense that the infant has done what the mother did. Yet the infant is seeing his mother's palms, not the back of her hands. Why doesn't he put the back of his hands against the palms of her hands, and in that way be able to see his own palms just as he saw hers? That is just what many autistic children do. Normal infants have imitated from within the mother's point of view, which they participated in. Autistic children have imitated from their own point of view, with only partial participation in the mother's experience.

The existence of autism is not in itself evidence for the intersubjective matrix. However, the picture of people living without being immersed in an intersubjective matrix gives a perspective on the matrix we normally live in. This matrix is like oxygen. We breathe it all the time without noticing its presence. When confronted with autism, we can sense the world without oxygen, and it is a shock.

Support from Phenomenology

I had hoped to find a god or goddess from antiquity who held the gift of mindreading (not future-telling) and could offer it to a human. This gift would make others' minds transparent. I have yet to find such a deity. My colleagues knowledgable in such matters assured me that my search is in vain. At least in Western antiquity, the mind was not confined to and imprisoned in the head or in the heart of one person. The mind circulated more freely, constantly receiving input from nature and the gods. It did not belong to someone as secret, private property. There was little need for the gift of making other's minds transparent.

Historically, we, in the modern, scientifically-oriented West, have isolated the mind from the body, from nature, and from other minds. Our experience of our body, nature, and other minds has to be constructed privately and perhaps quite idiosyncratically within our own mind. Until recently this view has been dominant and largely unchallenged except by philosophers.

We are now experiencing a revolution, not back to the views of antiquity, but closer to them. This revolution has been inspired largely by the work of the philosopher of phenomenology, Edmund Husserl (1913 / 1962, 1930 / 1980, 1930 / 1989, 1931 / 1960, 1964). The phenomenological approach has been has been revitalized by contemporary philosophers and incorporated by some scientists into current alternative views of human nature that are rapidly gaining strength (e.g., Beer, 1995; Clark, 1997, 1999; Damasio, 1994, 1999; Freeman, 1999a, 1999b; Gallagher, 1997; Marbach, 1999; Sheets-Johnstone, 1999; Thompson, 2001; Varela, 1996, 1999; Zahavi, 1996, 1999, 2001).

This new view assumes that the mind is always embodied in and made possible by the sensorimotor activity of the person, that it is interwoven with and cocreated by the physical environment that immediately surrounds it, and that it is constituted by way of its interactions with other minds. The mind takes on and maintains its form and nature from this open traffic. The mind emerges and exists, from intrinsic self-organizing processes, interacting with other minds. Without these constant interactions there would be no recognizable mind.

One of the consequences of this view of "embodied cognition" is that the mind is, by nature, "intersubjectively open," as it is partially constituted through its interaction with other minds (Husserl, 1931 / 1960; Thompson, 2001; Zahavi, 1996, 2001). What this means is that human beings possess a mental primitive described as "the passive (not voluntarily initiated), prereflected experience of the other as an embodied being like oneself . . ." (Thompson, 2001, p. 12).

Neurobiologically speaking, this prereflective experience of intersubjective openness can be seen as emerging from mechanisms such as mirror neurons, adaptive oscillators, and other similar processes likely to be found soon. But at the experiential level, this intersubjective openness creates the conditions for the primary intersubjectivity (synchrony, imitation, attunement, etc.) seen in early infancy, and for the manifestations of secondary intersubjectivity (such as "true" empathy) seen later. It is in this sense, I believe, that Braten (1998a) wrote of the infant's being made by nature to encounter "virtual others." We are preprepared to enter into the intersubjective matrix, which is a condition of humanness.

Any consideration of the process of psychotherapy must take into account the above premises. The existence of an intersubjective matrix defines the psychological context in which the therapeutic relationship takes form. Transference and countertransference are only special cases of a constant process. The idea of a one-person psychology is unthinkable in this situation.

These considerations throw another light on present moments. Intersubjective meetings are of relatively short duration. They are created in one or several present moments. So the present moment remains a fundamental process unit in the cocreation of the intersubjective matrix.

Chapter 6.

INTERSUBJECTIVITY AS A BASIC, PRIMARY MOTIVATIONAL SYSTEM

INTERSUBJECTIVITY is a condition of humanness. I will suggest that it is also an innate, primary system of motivation, essential for species survival, and has a status like sex or attachment.

The desire for intersubjectivity is one of the major motivations that drives a psychotherapy forward. Patients want to be known and to share what it feels like to be them. Granted, this desire is partially counterbalanced by various trepidations. When we look at the therapeutic process closely we find that it is more easily understood as the regulation of the intersubjective field between therapist and patient. This desire to be known and the ongoing regulation of the intersubjective space are also essential features of any intimate friendship.

These considerations have led me to examine intersubjectivity from an even larger perspective than psychotherapy and to see if it is best viewed as a basic human need. A basic motivational system should be a universal tendency to behave in a way characteristic of a species. This tendency should strongly favor species survival. It should be universal and innate, though it can require important environmental shaping. It must have a preemptive quality so that its value to the organism can take precedence, and behaviors can be enlisted, assembled, and organized as needed. It is not a constant pressure but can be activated and deactivated. To what extent does intersubjectivity meet these criteria?

CONFERRING SURVIVAL ADVANTAGE

Intersubjectivity makes three main contributions to assuring survival: It promotes group formation, it enhances group functioning, and it assures group cohesion by giving rise to morality. The same impulse that contributes to species survival can also serve to make psychotherapy and psychic intimacy among friends possible.

Group Formation

Humans are a relatively defenseless species. We survive because of our brains and coordinated group activity. Human survival depends on group formation (families, tribes, societies) and almost constant group cohesion. We are the most hypersocial and interdependent of all mammals. Many different capacities and motivations act together to form and maintain groups: attachment ties, sexual attraction, dominance hierachies, love, sociability. Intersubjectivity must be added to the list.

Regardless of how we define intersubjectivity, it must operate for groups as well as dyads. The couple is a subsystem of the basic units of evolutionary adaptiveness: the family and the tribe. In this regard, the work of Fivaz and the Lausanne Group (Fivaz-Depeursinge, 2001; Fivaz-Depeursinge & Corboz-Warnery, 1998) takes on particular importance. They have demonstrated that in the early phases of family formation, when the baby is only 3 to 6 months old, one starts to see the beginnings of a three-way intersubjectivity among mother, father, and baby. Intersubjectivity must exist among three as well as two in order to forge a psychological triad with reciprocity, even if asymmetrical—in other words, an intersubjectively intimate family.

These authors have shown, for example, that when a 3- to 6-month-old baby, mother, and father are seated in a triangle, a fascinating three-way interplay may occur that suggests triadic intersubjectivity. For instance, as they play together as a threesome, the baby is likely to rapidly alternate her orientations and affect signals between her parents, as if to share her pleasure and interest, or frustration, with both. Or, as she plays with, say, the father and something exciting and pleasurable transpires between them, she is likely to turn to look at the mother, as if to say: "Did you see that?" Most interestingly, if something unexpected or strange has happened between the baby and one of the parents, the baby is likely to turn to the other parent, with a look as if to say: "What is that about?" Here we may be witnessing an early form of social referencing.

By 9 months, three way (triangular) social referencing has been differentiated; the baby will regularly "consult" the faces of her parents about what is happening between them or in the environment. The processes by which they respond—reading her mind, affectively attuning to her feelings, sometimes hitting it right, sometimes missing—will remain in the implicit mode and may constitute key moments of creating meanings as a threesome.

The domain of the family's intersubjective experience grows with time in the life of a family. It takes on new dimensions with development (for instance, with the advent of moral emotions and then co-narratives) and also with the size of the family. The very same phenomena observed in the triangle emerges in the family unit when it enlarges to a foursome or more (F. Frascarolo, personal communication, April 8, 1998).

This shared history is part of the glue that defines the family's identity and status as a unique unit. Families may, in fact,

achieve remarkable levels of intersubjective richness and sub-
tlety. This is often apparent when an "outsider" sits in on a
lively family dinner. Language flirts around the edges of the
family's shared past experience, making only fleeting references. Short circuits, ellipses, and code words abound. The
family members immediately grasp what is in the mind of the
other family members. And the outsider, although having
understood the face meaning of each word, cannot compre-
hend those moments when the whole group bursts into laughter or when a shift in affective tone occurs.

Broadly speaking, the intersubjective motivational system
concerns regulating psychological belonging versus psychological aloneness. The poles of this spectrum are, at one end cos-
mic loneliness, and at the other, mental transparency, fusion,
and disappearance of the self. The intersubjective motivational
system regulates the zone of intersubjective comfort somewhere between the two poles. The exact point of comfort
depends on one's role in the group, whom one is with, and the
personal history of the relationship leading up to that moment.
The point on the continuum must be negotiated continually
with second-to-second fine-tuning. Too much is at stake for it
not to be.

What is at stake is psychological intimacy and belongingness, which play a powerful role in group formation and main-
tainance. Psychological belongingness is different from
physical, sexual, attachment, or dependency ties. It is a separate order of relatedness. It is a form of group belonging that
is either unique to humans or has taken an enormous quan-
tatative and qualitative leap in our species. One might argue
that the leap is language. But without intersubjectivity, language could not develop.

The intersubjective motivational system can be considered
separate from and complementary to the attachment motivational system—and equally fundamental. Clinically, we see

sexual or attachment behaviors in the service of intersubjective belonging (and vice versa). (For a more detailed discussion of these issues, see Dornes, 2002; Lichtenberg, 1989; and McDonald, 1992.) In attachment theory, there are two opposite motives and poles: at one end, proximity / security, and at the other, distance / exploration-curiosity. The attachment system mediates between these two poles. The basic survival advantage is in physically staying close together for protection against environmental dangers, be they tigers, automobiles, electric plugs, or other people, and at the same time permitting exploration to learn about the world. The attachment system is designed for physical closeness and group bonding, rather than for psychological intimacy. Many people who are "strongly" attached do not share psychological closeness or intimacy (in fact, it's the opposite). The system of intersubjectivity is needed for that.

I am drawing a clear distinction between the motivational systems of attachment and intersubjectivity, even though they can support and complement one another. Autism provides some evidence for this distinction. Autistic children show greatly impaired intersubjective skills but are attached to their parents. Shapiro, Sherman, Calamari, and Koch (1987) and Sigman and Capps (1997) reported that autistic children show clear and identifiable attachment behaviors even if the patterns of attachment are deviant. Attachment research does not measure the strength of attachment, only the behavioral patterns used to attach, but no one suggests that the autistic children appear unattached or more weakly attached.

Separating the two motivational systems is important both theoretically and clinically. People can be attached without sharing intersubjective intimacy, or can be intersubjectively intimate without being attached, or both, or neither. For the fullest connection between people, attachment and intersubjectivity are needed, plus love. In the clinical situation, inter-

101

subjectivity is essential, attachment and love less so. Nonetheless, there is usually a mix of the three, the proportions varying widely.

In any event, attachment and intersubjectivity support each other. Attachment keeps people close so that intersubjectivity can develop or deepen, and intersubjectivity creates conditions that are conducive to forming attachments. In development, it is hard to say which arises first. We know that the caregiver's sensitivity and responsiveness in the first months of life are both a manifestation of intersubjectivity and a precondition for secure attachment (Fonagy, 2001). The two motivational systems act in concert to assure the group cohesion necessary for survival. Although greatly facilitating one another, they remain independent systems.

In some societies the individual mind is not seen as private, unique, and independent. The concept of the self is less individualistic and more connected to the group's intersubjective matrix. In these situations, belongingness is maintained more through group ritual and activity (group dancing, moving, singing, storytelling, chanting) than it is through isolated verbal dyadic intersubjective exchanges. In such situations, physical expulsion or marginalization from the group causes an alienation that is a mix of broken attachment and psychic loneliness.

In most Western cultures, psychic belonging is achieved in large part through dyadic and family intersubjective contacts. We are not only a very social species, we also are a very intimate species, where mental intimacy is the key to relationships. In most of our modern Western conceptions of love and friendship, intersubjectivity is perhaps *the* indispensible element. With development, the persons with whom one most avidly seeks intersubjective relatedness changes, from parents, to peers in adolescence, to a loved one in early adulthood. And when one is suffering mentally, turns to a therapist for inter-subjective relatedness, which at times may mean survival.

Group Functioning

Humans need to act together to survive. The ability to read other people's intentions and feelings allows for an extremely flexible coordination of group action. The ability to communicate quickly and subtly within the group, through the use of intentional movements, signals, and language, expands the group's efficiency and speed of action—in other words, its adaptability. Language itself could not arise if it did not have an intersubjective base. You do not talk to someone unless you believe that they can share your mental landscape and act accordingly. This is presumed to be one of the reasons autistic children have such difficulty with language acquisition.

In addition to language, humans have the most highly developed and richest repetoire of facial and vocal (paralinguistic) expressions. These, too, assume an intersubjective capacity within the group that goes beyond simple sign decoding or instrumental communication.

Humans also spend an enormous amount of time becoming proficient in intersubjectivity and practicing it developmentally. We are the most imitative species. Nadel (1986) reported that reciprocal imitation constitutes the main form of play between children up to 3 or so years of age. (It continues after the age of 3, but at a lesser frequency.) At the same age, teasing, kidding, tricking, and so on become a major childhood activity (Dunn, 1999; Reddy, 1991). These behaviors also have an intersubjective base (see Nadel & Butterworth [1999] for studies of three-way communication in early childhood). We are the most playful species and spend years refining these skills. As would be expected, autistic children, with their relative intersubjective deficit, have difficulty teasing, tricking, "mucking around," and in general playing with others. They are less able to enlarge their greatly diminished intersubjective capacity.

What about intersubjectivity within groups? It is easier to see how dyadic intersubjectivity arises than it is to see group intersubjectivity. With groups there are two aspects: how they act together in concert or even in synchrony, and how they are read as a unit, even in one sweep of the eyes. We read groups as a unit in our everyday life. For instance, in a group discussion or in a family therapy session, checking whether everyone is "there," attending to the conversation, and sharing in the group's affective communication is easily done in seconds. Family therapists have developed theories and techniques for enhancing a family's intersubjective sharing, in particular by reintroducing rituals in family life to help resolve difficult transitions or losses (Imber-Black & Roberts, 1992). But the complexity involved in group communication has impeded research, in spite of the pioneering work of Scheflen (1973), Kendon (1990), and Reiss (1981). (For an application to couple therapy, see de Roten, Fivaz-Depevrsinge, Stern, Darwish, & Coboz-Warnery [2000].) It is beyond the scope of this book to pursue these questions further, except to say that group intersubjectivity happens and that species survival via the group is at stake.

Also, consider the role of altruism in species survival. This is a complex subject, but aspects or steps in altruistic behavior among humans may rest on the basis of intersubjectivity.

Cohesion Through Moral Pressure

Cohesion within human groups is greatly enhanced by moral suasion. I will argue that intersubjectivity is the basic condition for morality. The "moral emotions" (shame, guilt, embarrassment) arise from being able to see yourself in the eyes of another—in other words, you sense that the other sees you. Freud's account of the origin of morality via the super-ego—the internalized regard of the parent—makes the same assumption.

Intersubjectivity plays an essential role in the appearance of reflective consciousness. The idea of reflective consciousness as originating in social interaction is not new. Some form of an "other" is the essential feature. The other can be external or internal, but the primary experience must be shared from a second point of view. (Chapter 8 deals with this problem in creating reflective consciousness.)

The advent of reflective consciousness, along with language is considered key to the evolutionary success of the human species. Reflective consciousness and language enhance adaptability by giving birth to new options that can transcend fixed action patterns, habits, and some past experience.

In brief, intersubjectivity contributes to group survival. It promotes group formation and coherence. It permits more efficient, rapid, flexible, and coordinated group functioning. And it provides the basis for morality to act in maintaining group cohesion and language to act in group communication.

INTERSUBJECTIVITY AS A MOTIVE WITH PREEMPTIVE VALUE

A motivational system must contain subjectively felt motive(s) that organize and direct behaviors toward a valued goal. As one searches for and moves toward the goal, there is a subjective experience of preemption, felt as desire or need. When one achieves the goal, there is a subjective feeling of gratification or relative well-being or, minimally, a deactivation of the motivation. Can we speak of an intersubjective motive with the subjective quality of preemption?

There are two such intersubjective motives. The first is a

need to read the intentions and feelings of another. This is in the service of figuring out "Where you two are at?"; "What is going on?"; "Where do things stand?"; "Where are they likely to go?" This sounding of the immediate dyadic or group situation and its possibilities occurs upon meeting and then is continually updated, often second-by-second or minute-by-minute as needed. It is a form of orientation. If we can not orient ourselves in time and space, we become confused and anxious, and searching behaviors are put in motion to solve the discomfort. The same is true for intersubjective orientation in psychic space. We need to know where we stand in the intersubjective field with an individual, family, or group. "Intersubjective orientation" is also a vital ongoing event in psychotherapy. It is sought after and has a high affective value.

Each of the maneuvers to search and adjust the intersubjective orientation are present moments. They are moments of kairos because the intersubjective state needs to be acted upon; one must probe the intersubjective field to discover / create "where you are." The need to be intersubjectively oriented is felt as a preemptive "force" that mobilizes behavior. Motives are put into action. This is discussed in great detail in Part III.

Intersubjective orientation is a basic need in the context of direct social contact. When we are not intersubjectively oriented, anxiety arises and coping or defense mechanisms are mobilized. This anxiety could be called *intersubjective anxiety*. Dynamic and other psychologies have richly explored what are best called the "basic fears or anxieties." Being alone is always on the list, but it is usually not clear whether this is physical loneliness or mental loneliness. Clearly they are two different fears. The fear of psychic loneliness belongs to our intersubjective condition.

This sounding out of the state of the dyad is a form of "psycho-ethology." Imagine two dogs meeting. They engage in a rich repetoire of signals and behaviors to explore and establish their immediate relationship (e.g., sexual, aggressive, playful, dominant, and a nuanced mixture thereof). Now imagine that the two dogs are two people "tied" (by convention) into their separate chairs in a consulting room, or standing still, politely, at a cocktail party. Most of the acts of exploration and establishment of the current status between them will have to be in the form of behaviors that have been mentalized and not put into action. There are also signs and signals (e.g., body language and tone of voice) that can be clearly read with one-way intersubjectivity (one person reading another). When two-way intersubjectivity (two people reading each other) is added, the reading gets finer, affectively hotter, and more nuanced. And there is another feature: The status of the relationship being created is revealed in the act of its creation.

A second felt need for intersubjective orientation is to define, maintain, or reestablish self identity and self-cohesion—to make contact with ourselves. We need the eyes of others to form and hold ourselves together. Here, too, the need for the other's regard can be preemptive. Male prisoners in solitary confinement with very long or life sentences present an interesting example. Talking will not get them early parole or absolved them, and there is no environment under their control that they need adapt to. Yet they often want to talk to someone, to share their inner world. Why? One reason may be that they need intersubjective encounters to remain in contact with themselves. Under the isolation of prison, where so little of their own making or choosing surrounds them, they need the intersubjective regard of the other to refind and maintain their identity (Colette Simonet & Phillip Jaffe, personal communications, February 23, 2000 & April 27, 2000)).

Without some continual input from an intersubjective matrix, human identity dissolves or veers off in odd ways. It does not matter whether this contact is in the form of dyadic mind-sharing, group rituals, or some other form. We are familiar with the idea of multiple selves or distributed selves that shift somewhat, depending on whom one is with or on the prevailing context. This is considered normal. But when does the compass needle point to the "true self"? Or is this a meaningless question? In any case, the regard of the other helps fix one's relative self-position and find one's sense of a true self (even if that sense is illusory). In Western culture, the sense or even illusion of a more or less true self can be a vital condition for functioning.

In this regard, it is fascinating to consider that the majority of children age 6 to 12 in the several Western cultures studied have "imaginary companions" (Pearson et al., 2001). The figure is higher for girls but there probably is underreporting for boys. Why so many? Most often there is some form of dialogue with these companions. They seem to be created to complement, stabilize, validate, or orient the child's identity by way of an *inter-intra* subjective relationship.

Falling in love provides another situation for exploring the power of the intersubjective push. Falling in love has wide cultural and historical variability. Nonetheless, it is sufficiently pervasive with enough common features to warrent examination. First of all, it could be called a special state of mental organization because it pulls together so many diverse behaviors, feelings, and thoughts into an integrated assembly that is readily recognized. In fact, the "diagnosis" of someone falling in love is far more clear-cut than most categories in *Diagnostic and Statistical Manual-IV* and is probably composed of an equally specific mental organization with characteristic "neural representations." Following are some of the elements of falling in love that are driven by an intersubjectve motive (many of these are shared both by lovers and by parents with their young babies): Lovers can look into each other's eyes, without speaking, for minutes on end—a sort of plunging through the "window of the soul" to find the interior other. Nonlovers (in this culture), on the other hand, cannot tolerate the mounting intensity of a silent mutual gaze for more than 7 to 9 seconds without fighting, making love, or turning away. There is also an exquisite attention to the other's intentions and feelings, not only to read them correctly but even to anticipate them. There is a playfulness that involves much facial, gestural, and postural imitation. And there is the creating of a private world, a sort of privileged intersubjective space to which they alone have the keys. The keys are special words with specific meanings, secret abbreviations, sacred rituals and spaces, and so on. All these things create a psychological niche in which intersubjectivity can flourish.

Person (1988) has pointed out that in this process one creates a two-person world in which a couple forms and one also recreates oneself. One is thrown into a turbulent process of self-change (permanent or not is another question). The situation is almost the opposite of that of the life prisoner, where nothing can change and he can just stay the same, with effort. The lover, too, needs the eyes of the other to verify and validate his metamorphosis, to keep him in contact with himself, with his shifting identity. The regard of the other also helps maintain self-cohesion in the face of the desire for communion and fusion.

The power and frequent enlistment of intersubjective contact to situate and confirm one's identity is not sufficiently appreciated. For instance, the participation in rituals, artistic performances, spectacles, and communal activities like dancing or singing together all can result in a transient (real or imagined) intersubjective contact. All participants assume that others experience what is happening roughly as they do. They (even strangers) look at each other, and an imagined intersubjective contact passes between them, and along with it a sense of psychic belonging. They have not only enjoyed an event, but also have been immersed in the human intersubjective matrix and confirmed their self-identity.

INNATENESS AND UNIVERSALITY

A basic motivational system must be innate and universal, albeit diverse in its modes of expression. The evidence presented in Chapter 3 about the neurobiological and developmental foundations of intersubjectivity go a certain distance in addressing the issue of innateness—at least of the human capacity for intersubjectivity. The way the capacity is used in any society or culture is a fascinating subject not taken up here. Suffice it to say that I cannot imagine the capacity not being used in some adaptive form in all societies.

In modern Western societies there are large individual and cultural differences in intersubjective talent. Clearly there are constitutional factors. The case of certain forms of autism makes that clear. Are there sensitive periods? Gunnar (2001) suggested that children who have been massively socially deprived during the first year of life as seen in some orphanages, suffer affective consequences in later childhood, including diminished intersubjective abilities such as empathy.

Some might argue that intersubjectivity is a human condition and not a motivational system in itself, because intersubjectivity is nonspecific and is brought into play in the service of almost all motivational systems. In this sense the intersubjective motive would be more equivalent to "mastery motivation"

My counter argument is that although intersubjectivity can be in the service of other motivational systems, it is strongly activated in highly specific and important interhuman situations where it is the goal state unto itself. These situations are: when the threat of intersubjective disorientation arises, with accompanying intersubjective anxiety (e.g., when one's place or position in a group is thrown into question or becomes unclear); when the desire for psychic intimacy is great (as in falling in love); when rapidly coordinated group functioning is needed and the coordination must be spontaneously, rapidly, and flexibly altered from moment to moment (e.g., hunting a dangerous wild animal); and when self-identity is threatened and dipping into the intersubjective matrix is needed to prevent self-dissolution or fragmentation. In these situations, intersubjective contact becomes specific and primary.

For our purposes, the intersubjective motive is also at play in directing the second-by-second regulation of the therapeutic process, where the sharing of mental landscapes is desired and must be negotiated. It is in this context that the present moment takes on its role and relevance as the basic negotiating move or step to establish the nature of the intersubjective space in psychotherapy.

Chapter 7

IMPLICIT KNOWING

BECAUSE THE PRESENT MOMENT IS mentally grasped as it is still unfolding, knowing about it cannot be verbal, symbolic, and explicit. These attributes are only attached after the moment has passed. In what form, then, is the original moment apprehended? It falls into a domain called "implicit knowing."

During the 1990s, psychology began to place more emphasis on implicit knowledge compared to explicit knowledge. (Bucci, 1997; French & Cleeremans, 2002; Lyons-Ruth, 1997, 1998; Lyons-Ruth, Bruschweiler-Stern, Harrison, et al., 1998; Schacter, 1994, 1996). This emerging view of implicit knowing has been greatly enriched not only by observations of infants, but also by considerable previous work on nonverbal communication that prepared the way (Bänninger-Huber, 1992; de Roten et al., 2000; Frey et al., 1980; Frey et al., 1983; Gendlin, 1981, 1991; Kendon, 1990; Krause & Lütolf, 1988; Krause, Steimer-Krause, & Ullrich, 1992; Scheflen, 1973; Scherer, 1992; Steimer-Krause, Krause, & Wagner, 1990). This change alters how we see the present moment, as well as how we think about consciousness and the unconscious. The implications for therapeutic theory and practice will be immediately evident.

First, however, the distinction between the implicit and explicit must be clarified. Most simply, implicit knowledge is nonsymbolic, nonverbal, procedural, and unconscious in the sense of not being reflectively conscious. Explicit knowledge is symbolic, verbalizable, declarative, capable of being narrated, and reflectively conscious. I will elaborate on these points shortly.

Years of observational research on infants and their mothers, in parallel with the practice of adult psychotherapy, have made us sensitive to the importance of implicit knowledge. Babies do not communicate in the verbal explicit register until after 18 months or so, when they begin to talk. Accordingly, all the rich, analogically nuanced, social and affective interactions that take place in the first 18 months of life occur, by default, in the implicit nonverbal domain. Also, all the considerable knowledge that the baby acquires about what to expect from people, how to deal with them, how to feel about them, and how to be-with-them falls into this nonverbal domain. (Nature was wise to not introduce babies to symbolic language until after 18 months so they would have enough time to learn how the human world really works without the distraction and complication of words—but with help of the music of language [Stern, 1977, 1985].)

This knowledge has made us sensitive to the implicit domain, even when it is interwoven with the explicit world of language. It accounts, in part, for our placing primacy on the implicit happenings that occupy the present moment in the therapeutic process which have been less studied.

What, then, is the implicit domain of knowledge and what does it contain? Many view the implicit and explicit domains as two separate, parallel, and partially independent systems of knowledge and memory that emerge together. Rather than implicit knowing shifting into explicit knowledge with development, the two live side by side and grow throughout life (Fischer & Granott, 1995; Marcel, 1983).

Implicit knowledge is not restricted to only the rich world of nonverbal communication or body movement and sensation, but rather applies to affects and words as well, at least what lies between the lines. For instance, if someone repeatedly says, "Yes, but . . ." you quickly grasp that the "yes" is a Trojan Horse to get inside your walls. The "but" releases the soldiers. (The person could have imparted the same implicit message with a toss of the head.)

Implicit knowing is often thought to be more limited and primitive than explicit knowledge. Earlier notions of implicit knowledge equated it with physical procedures or sensori-motor intelligence, (e.g., getting your thumb to your mouth). Implicit knowledge was thought to dominate earlier developmental phases and then be largely overtaken by, and transposed into, verbal, symbolic knowledge as development (i.e., language acquisition) proceeded. Our current view is different. We now see implicit knowing as extremely rich and not solely concerned with motor procedures. It also includes affects, expectations, shifts in activation and motivation, and styles of thought—all of which can happen during the few seconds of a present moment. For example, the attachment patterns seen between mother and infant at only 12 months of age (well before speech) were evaluated at the moment of reunion when the mother returned after a short separation (Ainsworth, Blehar, Waters, & Wall, 1978). The infant implicitly knew what to do with his body, face, feelings, expectations, excitation, inhibitions, redirection of activities, and so on. He "knew whether" to approach her, lifting his arms for an embrace and body contact, or whether to not move and pretend that her return is a non-event, or whether to exaggerate his desire and need for contact to get more from her. He "knows" whether to drop what he was playing with, or to continue to focus on the toys, even half-heartedly. He "knew" if he should anticipate physical-psychological gratification or tolerate a state of

stress. He "knew" when to approach her, if he did not immediately, and at what speed, and with steps that were not so
large or so fast that she would reject him. That is a rich package
of implicit knowing (e.g., Lyons-Ruth, 1997). Bowlby's (1969)
"working model" of attachment which is the representation of
what the nonverbal infant will expect, do, feel, and think when
he is threatened in any way, is implicitly known.

Similarly the notion that implicit knowing will be translated
during development into explicit verbal knowledge when language arrives on the scene is questionable. It is more likely that
the majority of all we know about how to be with others
resides in implicit knowing and will remain there. This is especially so if we assume two relatively independent parallel systems, as suggested previously.

Two interesting suggestions have been made to repartition
the implicit / explicit domains. Bucci (1997, 2001) reparti-
tioned them into three categories: the subsymbolic, nonverbal
code (consisting of continuous, analogic experiences such as
how to paint a picture); the symbolic, nonverbal code (consisting of nonverbal experiences and information such as the
imagic knowing of someone's face); and the symbolic, verbal
code (consisting of words). This redrawing of the boundaries
is most useful and will be used in this book periodically. For
the most part, however, we will stay with the cruder established division into implicit and explicit. Fogel (2001, 2003)
has proposed another interesting and useful division of implicit
memory into two types. The first is a "regulatory implicit memory" that permits us to negotiate, nonconsciously, our
responses to the sensory, motor, and affective aspects of our
physical and social environment. This is involved, for example,
in attachment patterns (Siegel, 1999) and in the formation of
a "core" self (Stern, 1985), a "primary" self (Damasio, 1999),
a "dialogical self" (Fogel, de Koeyer, Bellagamba, & Bell, 2002);
or an objective self (Rochat, 1995), as well as in the formation

115

of the affective origin of the self (Schore, 1994) Fogel's second category is "participatory memory" which is activated in specific contexts and brings to life an implicit memory that is from the past but is experienced as happening in the present. A traumatic memory would be an example (Siegel, 1995, 1996).

Most of the time there is no reason to put the implicit into words. It remains silent unless events force a verbal rendering. And then only a small portion of the whole implicit knowledge base is transposable into words. Bollas (1987) has coined the term "the unthought known" as a major clinical reality. This is a felicitous label because implicit knowledge, although nonconscious, usually is potentially conscious and thus potentially verbalizable. (These distinctions will be made clearer later.) For this reason, I use the term implicit *knowing* instead of *knowledge*. The participle *knowing* offers constructive vagueness. It also offers a more dynamic concept of ongoing knowing as opposed to static knowledge, which can be seen as being in the past. Stolorow and Atwood (1992) used another felicitous term well-known to clinical psychology; *the prereflective conscious* (however, it need not be considered "pre" in any developmental sense).

THE RELATIONSHIP TO THE UNCONSCIOUS

The clinical relevance of implicit knowing looms large. Implicit knowing is "descriptively (topographically) unconscious." The term "unconscious" should be reserved for repressed material where there is a defensive barrier to entering consciousness. More precisely, implicit knowing is nonconscious. It is not repressed. In contrast, the psychoanalytic "dynamic unconscious" is not conscious because the force of repression actively keeps it out of consciousness. Repression is presumably not acting on implicit knowing. Accordingly, the implicit is simply nonconscious whereas repressed material is unconscious.

The implicit includes a vast array of knowing that everyday social life is based upon. For instance, what do you do with the direction of your gaze when you are listening to another? when you are talking? What do you do with your body and tone of voice when speaking to an authority figure or to a therapist for the first time? How do you let someone know you are about to terminate a discussion without saying so, or that you disagree with the person but do not want to go into it? How do you know when someone likes you? How do you know that the person knows that you like him or her?

Much of this implicit knowing is not even transposable into words. Clinical examples abound. For instance, patients when describing their childhood may mention extended family dinners every Sunday. What happened each Sunday was implicitly known: the roles of each family member, the seating, how the action flowed, how fights arose and how they were aborted or resolved, who played the fool for comic relief and when—in other words, the family script (see Byng-Hall, 1996; Reiss, 1989). In therapy, such a patient and therapist could spend hours over weeks or months to piece it all together into a coherent, complete, consistent, and continuous narrative form. This requires much work. And the final version will only be adequate for certain highlighted aspects of narrative-making and interpretation; the rest will remain implicit.

A quotation from novelist Alessandro Baricco (2002) goes more directly to the heart of the matter (read *implicit knowings* in place of *ideas*):

Ideas are like galaxies of little intuitions, a confused thing . . . which is continually changing . . . they are beautiful. But they are a mess . . . in their pure state they are a marvelous mess. They are provisional apparitions of infinity. Clear and distinct ideas are an invention of Descartes, are a fraud, clear ideas do not exist, ideas are obscure by definition, if you have a clear idea it is not an idea. . . . Here's the trouble. . . . When you express an idea you give it a coherence that it did not originally possess. Somehow you have to give it a form that is organized and concise, and comprehensible to others. As long as you limit yourself to thinking it, the idea can remain the marvelous mess that it is. But when you decide to express it (in words) you begin to discard one thing, to summarize something else, to simplify this and cut that, to put it in order by imposing a certain logic: you work on it a bit, and in the end you have something that people can understand. A 'clear and distinct' idea. At first you try to do this in a responsible way: you try not to throw too much away, you'd like to preserve the whole infinity of the idea you had in your head. You try. But they don't give you time, they are on you, they want to know. . . . (pp. 206–207)

(Note that Baricco's notion of an *idea* is a loose concept embracing the implicit, the wordless capturing of some essential aspects of our life or universe. For this reason I feel free to substitute *implicit knowing* for *idea*.) Present moments as experiences in the implicit domain are like Baricco's ideas.

From the clinical perspective, we need to examine this view of the implicit mode because the regulation of the intersubjective field, in therapy, present moment-by-present moment, occurs largely nonverbally, nonconsciously, and implicitly. Much of transference falls into the category of implicit knowing of one kind or another. Only some of it can and will be made verbal, when needed. In mother-infant therapies, it is very common for the therapist to leave a great deal of the mother's transferential implicit knowing just where it is, and not try to interpret it to make it explicit and conscious. The particular psychological nature of early motherhood argues for this therapeutic solution as the most helpful (Stern, 1995).

This new view of implicit knowing poses a major problem for traditional psychoanalysis. This is because implicit knowing is not dynamically unconscious and thus is not withheld from consciousness by resistances. It is nonconscious for other reasons. The concept of resistance or repression does not apply here. It appears that the lion's share of descriptively nonconscious material remains unverbalized for reasons other than resistance. Accordingly, "resistance" is restricted to only those situations where repressed dynamic unconscious material is involved—that is to say, a minority of the therapeutic work. This constitutes a considerable limitation for a major aspect of the psychoanalytic endeavor. This limitation takes on even greater importance when we consider the enormous scope of implicit knowing both in everyday life and in pschotherapy. Implicit regulatory memories and representations play a constant role in shaping the transference and the therapeutic relationship, in general, as well as in making up much of our lived past and symptomatic present.

There are two main agendas in the clinical situation. The first concerns the explicit verbal content that arises in the session. In "talking therapies" this is what the patient talks about: the past, the future, dreams, phantasies, problems outside of the consulting room (e.g., work, family, negative feelings, disturbing thoughts). This is the traditional subject matter that takes precedence most of the time. One could also call this the narrative agenda. We will call it the "explicit agenda." When dealing with the explicit agenda, the therapist and patient stand side by side, so to speak, looking at a third thing—the content external to their immediate relationship. The search is for meaning, coconstructed by patient and therapist in a narrative format.

In body, movement, expressive, Gestalt, and drama therapies the explicit agenda can also be appreciable. For instance, the responses to probes such as "What are you feeling right now?" or "Where in your body do you feel that?" are verbal. The verbal content arises from implicit, nonverbal sources, but then is plugged into the explicit agenda of narrative-making.

The second agenda concerns the regulation of the implicit state of the relationship between the therapist and patient. This includes much of the therapeutic alliance, the holding environment, the working alliance, the transference / countertransference relationship, and the "real" relationship. Cocreating and regulating these relationships out of awareness constitutes the "implicit agenda."

The regulation of the immediate intersubjective field is the aspect of the implicit agenda that most interests us. The implicit agenda is fundamental in the sense that it contextualizes the explicit agenda. It constrains it and determines what can be talked about—in other words, its degrees of freedom.

In psychotherapy, the main implicit task is to regulate the immediate intersubjective field. This is accomplished in the sequence of moments and present moments that are the small steps in negotiating and fine-tuning the intersubjective field. In each present moment one carries out the regulation by probing, testing, and correcting the reading of the other's mental state in light of your own. This dyadic process of parallel, simultaneous reading of patient and therapist occurs largely nonconsciously. Present moments are thus devoted to intersubjective questions such as: "What is happening here and now between us?"; "What do I sense or know about how you experience me, now?"; "What do you know about how I now experience you?"; and so on. At more local level, these issues boil down to smaller questions: "Did you understand what I just said?"; "But did you really understand?"; "I don't want to go any further with that subject, now, not just yet"; "I feel you didn't like what I said and took a step back"; "You're getting too close, please do nothing"; "Stop pushing me"; "Are you there?"; "You didn't fully respond"; "Do I understand what you mean?"; or "We don't really know what to do now, do we?" In dealing with this relational-process agenda, the patient and therapist are no longer standing side by side looking at a third thing. They are either face-to-face looking at each other, even if it is out of the corner of an eye, or they are standing side by side looking at themselves, looking at each other, or alternating between these two positions.

From a clinical point of view, any implicit knowings about the relationship will influence the explicit agenda and vice versa. Neither one can be considered independent from the other. This book, however, focuses heavily on the implicit domain of knowing, in particular on the intersubjective field between therapist and patient, and more specifically on how this field is regulated moment-by-moment during present moments—our basic unit of subjective experience. In therapy, it is this area that has not been treated as deeply as the explicit.

The fact that implicit knowing is not reflectively conscious and is also not dynamically unconscious leads us to consider the distinction between conscious and nonconscious, in relation to the implicit and explicit, to which we now turn.

Chapter 8

THE ROLE OF CONSCIOUSNESS AND THE NOTION OF INTERSUBJECTIVE CONSCIOUSNESS

HERE IS THE PROBLEM: Forming the present moment as it unfolds is an implicit process, yet for an experience to qualify as a present moment it must enter awareness or some kind of consciousness. But what kind? A look at the general question of consciousness and its background seems necessary at this point.

BACKGROUND

Historically, academic psychology has been only periodically interested in consciousness until recently. Psychodynamic theories have been far more interested in the unconscious. Freud (1926 / 1959) assumed that consciousness need not be discussed because it was evident and beyond all doubt. He then went on to explore the structure of the dynamic unconscious, which, at the time, was not as evident and accepted as it is today. This approach neglected the present moment and phenomenal experiences in general, as they are intertwined with consciousness. But an emphasis on the present moment brings us face-to-face with the question of consciousness. After all, the present moment is the phenomenal content of a bounded stretch of awareness or consciousness. It exists only during a moment of awareness. Or must it be a moment of consciousness? And what is the difference?

There are several different ways to think about awareness and consciousness. *Awareness* concerns a mental focusing on an object of experience. *Consciousness* refers to the process of being aware that you are aware, or meta-awareness.

Developmentalists have been forced to define different types of consciousness in order to describe the ontogeny of consciousness from infancy on. Using a model he calls the Levels of Consciousness Model, Zelazo (1996, 1999) listed the first three levels as follows: minimal consciousness (usually called "awareness"), reflective consciousness (sometimes called "secondary" or "recursive" consciousness), and self-consciousness. The distinction between awareness (minimal consciousness) and consciousness (reflective consciousness) is what most concerns us. Developmentally, awareness is assumed to be a primitive form of consciousness confined to the boundaries of the present moment in which the experience is occurring. As Zelazo put it, "An infant is conscious [read: aware] of *what* he or she sees, but he or she is not conscious of *seeing* what he or she sees, let alone that *he or she* (as an agent) is seeing what she or he sees" (1999, p. 98). The experience is thus not reflected on, is present-bound, remains unrelated to the self, and does not enter memory. Therefore it is unrecoverable. Consciousness, on the other hand, is reflective—in other words, it is aware that it is aware. Thanks to reflectivity, this type of consciousness can be remembered, enters into explicit memory, and can be verbalized. (For the moment I will stay at the mental and behavioral level, while trying to untangle these terms, and ignore the neuroscientific accounts.)

Philosophers have struggled with similar distinctions expressed differently. The distinction between awareness and consciousness is recast as the distinction between phenomenal consciousness and introspective consciousness. Phenomenal consciousness concerns direct experience, "the raw feel" (Rorty, 1982), the way things seem to be on the mind's "stage," "what it is like" (Nagel, 1998), and the experience of qualia (e.g., *redness*). Introspective consciousness, or access consciousness (Block, 1995), is the awareness of having the phenomenal experience. (See Block, Flanagan, & Guzeldere, 1997, for a full discussion of these distinctions from many points of view.) In the philosophical debates the distinction between awareness and consciousness is less evident, in part because one can have a phenomenal conscious experience of which one is not aware (Dretske, 1998). The boundary between these two types of consciousness is not so clear. However, one can argue that reflective consciousness is necessarily in a different time frame than awareness because it is after-the-fact. Descriptions of the flow of consciousness in literature do not clarify the soft boundaries between consciousness and awareness.

A problem with the conscious / nonconscious distinction as applied to the clinical situation is that the patient and therapist are dealing at all times with two simultaneous agendas that interact. There is the explicit agenda of the content of what they are saying and its meaning. This is clearly reflectively conscious material because it is accessed verbally. Many clinical notions of consciousness lean heavily on language as the indispensable element. Stated in extreme form, there can be no reflective or introspective consciousness without a label for the objects of experience in the form of language or symbol. Most psychoanalytic theory has embraced this idea, at least loosely. This reliance on language, however, is problematic because much clinical action involves nonconscious "objects of experience"—namely, enactments and the implicit agenda that micro-regulates the therapeutic intersubjective field.

Usually talking therapies stress introspective or reflective consciousness, which is almost always synonomous with verbal access. In movement, drama, and existentially-oriented therapies, on the other hand, phenomenal consciousness is stressed and is usually synonomous with enactments.

INTERSUBJECTIVE CONSCIOUSNESS

I return to the central question: How can a present moment that is implicitly grasped become conscious? And with what kind of consciousness? The solution I propose here involves a new form of consciousness that I will call *intersubjective consciousness*. It is well-suited for the intense dyadic contacts characteristic of psychotherapy.

When two people cocreate an intersubjective experience in a shared present moment, the phenomenal consciousness of one overlaps and partially includes the phenomenal consciousness of the other. You have your own experience plus the other's experience of your experience as reflected in their eyes, body, tone of voice, and so on. Your experience and the experience of the other need not be exactly the same. They originate from different loci and orientations. They may have slightly different coloration, form, and feel. But they are similar enough that when the two experiences are mutually validated, a "consciousness" of sharing the same mental landscape arises. This is *intersubjective consciousness*. It is what happens during special present moments in psychotherapy. Tronick (1998) has called attention to a similar phenomenon seen in the mother-infant and patient-therapist relationship. He called it, "expanded dyadic consciousness." This refers more to the enlarged scope of the sharing, as if it were a growing joint knowledge base that exists without specifying when it is existing in actual consciousness and when it is just a potentially usable piece of shared knowledge. It is a sort of potential consciousness. This confuses dyadic consciousness with dyadic implicit knowing, or implies that they are synonomous. In contrast, I am using "intersubjective consciousness" to refer only to what is happening *now* in a specific present moment, not as a potential space of shared knowing. Consciousness does not extend beyond now. So intersubjective consciousness can only be created now—not expanded in a future (even one close at hand) that is not yet in consciousness. It is only the intersubjective field of implicit knowings that can be expanded by acts of intersubjective consciousness.

Before defining intersubjective consciousness further, we must examine it from several perspectives. Recall that the neuroscientific explanations of consciousness are from an intrapsychic perspective. Within one brain, an initial neuronal grouping gets activated by an experience. This grouping then activates a second neuronal grouping in the same brain, which then reports back to the initial grouping, reactivating it and creating a reentry loop. Such loops can extend to other neuronal groupings that reactivate one another, creating a recursive network. The original experience thus gets treated from different perspectives (in terms of neural circuitry). This multifocused reiteration (a form of meta-activity) gives rise to a higher experience at the mental level—namely, consciousness.

In contrast, intersubjective consciousness is viewed as an interpsychic event requiring two minds. An experience is had by one individual. This is felt directly. It activates almost the same experience in another individual, via intersubjective sharing. This is then reflected back to the first individual in the regard and behavior of the second individual. As they encounter each other in this shared present moment, a reentry loop is created between the two minds. Mutual gaze in particular lets the intersubjective reentry loop reverberate and remain activated for the several seconds needed for the present moment to do its work. This intersubjective recursion involving the perspectives of two people gives rise to a "higher" experience in both of them (just like the neurological reiteration gives rise to a higher experience). This higher experience is intersubjective consciousness.

I am suggesting a more social view of consciousness. What concepts and evidence lead in this direction? In consciousness research, there is a long-standing question about whom or what brain structure our experience is being reported to to make it conscious. Earlier Cartesian ideas implied that a humunculus in the head watched objects of experience pass across some kind of mental stage. The work of many has made it abundantly clear that such solutions are not tenable (e.g., Block, 1995; Chalmers, 1996; Damasio, 1994; Dennett, 1998; Nagel, 1998). Still, the question of whether a reportee exists persists (e.g., Cotterill, 2001).

The neurobiological perspective asks the modern version of Decartes's question: What brain structures "receive the report" to somehow make it conscious without the intervention of an humunculus? As yet, there is no accepted central site of consciousness in the brain. And many have suggested that none exists—rather, that consciousness is a collective attribute of the entire body in its motoric and mental engagement with the environment (e.g., Cotterill, 2001; Freeman, 1999b; LeDoux, 1996; Sheets-Johnsone, 1999). An engagement with the environment includes, importantly, interactions with other people's minds, as well as with the culture.

This line of reasoning leads to a more social perspective, where the question "Who receives the report?" is opened up beyond one person's mind or brain. It is in this light that social mirror theory suggests that reflective consciousness is social in origin and depends on a shared experiential world and social reflectivity (e.g., Whitehead, 2001). As Whitehead pointed out, these ideas are based on a long tradition established by Dilthey (1976), Baldwin (1895), Cooley (1902) and Mead (1934 / 1988). In a similar vein, Vygotsky (1934 / 1962) argued that language is socially constructed—that its acquisition occurs only in interaction with other language speakers, that public language precedes private language, that language use is inevitably immersed in cultural participation. Bruner, Olver, and Greenfield (1966) came to the same conclusion about meaning-making. Meanings are coconstructed from the interaction with minds and artifacts of the surrounding culture. Feldman and Kalmar (1996) made a strong argument that identity is socially constructed. Even autobiographical memories that are told and retold to others in narrative form are socially shaped. So we can add intersubjective consciousness to the list of phenomena that appear to have a very considerable social origin.

These suggestions open up a wider scope of questions for the neurosciences. How do we account for recursive loops that are set up between two brains?

Social mirror theory argues that that there cannot be mirrors in the mind if there are not mirrors in society: We become aware of our own internal states as we discover that others have them. Even more, another can perceive a state existing within us and express that perception from their viewpoint (Whitehead, 2001). Reflective consciousness will not occur unless there is an "other" present to witness our having a phenomenal experience—in other words, to play the role of the humunculus sitting in the theater of the mind. The reentry is by way of your experience of the other's experience of your experience (where the other's experience is grasped intersubjectively).

The other must be different from the self-who-is-undergoing-the-experience. There are several "others" who can serve this function. One can share it with other aspects of the self. It is now largely accepted that there are multiple (context-specific) selves that can interact with each other, observe each other, and converse together out of consciousness. This is normal, not limited to pathological dissociative states. In psy-

choanalytic terms, the observing ego witnesses the experiencing ego, or the superego watches and judges the experiencing
ego. There are also other observers within one's mind, such as
"evoked companions" (Stern, 1985) and imaginary friends. So
aspects of the self (who are not directly experiencing) can act
as the other, or a virtual other can be imagined or phantasized
as witness or participant. In the latter situations, reflective consciousness is social-once-removed, so to speak.

But the situation is very different and much more social in
a psychotherapy. The other is very real. He or she is interacting
with you. Together, you cocreate experiences. Your phenomenal experience includes your direct experience of the other's
phenomenal experience. The setting is not only social, it is
quintessentially intersubjective. Recent research has taken up
some of the fundamental issues involved in such a situation
(see Boston CPSG, Report No. 3, [2003]; Boston CPSG, Report
No. 4 [in press]).

The idea of a real other acting as the reflector (mirror) of
the self's experience is given support by the growing consensus
about the pervasive sharing of direct experience with others.
The behavioral, developmental, and neuroscientific evidence
for such sharing or matching is impressive, as described in
Chapter 5.

Returning briefly to the mirror neuron story, there is one
other finding of interest. Under certain conditions, when we
act, some sets of our own mirror neurons fire. It is as if we are
mapping our own actions as we would those of another. For
whom are we doing this? Perhaps it is for the others who are
members of our own family of multiple selves. This would permit intersubjective traffic within ourselves and give a basis for
reflective consciousness founded on two views from two selves
operating within one person.

We can now return to the developmental view of consciousness. Zelazo (1996, 1999) noted that around 9 to 12 months

of age, a whole set of new capacities appear. Infants start to label with words. They also point to show something to another, search for hidden objects, display deferred imitation, seek joint attention, and socially reference (look toward the face of an adult when a situation is emotionally uncertain to help them know what to do or feel). Are all of these nonverbal actions also reflectively conscious? (Their *consciousness-ness* is less obvious.) Zelazo implied that yes, they are all the manifestation of the new neurophysiologically based mental capacity for recursiveness. Recursiveness within one mind is, in his view, the developmental leap that creates the necessary condition for being conscious.

Zelazo (1996, 1999) gave a neurophysiological explanation for the developmental appearance of the various behaviors, but there is, as yet, no evidence for such a developmental leap in neurophysiological processing at this age. He appears to have reasoned backwards from behavior to neurophysiology. Is there another way to imagine how all these behaviors come about at the same time that is not based on word acquisition or on the proposed shift in neural circuit functioning? We now have a suggestion at the phenomenal level. Around 9 to 12 months of age, infants are capable of secondary intersubjectivity (Stern, 1985; Trevarthen & Hubley, 1978). I propose that the crucial leap that gives rise to the appearance of these new behaviors in infants is their capacity for intersubjectivity. What Zelazo called recursive or reflective consciousness begins as intersubjective consciousness.

Returning to our main concern, the clinical situation, there are, practically speaking, three types of consciousness at play (their boundaries are not always so clear in real life).

1. *Phenomenal consciousness.* This concerns experiences that one is aware of only as they are happening. They do not enter into long-term memory, only into short-term

(working) memory. After that, they disappear. Much of what happens in the second-by-second process of therapy falls into this category.

2. *Introspective consciousness.* This concerns phenomenally conscious experiences that are reflected upon (as described previously) and get attached to a symbolic or imagistic label so that they can be verbally accessed by introspection. The majority of the content agenda of talking psychotherapy operates with this form of consciousness. In therapy, one could, for all practical purposes, call *introspective consciousness,* "verbal consciousness," even though access symbols are not exclusively linguistic. (The operation of repression or other defenses against this kind of consciousness do not require modifications in the basic concept.)

3. *Intersubjective consciousness.* This concerns phenomena that only happen in relatively intense interactions such as those that prevail in therapy and in special present moments. Here, an experience is cocreated and there is matching or at least great overlap in the phenomenal consciousness of each partner, but from a different center of orientation. In addition to each member's having a similar phenomenal experience, there is a direct awareness of the other's experience and awareness of the concordance with his own. For this to work, self-consciousness must also be operating so there is no confusion about who owns which phenomenal experience. The two experiences are intermingled but also separate. Two are needed. Because this is a mutual process, the shared experience becomes "public." A form of social reflectivity results in intersubjective consciousness.

A negative form of intersubjective consciousness can also exist, in which there has been a failure to cocreate an expected experience or a failure of matching or fittedness.

131

In this situation, the desired and expected cocreating or matching is felt as an absence. The absent social reflection is only imagined, but that is sufficient to render it intersubjectively conscious and lock it into memory.

To summarize, phenomenal consciousness is perceptually based. Introspective consciousness is verbally based. And intersubjective consciousness is socially based.

I am suggesting that during the moment-to-moment process of therapy, experiences are cocreated during an intersubjective present moment. When that happens, the conditions for social reflectivity are met and the experience becomes intersubjectively conscious. It is essential that the intersubjective meeting occur in the here and now (i.e., in a present moment) so that the two takes on the experience (that from the self and that reflected from the other) occur simultaneously and together become part of the same structure. This structure includes the temporal unfolding of the lived story, which is experienced by both partners. They have done something and been through something together. This sharing is the content of the present moment that is intersubjectively conscious. It can then enter into long-term memory, become part of associative networks, and perhaps become sufficiently verbalized for therapeutic purposes—with much work. The intersubjective consciousness that gets attached to present moments is well-suited to dealing with the rich implicit knowing that accumulates in psychotherapy and works to change people.

Part III
VIEWS FROM A
CLINICAL PERSPECTIVE

Chapter 9

THE PRESENT MOMENT
AND PSYCHOTHERAPY

I AM NOT PROPOSING a revision of psychotherapeutic theory, or a new and different overall technique. Rather, I am suggesting that we look at psychotherapy differently, through the magnifying glass of the present moment and from a phenomenological perspective. This altered vision will lead to changes in how we think about our work and what we do from moment to moment. Which of these changes will be most important and lasting is not yet clear. To indicate some of the implications of this material for the clinic, a brief review of the nature of the present moment and its relationship to implicit knowing, intersubjectivity, and consciousness is in order.

One of the more far-reaching ideas proposed is that we view intimate human relations and psychotherapy at a micro level made up of moments that occupy a subjective *now*—what we call *present moments*. The only thing new about these units is that we treat them as the very starting point of our inquiry. On phenomenological grounds, we consider them to be the smallest chunks of psychological experience that have a clinical sense, and as the basic units for examining the psychotherapeutic process. The present moment is seen as the lived material from which verbalizations, interpretations, representations, generalizations, and metapsychology are all derived abstractions. One could well ask, "Why, then, has a unit consisting of the subjective now not played a more central role in our psychologies?" This is exactly what I am trying to achieve.

In general, the present moment both as a subjective and as a micro-process unit has been neglected. In spite of the aforementioned work of James, Fraisse, Koffka, William Stern, Merleau-Ponty, Varela and others, the subject has not entered into the mainstream of academic psychological concern. Nonclinical psychology has defined itself as an objective science, and, until very recently, turned away from the subjective and phenomenological. This relative neglect has historical reasons. Attempts to render subjective experience objective have met with limited success, so far. The introspectionist school of psychology, in the early part of the twentieth century, never fullfilled its promise. The realization that introspection was at best early retrospection seemed to doom objectivity. Also, phenomenological accounts of experience are limited to single case studies where replication poses major problems.

Toward the end of the twentieth century, a shift took place. Some thinkers (e.g., Marbach, 1988, 1993, 1999; Naudin, Gros-Azorin, Mishara, et al., 1999; Varela & Shear, 1999; Zahavi, 2001) have suggested interesting ways that a phenomenological approach could be useful to objective psychology. With the advent of new brain-imaging techniques, self-reflective accounts took on a new importance (e.g., Cabeza, 1999; Gardiner, 2000). Actually, they were always important but passed unexamined. For example, Silbersweig and Stern (1998) determined that the electrical activity in the auditory cortex of a paranoid patient during an auditory hallucination was similar to that seen when the patient was actually listening to someone talking to him. But the patient had to tell the experimenters that he was hearing voices and when. Subjective experience is at the beginning and at the end of much objective science. It is the taken-for-granted initiator and final arbiter of what happened. Its "reality" is not questioned or examined. We know it too well.

Although accepted, the findings of Gestalt psychology, which rely heavily on subjective experience, have not played as central a role as they might.

In a similar vein, contemporary psychology has been able to live with *chronos* as its time concept and use it productively. For instance, if one is interested in the notions of *before and after*, the estimation of *time intervals*, the temporal limits of *perceiving simultaneity* or *continuity*, most studies of *memory*, or even how *narratives* or the *real* world is constructed in the mind, there is no need for a present moment that is any thicker than a point, no need for subjective units of time, and certainly no need for present moments that unfold with characteristic time contours.

In short, until recently, mainstream academic psychology has had no pressing need to pay attention to the nature and structure of subjective experiences such as the present moment. Psychology's new alliance with the neurosciences has changed that and a more fruitful dialogue is now taking place.

There has also been a general neglect of the present moment from psychoanalysis and psychodynamic psychotherapies. From a psychodynamic perspective, meaning and the narrative coherence of a life story are the primary concerns. Broadly speaking, psychoanalysis is interested in the relationship between pieces of current experience, past experiences, and preformed structures that together forge meaningful patterns. The timing between these pieces (a perspective from *chronos*) is important for psychoanalysis, but not the timing within the individual pieces, especially the present. (Green's [2000] notion of fragmented psychic time is only a partial exception.) However, it is the micro-diachronic world of the present that is our main focus.

In the following exploration of the present moment in therapy, I am, of course, speaking of the present moment as recalled verbally, where the telling takes place after (even just moments after) the lived experience. It has been refashioned by language. What, then, makes this examination of the present moment any different from the usual psychoanalytic process of exploring subjective experience? There are two differences.

The first lies in the assumption that the present moment (even as told) reveals a "world in a grain of sand" clinically worth examining in and of itself. In contrast, the more traditional assumption is that the present moment, as told, serves mainly as the raw material from which an associative thread can be picked up to create an associative network. It is then the associative network that contains "the world in a grain of sand"—the sought-after meanings. The actual experience-as-lived does not have to be exhaustively examined to permit the operation of free association and then interpretation. Often when the (psychodynamically well-trained) patient starts to tell about a present moment, as soon as he comes upon a sensation, feeling, image, or word that leads to an associative pathway, he is likely to take that path. This means that the exploration of the experienced-as-lived gets interrupted by associative work that leads away from the original present moment. The patient may or may not return to it and pick it up where he left off. Usually he doesn't, but rather jumps ahead to another element of the experience or to another experience that seems promising for a related associative side-trip that may enlarge the meaning.

Technically, these are not side-trips. They are the essence of the psychoanalytic work, because it is the associative network that reveals the meanings, not a detailed description of the subjective experience-as-lived in any one present moment.

The point I wish to make is that the longer the therapist can stay with the present moment and explore it, the more different paths to pursue will open up. I suggest that there is great clinical value in a more lingering interest in the present moment. This is not to say that associative networks need to be replaced by a focus on the present moment, or that the two are theoretically in competition. They are different and complementary. Which one to follow at what moment is a technical decision. Many therapists say they do use explorations of the present moment. But how can they use it well when they have a minimal sense of the nature and structure of the present moment, and fail to understand what makes it a psychodynamically fascinating package of experience in itself? When therapy is viewed micro-analytically with the present moment and sequences of present moments as the focus, one starts to see it unfolding somewhat differently than we usually do. The understanding of process moves closer to the foreground, and the search for meaning moves more to the background. The result is a greater appreciation of experience, and a less hurried rush to interpretation.

Under special and periodic conditions, psychoanalysis does make a full, prolonged, direct confrontation with present moments that are being verbalized almost as they are happening: during the emergence of transference / countertransference material onto the mental stage as it occurs in the here and now. This aspect of psychoanalysis stands out as quite different from psychodynamic inquiry in general. The enactment of the transference and countertransference requires an approach that is far more phenomenological. There is almost a century-long tradition behind this. It is addressed squarely in the work of some psychoanalysts (e.g., Ehrenberg, 1992; Knoblauch, 2000). It is for this reason that the Boston CPSG has worked so intensively on understanding intersubjective meetings in the present moment.

In most clinical practice, however, the focus on the transference relationship in the present moment is maintained only long enough to be interpretable at the right time. Theoretically, after the interpretation, the piece of the transference explained in terms of the past falls away. The therapist then leaves the phenomenological present of the relationship to return to the past, to the quieter historical and narrative aspects of the psychodynamics. The relationship as it exists in the here and now is abandoned and the treatment continues on another plane.

In short, in most psychodynamic treatments there is a rush toward meaning, leaving the present moment behind. We forget that there is a difference between meaning, in the sense of understanding enough to explain it, and experiencing something more and more deeply. I will return to this vital distinction later.

The second difference between my pursuit of the present moment and the usual psychoanalytic process of exploring subjective experience concerns the issue of revision after the fact (the "après coup" or deferred action)—in other words, the problematic relationship between a lived experience (a present moment) and its later linguistic (re)construction. This has always been a major preoccupation for psychoanalysis. Usually psychoanalysis is more interested in the (re)construction than in the happening (if knowable). After all, it is the (re)construction that revises and changes the happening into a psychodynamically pertinent psychic reality. In a sense, psychoanalysis is so focused on the verbally reconstructed aspect of experience that the phenomenal gets lost. Everything in treatment is after the fact. It is as if intellectual and linguistic functions always operate on what might happen or on what did happen, but never on what is happening (Merleau-Ponty, 1945 / 1962).

It is worth unpacking the concept of revision-after-the-fact so that we can better see the present moment, which otherwise seems to disappear after it is revised. I think of revision as falling into four categories or levels. The first is a "rolling revision," which takes place as the present moment is still unfolding. Each subsequent instant of the passing present moment revises the immediate past-of-the-present-moment. (Recall Husserl's three-part present.) This is an ongoing process, terminating when the gestalt of the present moment is seized. In other words, the "après coup" operates on the extended present, *in the present*, not only later. Language is not needed to effect this continual rolling revision. This makes revision a more general process. All experience is being constantly, successively revised instant by instant. This is not an unusual or periodic occurrance; it is how the mind works.

The second type of revision-after-the-fact is that brought about by the transposition of experience into language—revision through verbalization.

The third type is what was originally meant by deferred action—namely, where a later experience significantly changes the past understanding of a prior event. It is a sort of reappraisal that could be called a "conceptual" revision.

The fourth type of revision is that which comes about during the micro-analytic interview. (See the Appendix for greater detail.) In brief, this is not a simple, one-shot, linguistic rendering of a present moment. It is a detailed composing and integrating of layers to arrive at what the experience of the present moment felt like. It aims for life verisimilitude—not meaning. Much of the data for the chapters that follow were collected using aspects, modifications, or abbreviations of this last type of revision. Many therapists believe that they do something quite similar at points in their treatment or over the course in time. I strongly question this assertion.

This last type of revision is not psychotherapeutic business as usual. The basic assumptions guiding it are different, the knowledge about the nature of a present moment is different, the method is different, the goal is different, and the resultant descriptions are different.

In brief, psychoanalysis treats happenings as they unfold in the present moment as events displaced in time and person (transference), as yet another instantiation of past patterns, as springboards for free associations, or as only surface events like the manifest content of dreams. Much is lost.

Some psychotherapies are particularly attentive to the "here and now," especially schools of existential, Gestalt and relational psychotherapy, as well as movement, dance, music, and expressive therapies. They try to stay focused, as much as possible, on what is unfolding at the present moment in the relationship. This present-centered interaction is viewed as the main context for the emergence of material to work on. Systemic therapies also have traditionally focused much attention on the present. Many of the traditional theraputic maneuvers try to alter the prevailing context, physical or psychological, so that the patients find themselves in a changed present. In this altered context, new behaviors, thoughts, and feelings emerge and are used therapeutically.

But although the present has been used clinically, there has been no systematic attempt to explore and describe the phenomenology of experience in the present moment. Likewise, in many of the body and movement therapies, although the present action is unfolding in temporally dynamic contours, there is little attempt to conceptualize this micro-diachronic aspect. So many of these "beyond talking" therapies use their powerful techniques to evoke material that is then represented verbally and used psychodynamically. In other words, what makes them most different from "talking" therapies is the method used to evoke the material and the source of the material. How the evoked material as finally used does not differ greatly from the talking therapies. Although these therapies pay much attention to the micro-temporal structure of the process in practice, they pay less attention to its detailed description and conceptualization.

The nature and enlarged scope of implicit knowing has several implications for the clinic. One of the more inclusive concepts used in traditional psychoanalytic treatment is that of resistance. A simple and broad definition of resistance comes from Laplanche and Pontalis: "the name 'resistance' is given to everything in the words and actions of the analysand that obstructs his gaining access to his unconscious" (1967 / 1988, p. 394). *Unconscious*, here, refers to the repressed dynamic unconscious. In Freud's thinking, repression and resistance were essentially the same in that they both obstructed the dynamic unconscious from gaining consciousness. According to Laplanche and Pontalis, Freud came to see resistance as a broader concept, as can be seen in his description of five different kinds of resistance: repression, transference resistance, resistance because of secondary gain (all of these are ego defenses), resistance from the super-ego stemming from unconscious guilt and the need for punishment, and resistance stemming from the id in the form of the repetition compulsion.

The problem now facing us is that implicit knowing is not dynamically unconscious and is thus not withheld from consciousness by resistances (repression). It is not conscious for other reasons I have mentioned. The concept of resistance does not apply to implicit knowing. This limitation takes on even greater importance when we consider the enormous scope of implicit knowing in both in everyday life and in psychotherapy. Implicit regulatory memories and representations play a constant role in shaping the transference and the therapeutic relationship, in general, as well as in making up much of our lived past and symptomatic present.

It appears that the majority of descriptively unconscious material does not need the concept of resistance, which must now be confined only to situations where repressed dynamic unconscious material is involved. Enactments, which are receiving much needed attention, fall into a gray zone between dynamically unconscious and implicitly nonconscious.

Can Freud's early typology of resistances be of help in understanding the difficulties in going from the implicit to the explicit? The issue of violating some kind of wholeness and purity comes up. Recall the Alessandro Baricco quote in Chapter 7 that described the pure state of an unverbalized idea as a "beautiful mess," an implicit knowing. This is commented on in Stern's (1985) description of the language-learning child whose comfortable, rich, implicit, pre-verbal world is fractured into unrecognizable pieces by attaching language to his implicit experiences. In the *Diary of a Baby* (Stern, 1990, p. 122), a fictional 9-month-old infant plays in a patch of sunshine falling on the wooden floor. It makes a rich, multimodal sensory-feeling world for him. He tries to lick the sunshine on the floor. His mother stops him abruptly and says, "That's just sunshine, honey. It's just to look at. It's only light on the floor. You can't eat this sunshine. It's dirty."

If the fictional child could have understood her words he would have thought something like: "Each of her words is a muffled blow that cracks my space into pieces. 'Just sunshine'—but it was my pool, a special pool! 'It's just to look at'—I heard it. I felt it too! 'Only light on the floor'—How? 'It's dirty'—I was in it."

When she stops talking the pieces of his world lie scattered all around. That original world is gone.

Something is gained and something is lost when experience is put into words. The loss is of wholeness, felt truth, richness, and honesty. Is there some kind of resistance operating to counter this loss—a resistance that keeps some experiences protected in their richly complex, nonverbal, nonreflectively conscious state? Perhaps it is an aesthetic and moral true-to-self resistance, an existential resistance against the impoverishment of lived experience. In any event, with the realization of the nature and reach of implicit knowing, the scope and applicability of the concept of resistance has been significantly curtailed.

Another crucial implication of better understanding the domain of implicit knowing concerns psychotherapeutic change. We in the Boston Group (BCPSG) and many others have realized that to effectuate therapeutic change it is not always necessary to interpret in the explicit domain. Change can come about through shifts in implicit knowing.

A different implication for clinical theory concerns the place of action versus language. The more salient implicit knowing becomes, the more importance the nonverbal assumes. All present moments involving intersubjective contact involve actions, be it a mutual gaze, a postural shift, a gesture, a facial expression, a respiratory change, or a change in vocal tone or strength. One forgets that all paralinguistic contouring of speech sounds are motor acts that are felt by a listener who is participating in the vocal proprioceptive experience of the speaker. Knoblauch (2000) described this beautifully in the clinical situation. Recall that the clinical vignettes used as examples of present moments in Chapter 1 all have an action base—for example, the two-handed handshake and accompanying mutual gaze.

Am I giving action (or joint action) precedence over thought? Yes and no. Such a question makes no sense from the contemporary perspective of an embodied mind and the capacity for other-centered-participation. The recent paradigm shift in the cognitive sciences proposes a mind that is not an independent disembodied entity. Rather, thinking itself requires and depends upon feelings emanating from the body, as well as upon movements and actions (see Clark, 1997; Damasio, 1999; Sheets-Johnstone, 1999; Varela, Thompson, & Rosch, 1993). Present moments involving intersubjective meetings are based on people with embodied minds who act and react physically as well as mentally.

Before this conceptual shift, when mind and body were still separated, it was pertinent to ask, "Are we giving precedence to action over thought?" The answers determined both theory and practice. For instance, Freud was Cartesian in separating the mental from the physical. He conceived of thought as a derivative from (secondary to) inhibited action. Action was primary for him. One often forgets this. His classic example was a hungry baby who could not engage in the "specific action" of the drive (sucking to satisfy the desire) because mother was not present. Accordingly, the psychic energy normally directed to the motor and sensory functions of the mouth was redirected and channeled to the perceptual part of the mind to create a hallucination of sucking-drinking. Inhibited action turns into a derivative product, mental phenomena.

Similarly the technique of the couch and the prohibition against "acting in or out" were to force psychic energy into expression via thought, where it could be followed with free association and the "talking cure." The technical and theoretical prohibitions against action, especially acting in, were also originally put in place by psychoanalysis to contain and redirect potentially disruptive enactments of transference and countertransference toward the mental. How, then, are we to view the fact that we now see therapy, even psychoanalysis, as greatly based on action in the implicit domain, even when we are just speaking and listening?

The real problem is not action itself but rather certain kinds of actions that permit possible (mis)interpretations. A patient's expression of love toward his therapist that is carried in the tone of voice, gaze, and manner of moving rather than enacted in a clear and undeniable form is permissible (Stern, 1992). Why? Because the actions are deniable? Unconscious? Nonconscious? Hardly real actions? Technically able to be handled and useful? The dividing line between permissible and non-permissible actions thus becomes technical or moral and legal rather than theoretical.

These considerations raise long-standing questions about the division between the more psychoanalytic therapies and the body, action, movement, and expressive therapies. Given the traditional position of psychoanalysis, with its concentration on the verbal, it was inevitable that therapies privileging the physical would arise. At this point in time, no one can claim a royal road to the unconscious. The dream, free association, the present moment, body sensations or expression, and actions are all, if not royal, still good enough routes into the mind, including the unconscious and the implicit.

Another major implication concerns viewing intersubjectivity as a major motivational system, as described in Chapter 6. How many major and minor motivational systems are there anyway? This question goes beyond the scope of this book, so we will only touch on it briefly (see Dornes, 2002; Lichtenberg, 1989).

At one extreme, psychoanalysis proposed only two overriding major systems (the life and death instincts). This tended to absorb all other important motivational systems, thereby blurring their boundaries and preventing them from being considered, in their own right. The case of attachment theory is instructive. For many decades psychoanalysis either rejected attachment theory, or assimilated it out of existence. In spite of the fact that this major motivational system originated in part from a psychoanalytic perspective. Only more recently is attachment theory taking a comfortable place in mainstream psychodynamic thinking. I see intersubjectivity as occupying a position similar to what attachment previously had.

At the other extreme, many motivational systems play different roles in species and individual survival. But without a clinically useful hierarchy, therapists would be greatly limited. At the present time we seem to be caught between these two extremes. The quantity and ordering of motivational systems that are clinically and theoretically satisfying is a work in progress.

Perhaps the two most important clinical consequences of intersubjectivity's being a major motivational system are: (1) that it affirms the idea that the therapeutic relationship is essentially a two-person, cocreated phenomenon (the intrapsychic has become subordinate to the intersubjective), meaning that therapy is a cocreated journey, and (2) that it is clinically helpful to view the desire to be known and achieve intersubjective contact as a major motive in driving psychotherapy forward. It also permits us to look at the therapeutic process as an attempt to regulate the intersubjective field. This provides us with an organizing perspective. This will become evident in the chapters that follow.

Finally, what implications flow from turning the inquiry away from the unconscious and toward consciousness? Consciousness is perhaps the real mystery, not the unconscious. Recall that the present moment, although formed intuitively and implicitly, reaches consciousness. Academic psychology began with consciousness as the problem and ignored the dynamic unconscious. Psychoanalysis began with the unconscious and dismissed consciousness as self-evident. Yet the psychoanalytic unconscious, at its most simple, is consciousness masked by repression. So the more crucial question is: What is consciousness and how does anything ever become conscious? How to mask this mysterious phenomenon is an important but secondary question. The turn toward consciousness is linked with the turn toward the present moment. They both stem from the same tendency.

Chapter 10

THE PROCESS OF MOVING ALONG

MOVING ALONG is the term the Boston CPSG uses for the everyday dialogue that moves a therapy session forward, at least in time. It is what the therapist and patient do together. What makes moving along special is the scale at which we look at the dialogue. It is the therapeutic process seen through a micro-analytic lens, where the units are of several seconds' duration. As we have seen, life between people is directly lived at a relatively small scale: a sentence, a pause, a facial expression, a gesture, a feeling, a thought. Of course, these can be strung together and assembled into overarching units. We will call this small scale the *local level*. It is where present moments emerge* (Boston CPSG, Report No. 3, 2003; Boston CPSG, Report No. 4, in press; Stern et al., 1998; Tronick, Bruschweiler-Stern, Harrison, 1998).

When an entire therapy session is reviewed after it is finished, it is easy to reconstruct its trajectory, see its main

---

* Many of the central ideas for this chapter and the two following it come from the work of the Boston Change Process Study Group (Boston CPSG). The collaborative work of this group has appeared in serial publications cited in the text. I take responsibility for the many changes from our collective formulations.

themes, and estimate where it fits into the overall course of the therapy. However, when the session is viewed from the inside, while it is still happening, its path appears less clear, simple, and directional. *Moving along* captures the often ambling, loosely directed process of searching for and finding a path to take, of losing the way and then finding it (or a new one) again, and of choosing goals to orient to—goals that are often discovered only as you go along. This is the view of the process at the local level as it is unfolding.

The perspective of the process from inside the therapy at the local level is what is unique about this approach. (The work of Labov and Fanshel [1977] is a pioneering study pointing in this direction.)

I will explore moving along at the local level in the form of several questions: What are the elements that make it up? What drives moving along forward and regulates its flow? What is the nature of the moving along process? And where does moving along move to?

WHAT ELEMENTS MAKE UP MOVING ALONG?

Two elements make up moving along: present moments of which one is simply aware and present moments that enter consciousness. The latter present moments are the units that chunk words, gestures, silences, and so on into meaningful groupings. They package the flow of behavior. I will call the present moments that are simply in awareness *relational moves*. One is aware of a relational move while it is being performed. But it does not enter into long-term memory and does not later show up in narrative accounts as a recalled auto-biographical event. It presumably has the same temporal architecture and lived-story structure as a conscious present moment.

150

Methodologically, the conscious present moment can be described as a first-person phenomenon open to introspection and co(re)construction. The relational move, on the other hand, because it does not enter into consciousness can only be described objectively, as a third-person phenomenon, even though it is a first-person experience while it is happening. The mental aspects of the relational move must be inferred.

Conscious present moments can be divided into three different groups. First, there is the *regular present moment* described in detail in previous chapters. Second, there is the *now moment*. This is a present moment that suddenly pops up and is highly charged with immediately impending consequences. It is a moment of *kairos*, heavy with presentness and the need to act. Third, there is the *moment of meeting*. This is a present moment in which the two parties achieve an intersubjective meeting. At this moment the two become aware of what each other is experiencing. They share a sufficiently similar mental landscape so that a sense of "specific fittedness" is achieved (Sander, 1995a, 1995b, 2002). Moments of meeting usually immediately follow now moments, that set them up. The moment of meeting then resolves the need for resolution created in the now moment.

WHAT DRIVES MOVING ALONG FORWARD AND REGULATES ITS FLOW?

Moving along is driven forward, in large part, by the need to establish intersubjective contact. This is why we consider the general intersubjective motive as particularly relevant to the clinical situation. There are three main intersubjective motives that push the clinical process. The first is to sound out the other and see where one is in the intersubjective field. This is what I have called *intersubjective orienting*. It involves the moment-by-moment testing, mostly out of consciousness, of where the relationship between patient and therapist is, and where it is going. This is a precondition of working together.

The second intersubjective motive is to share experience, to be known. This involves the desire to constantly increase the intersubjective field—in other words, the mental territory held in common. Each time the intersubjective field is enlarged the relationship is implicitly altered. That means that the patient is experiencing a new way-of-being-with the therapist and hopefully others. The change is implicit. It need not be made explicit and talked about. It becomes part of the patient's implicit relational knowing. An other consequence is that whenever the intersubjective field is enlarged, new paths for explicit exploration open up. More of the patient's world becomes consciously, verbally understandable.

The third intersubjective motive is to define and redefine one's self using the reflection of the self from the other's eyes. One's own identity is reformed or consolidated in this process.

These goals are realized at the local level by the sequences of relational moves and present moments that make up the session.

The following example illustrates a dialogue of relational moves and present moments that adjust the intersubjective field. It comes from the clinical experience of a member of the Boston CPSG. Compared to many clinical anecdotes, it is quite banal, it contains no dramatic happenings. This is true of most of the clinical examples I use. Recall that we are after process rather than content. Theoretically, we could jump into a session almost anywhere to glimpse some of the features of its process.

Relational Move 1 (opening of the session)

Patient: *I don't feel entirely here today.* (The intersubjective intention is to announce the immediate state of her position in the relationship. It establishes a certain distance and reluctance to do much intersubjective work, at least for the moment. She is saying that she is not yet available for or desiring such joint work.)

Relational Move 2

Therapist: *Ah.* (Said with a rise in pitch at the end. This serves as a recognition of the patient's declaration. It is not clear whether it is a full acceptance of the intersubjective state the patient has put forward, or a mild questioning of it, or both. In any case, it takes a small step forward toward working together—small but significant compared to a silence or even a "hmm" [with a terminal fall in pitch]. The "ah" is more open and questioning than a "hmm." It implies a future event.)

Relational Move 3.

Both: [*A silence of 6 seconds ensues.*] (The patient signals her hesitancy to rush to change the immediate intersubjective status quo. In letting the silence evolve the therapist puts forward an implicit intention not to change things, for the moment. It also is an implicit invitation and perhaps mild pressure on the patient to break the silence. Or both. Regardless, they are cocreating a sort of mutual acceptance of the immediate status quo—in other words, to do or say nothing. Whether it is a solid or unstable acceptance remains to be seen.)

Relational Move 4

Patient: *Yeah.* (The original intersubjective position is reinstated by the patient. She is not yet ready to move forward or closer. Yet she indicates that she wishes to maintain contact by saying something. She has not approached, but she has not withdrawn.)

Relational Move 5

Both: [*Again a silence intervenes.*] (The patient still does not take up the implicit invitation to continue from the last move. But because contact has been maintained with the "yeah," the silence can proceed without creating any important loss of intersubjective ground. The therapist is holding his ground, but because his exact position has been left unclear, the relationship can tolerate it. They are loosely being-together in this somewhat unstable state.)

Relational Move 6

Therapist: *Where are you today?* (The therapist now makes a clear move toward the patient in the form of an invitation to open the intersubjective field wider.)

Relational Move 7

Patient: *I don't know, just not quite here.* (The patient takes a step foward and a half-step back. The foward step is probably the larger because she does share something, namely, not knowing where she is today. [This later proves not to be true. She does know but is not ready to talk about it. The intersubjective conditions are not yet right.] Her "just not quite here" restates her first relational move. The patient also partially declines the therapist's invitation to enlarge the intersubjective field.)

Relational Move 8

Both: [*A longish silence.*] (The therapist indicates by silence that he does not intend another invitation, at least not now. Nor will he push her harder. He will wait for the patient's initiative. This, too, is a sort of invitation and pressure, weak or strong depending on their habitual pattern of handling silences. The patient keeps distance but also contact so that a sense of her deciding hangs in the air. It is clear their intersubjective position vis-a-vis one another is unstable. But they have signaled that they can tolerate this limited, temporary way of being-together for the moment. The sharing of this joint toleration, in itself, brings a slight shift in the intersubjective field.)

Now Moment

Patient: *Something happened last session that bothered me . . . [pause] . . . but I'm not sure I want to talk about it.* (The patient takes a big step foward toward the therapist in the sense of sharing experience and expanding the intersubjective field. There is also a hesitant step backward. The tension is broken and a new tension created. An opening has been made that promises to further expand the intersubjective field. This qualifies as a small now moment because it concentrates attention on new implication of the present moment and its resolution.)

Attempt at a Moment of Meeting

Therapist: *I see . . . so is the other place where you are now our last session?* (He validates what she said as now intersubjectively shared—namely, that she is not fully there, being still occupied by something unsettling that happened last session. He has moved closer to her but without pressing her.)

Relational Move 9

Patient: *Yeah. . . . I didn't like it when you said. . . .* (The patient explains what she didn't like in last session. A larger field of intersubjectivity now starts to be claimed and shared.)

I will stop the transcript here to avoid discussing the content belonging to the first agenda and to stay with the second agenda of regulating the micro-intersubjective environment.

So little seems to have happened so far at the level of content agenda, yet the patient and therapist are positioning themselves intersubjectively so that something can emerge at the content level. Even more important, from our point of view, they are establishing a body of implicit knowing about how they work together to get somewhere. They are establishing complicated implicit patterns, unique to them, of how to regulate their intersubjective field.

WHAT IS THE NATURE OF THE MOVING ALONG PROCESS?

Unpredictability

Moving along, while it is happening, is largely a spontaneous, locally unpredictable process. The therapist cannot know exactly what the patient is going to say next, let alone what he is going to say next, until he says it or does it. And the same applies for the patient. Even when the therapist knows in advance that the patient soon will have to talk about a certain subject, she cannot know when that subject will come up or the exact form that it will take. Often the theme at hand is well known, but one still doesn't know what will happen next. (If the therapist thinks she knows, she is treating a theory and not a person.) For this reason psychotherapy (as experienced from within) is also a very "sloppy" process.

"Sloppiness" and Cocreation: The Creative Virtues of "Sloppiness" in the Psychotherapeutic Process

Sloppiness results from the interaction of two minds working in a "hit-miss-repair-elaborate" fashion to cocreate and share similar worlds. Because the process of chaining together (sometimes very loosely) relational moves and present moments is largely spontaneous and unpredictable from move to move, there are many mismatches, derailments, misunderstandings, and indeterminacy. These "mistakes" require a process of repair. The term *sloppy* has become a legitimate concept in scientific discourse thanks to dynamic systems theory where such a phenomenon is crucial.

My observations of parents and infants have made me familiar with this process of constant derailing and repairing in dyadic interactions. There are many "missteps" every minute in the best of interactions, and the majority of them are quickly repaired by one or both partners. For certain stretches of interaction, rupture and repair constitute the main activity of mother and baby. I have described these derailments and slippages as "missteps in the dance" (Stern, 1977). Tronick (1986) has devoted even more attention to this phenomenon. We both have commented that missteps are most valuable because the manner of negotiating repairs, and correcting slippages is one of the more important ways-of-being-with-the-other that become implicly known. They amount to coping mechanisms. The rupture–repair sequence thus is one of the more important learning experiences for the infant in negotiating the imperfect human world. Missteps in the dance have also been described in the mother-father-infant triad (Fivaz-Depeursinge & Corboz-Warnery, 1998; Fivaz-Depeursinge, Corboz-Warnery, & Frascarolo, 1998). Other misstepps have been described in situations of medical consultation (Heath, 1988).

The more the Boston Group examined the moving along process the more we began to notice sloppiness in the moment-to-moment process of psychotherapy. (The Boston CPSG Report No. 4 [in press], is devoted to a far broader and deeper discussion of sloppiness. The present discussion is a summary.) We identified several sources or elements of sloppiness. First is the difficulty in knowing your own intentions, in transmitting them, and in another's reading them correctly. We call this *intentional fuzziness*. Second, there is unpredictablity. Third, there is great redundancy, most often with evolving variations. And finally, the moving along process is by its nature improvised.

Progressively, we began to appreciate the crucial role of *sloppiness* and view it not as error or noise in the system but rather as an inherent feature of interactions. The sloppiness of the process throws new, unexpected, often messy elements into the dialogue. But these can be used to create new possibilities. Sloppiness is not to be avoided or regretted but rather is necessary to understand the almost unlimited cocreativity of the moving along process.

Sloppiness would be of little value if it did not occur in a context of cocreativity. Both the sloppiness and its repair or unexpected usage are the product of two minds working together to maximize coherence. Note that I use the word *cocreate* rather than *coconstruct* because the latter carries the suggestion that a prior plan is being put in place with already-formed pieces being assembled according to a known model.

A fuller understanding of the role of relational moves and present moments in the moving along process is based on the idea that whatever happens is cocreated, or coadjusted. This is a deeply dyadic process embedded in an intersubjective matrix. Several ideas make that clear. First, each move and moment creates the context for the one that follows. So if the patient (or therapist) enacts a relational move, the following relational move by the partner has already been constrained and prepared for. This mutual context-creating goes on and on, one relational move after the next, such that the direction of where the moves go together is very largely dyadically determined. Second, each relational move and present moment is designed to express an intention relative to the inferred intentions of the other. The two end up seeking, chasing, missing, finding, and shaping each other's intentionality. In this sense also, the moving along process is cocreated.

To carry this line of thinking further, sloppiness in a two-person psychology can be seen as analogous to irruptions of unconscious material in a one-person psychology (free association, slips of the tongue). Along with other unplanned emergent events, they both create the surprise discoveries that push the dyad to its uniqueness. Potentially, they are among its most creative elements. After all, theory alone only provides the bones, sloppiness and irruptions of unconscious material are two different ways of providing the flesh.

The products of sloppiness are thus emergent properties that come into being from the roughly equal contribution of two minds. These products had no previous existence, even in a latent form. Accordingly there is nothing to analyze in a psychodynamic manner. Sloppiness creates something that needs to be lived through and worked out rather than understood. The traditional idea of an analysis of defenses is not applicable. A slip of the tongue is not sloppiness. This is not to say that some bits of sloppiness can not be dynamically determined. But not all are. They are more an inherent product of interacting than of psychodynamic functioning.

An example of sloppiness and its creative use follows.* You may find it somewhat confusing; after all, it is sloppy.

The patient had a history of childhood abuse. The issues of self-esteem, acceptance, and agency were paramount. The patient had two dreams, one a few days before the session (the "Friday dream") and one the night before it (the "Tuesday dream"). Also after the first session the therapist had offered an extra session and worried that the patient felt coerced to accept it.

---

* The material is from a case conducted by one of the Boston Group members. The full transcript and the events preceding and following it are included in Boston CPSG, Report No. 4 (in press). They greatly expand and add to the points made here.

Patient. *So there are two completely different . . . the dream that I had last night left me feeling really connected to you, and you know it made me feel . . . I don't know, I guess closer to you, that you would tell me you were not perfect.* (Two dreams have already been presented in the session. The patient decides to talk about the more recent one, Tuesday's. Did she decide on the spot? Although there may have been many reasons for her choice—being defensive, time proximity, etc.—this is an example of fuzzy intentionality. It also leaves the first dream, Friday's, not taken up, hanging somewhere in the air. The situation immediately becomes potentially more complex. And even within the choice she has made—the Tuesday dream—she introduces some minor uncertainties: "*I don't know, I guess. . . .*" These declarifications could be resistances, reluctances, or a real question at the moment about what she was saying. In any case, they add to the intentional fuzziness. The fact that they may be defensive does not take away the fuzziness. It only "explains it away.")

Therapist: *Uh-huh.* (This "means": "Go ahead because I'm with you. Because I have not yet understood enough and need to hear more. Because I don't have anything to say, yet. Because I don't even know where you're headed. Because I need more time. Because maybe the other dream is more important. Because perhaps all these things are in operation." The patient will get the general idea because of convention and their past history. Fuzziness is present but not too important yet.)

Patient: *Um.* (This means: "I'm not sure where I'm going to go with this. Or if I do know, I'm not sure I will go there. It looks like you're not going to help me much. Or are you?" [the therapist does help].)

Therapist: *You actually thought about calling me on Saturday about this other dream.* (Here we have the first surprise. The therapist suddenly shifts to the Friday dream even though the patient started with the Tuesday dream. In fact, the shift is not even to the dream but to what she thought of doing after the dream—calling him on the telephone. Why? He seems to have radically altered the direction of things. Did he know why at the moment of doing it? The word *actually* stands out. It is either a request for clarification that she really did think about calling him or a statement of his own surprise that she did. Or is it related to his concern that he had previously coerced her into accepting an extra hour? Or to his sense that the Friday dream is hanging in the air? In any case his intentions are probably multiple, and not yet well formed. The shift turned out okay, but that does not mean he knew what he was doing at the time. And we do not want to resort to his clinical intuition to clarify, after the fact, something that was at the time fuzzy. The therapist's abandonment of the Tuesday dream is also surprising because it appears to contain hotter transference material.)

Patient: *Yeah!* (She works through some of the fuzziness by focusing on only one piece of unclarity: Did she really think of calling him?)

Therapist: *Which would have been, uh, and the reason you were thinking of that, that kind of very real connection, was what?* (He is struggling here to find his way. He has suddenly switched directions again. He makes four incomplete and rapidly abandoned different sorties to find and express his intention. In so doing, he comes up, or rather comes back from a different orientation, to the words *real connection*, which she had used a few turns back in her first statement about the Tuesday dream. He has recontexualized the term. He is now starting to make a small and tentative bridge between the two dreams. This intention still remains fuzzy. But the term "real connection" is starting to become an enriched cocreated notion that will later help organize the session. The enrichment of this notion is a joint product of the sloppiness and of the attempts to work it through.)

Patient: *What are you referring to, the calling?* (She is doing some repair work here.)

Therapist: *Yeah, the calling.* (They trade attempts to reduce the sloppiness and discover / create less fuzzy intentions. Here we also see recurrences and variations to lock in clarifications.)

Patient: *Well, because I had seen you on Fri . . . and felt there was like a thread of consciousness that had flowed into that dream.* (She, too, vaguely senses some relationship between the two dreams. Their fuzzy intentions are starting to converge. The sloppiness between them concerning which dream to treat and the switching between dreams have made the theme of the relationship between the two dreams emerge. However, this was not the therapist's original intention, nor the patient's. It emerged in the process.)

Therapist: *Yeah.*

Patient: *It seemed kind of confusing to me that . . . I don't know how to say this exactly. It's like a throwback or something. To be dreaming about X [a group therapist from a previous therapy] and feeling that kind of pressure.* (Unsteadily, she goes back to the Friday dream. There is a disjunctive going back and forth. In this context, the "feeling of pressure" emerges. It rises up as a new interesting element but was not anticipated.)

Therapist: *Yeah.* (Read: "I'm not fully with you yet, go ahead.")

Patient: *Is what I don't quite get—I mean, I think.* (She is stumbling forward here.)

Therapist: *The pressure is there isn't it? Here we come into the issue of coercion, being made to do something. And in this dream you really are being pressured to say something more. And I guess I wonder how did it, uh, connect to the fact that we had that extra session on Friday.* (The new notion of coercion and pressure is now emerging. They now have to work through the fuzzy intentions that will compose and clarify this notion. He interrupts her by suggesting that the pressure is about the coersion of the extra session.)

Patient: *What it seems like to me is that . . . the dream was more connected to the idea of me feeling I have to measure up, come up with the right stuff . . .* (The therapist was partly right and partly wrong. For the patient, the therapist's suggestion that the dream was connected to the extra session was a wrong path. She does not pick it up. What is more important at this moment is that she is clarifying what pressure means— namely "to come up with the right stuff." The emergence of this crucial clarification on her part was facilitated by the therapist's error in the placement of emphasis and her attempts to repair and reposition the emphasis, for him and in her own mind. Another harvest from sloppiness.)

Therapist: *. . . uh, huh . . .* (Having been put back on her path, he is watching and encouraging this unexpected unfolding.)

Patient: *. . . than the feeling of coerced into coming here. Somehow there is a difference somehow in there from sort of making a link with . . .* (She is refining the clarification and stumbling forward. The level of sloppiness seems to have momentarily increased again.)

Therapist: *. . . yeah, uh, huh . . .* (He is urging her to continue to find and make her way, their way.)

Patient: *. . . feeling coerced to coming here on Friday, which I didn't feel at least consciously. Because what I was feeling had more to do with their [the group's] asking me—it was like I had to be sicker than I felt. And I think that's frequently a part of what my mindset is when I come here, that there is some sick part of my mind that I have to access.*

The therapist and patient stumble forward during the rest of the session to various interrelated topics including:

- The question: Does she have to be sick to get treated by the therapist?
- The fact that she now does not feel so bad about herself; she is okay, stronger.
- The Tuesday dream in which she felt equal to the therapist, thanks in part to his human fallabilities.
- The fact that that was why she didn't have to call him after the Friday dream.
- A feeling of equality and acceptance.
- A desire to sit up and face the therapist, which she did in the beginning of the next session.
- Her realization that she has her own agency in life and therapy, which permitted her to lie back down on the couch to continue working.
- A feeling of being "a lot more connected here."
- Working more freely and deeply in therapy.

Progressively they cocreated islands of intentional fittedness from the sloppiness. These then coalesced through the same process of utilizing the potential creativity of sloppiness to forge larger spaces of shared implicit relational knowing. The intersubjective field shifted and new paths opened.

It is important to emphasize that sloppiness is potentially creative only when it occurs within a well-established framework. Without that, it is only disorder. Accordingly, the therapist must work with a technique and theoretical guidelines in which he or she is comfortable and well-versed. I am not advocating "wild analysis" at all. Rather, I am pointing out that even within the normal boundaries of any approach there is plenty of room for sloppiness. Furthermore, within the idiosyncratic style that each individual uses when applying an approach, there is a wide degree of freedom for sloppiness to be cocreated.

Sloppiness has, indeed, surprised us. It has gone from a big problem in understanding treatment to one of the keys in grasping its enormous creativity. This insight would not have been possible without a dynamic systems theory perspective applied at the local level of present moments.

WHERE DOES MOVING ALONG MOVE TO?

The desire for intersubjective contact mobilizes the cocreativity of two minds working together at the local level (with short-term and long-term therapeutic goals in mind), to get somewhere. But where?

I will describe five different fates of the moving along process: (1) It results in sudden, dramatic therapeutic changes; (2) it results in failed opportunities for change with negative therapeutic consequences; (3) it results in progressive implicit changes in the therapeutic relationship that favor desired changes; (4) it prepares the way for new explorations of explicit material; and (5) it prepares the way for interpretations.

Dramatic Therapeutic Change

Moving along can lead to sudden, dramatic therapeutic changes by way of "now moments" and "moments of meeting." The intersubjective field can be dramatically reorganized at key moments. This occurs when the current state of implicit relational knowing is sharply thrown into question and basic assumptions about the relationship are are placed at stake. The shift is brought about by the unpredictable arising of an emergent property, that was being prepared for, unseen, in the moving along process. It threatens to throw the entire intersubjective field into a new state, for better or worse.

These moments capture the essence of *kairos*. A new state is coming into being or threatening to come into being, with consequences for the future. There is novelty and an "upset," as well as a mounting emotional charge. The situation emerges unexpectedly and something must be done (including the option of doing nothing). This confluence of elements results in the emergence of now moments and moments of meeting.

Examples of these types of present moments are needed at this point. I will start with the now moment. Suppose that a patient has been in analytic therapy on the couch for a few years and has expressed concern from time to time that she does not know what the therapist is doing back there—sleeping, knitting, making faces. Then one morning without warning the patient enters, lies down, and says, "I want to sit up and see your face." And with no further ado, she sits up and turns around. The therapist and patient find themselves staring at each other in startled silence. That is a *now moment*. The patient did not know she was going to do it—right before, certainly not that day, that moment. It was a spontaneous eruption. Nor did the therapist anticipate it, just then, in that way. Yet they now find themselves in a novel interpersonal and intersubjective situation. *Kairos* hangs heavy. (This is a clinical anecdote from a case conducted by Lynn Hofer, a psychoanalyst in New York [personal communication, February 23, 1999].)

Or suppose a patient is being treated in face-to-face psychotherapy. And one day he says, "I'm sick of looking at your face all the time. I can't think without knowing or wondering how you are reacting. I'm going to turn my chair around and face the wall. Right now." And he does. The patient is now facing the wall and the therapist is facing the patient's back. A silence falls. That, too, is a now moment.

Or a patient says something very funny and the therapist breaks into explosive laughter, which never happened before.

Or the therapist goes to the movies and finds herself on the ticket line, just behind a patient. There are many now moments, within, outside of, and at the edges of the therapeutic frame. A clear frame is crucial for the process. One cannot overemphasize the need for a clear frame for these events to take on meaning.

When such a major emergent property declares itself, it immediately occupies the center stage. A now moment is so-called because there is an immediate sense that the existing intersubjective field is threatened, that an important change in the relationship is possible (for good or ill), and that the pre-existing nature of the relationship has been put on the table for renegotiation. These realizations (most often felt rather than verbalized) make the dyadic atmosphere highly affectively charged. The therapist feels disarmed and the level of anxiety rises because he or she really does not know what to do. Also, in such moments the participants are pulled fully, even violently, into the present moment that is now staring them in the face. Often in therapy, one is not fully "there" in the present. One is evenly hovering in the past, present, and future. But as soon as a now moment arrives, all else is dropped and each partner stands with both feet in the present. Presentness fills the time and space. There is only *now*.

The essence of the now moment is that the established nature of the relationship and the usual way of being-with-each-other is implicitly called into question. Such moments could be dismissed as various forms of "acting out or in," but that misses the central point (even when partly true). All therapists and patients, regardless of their theoretical approach and regardless of the body of acceptable techniques they adhere to, establish a way of working together. Much of this style is unique to the therapist and to the dyad. It provides the customary framework in which the work is done and the relationship is defined. In a dynamic system such as therapy, it is inevitable that the usual framework of the individual style is bumped up against and even temporarily broken through—even when the broad technical guidelines of the approach are respected. This may signal the need to redefine their way of working together or their implicit relationship. It can be extremely positive when used well. Much of the work directly involving transference and countertransference falls into this category. But here we are talking about more than traditional transference–countertransference material.

When a now moment occurs the therapist is confronted with a difficult task for which he is not necessarily prepared. The nature of a now moment usually demands something beyond a technically acceptable response: It demands a moment of meeting. The moment of meeting is the present moment that resolves the crisis created by the now moment. (Recall that this is just a special form of present moment.) Intersubjective "fittedness" is sought, where both partners share an experience and they know it implicitly. It requires an authentic response finely matched to the momentary local situation. It must be spontaneous and must carry the therapist's personal signature, so to speak. In that way it reaches beyond a neutral, technical response and becomes a specific fit to a specific situation.

Take, for example, the patient who suddenly sat up to look at her therapist. Right after the patient sat up, the two found themselves looking at each other intently. A silence prevailed. The therapist, without knowing exactly what she was going to do, softened her face slowly and let the suggestion of a smile form around her mouth. She then leaned her head foward slightly and said, "Hello." The patient continued to look at her. They remained locked in a mutual gaze for several seconds. After a moment, the patient laid down again and continued her work on the couch, but more profoundly and in a new key, which opened up new material. The change was dramatic in their therapeutic work together.

The "hello" (with facial expression and head movement) was a "moment of meeting," when the therapist made an authentic personal response beautifully adjusted to the situation immediately at hand (the now moment). It altered the therapy markedly. It was a nodal point when a quantal change in the intersubjective field was acheived. In dynamic systems theory it represents an irreversible shift into a new state.

After a successful moment of meeting, the therapy resumes its process of moving along, but does so in a newly expanded intersubjective field that allows for different possibilities.

The "hello" was a specific fitted match. It was shaped to the immediate local context. This is why most standard technical maneuvers do not work well in these situations. Imagine that instead of saying "hello" the therapist had said to her patient, "Yes?" or "What are you thinking now?" or "What do you see?" or "Do you see what you expected?" or "Hmmm?"—or let the silence continue. All of these are technically acceptable (though not necessarily optimal) within a psychoanalytic framework. They may lead to interesting places, but they feel inadequate for the specific situation.

One of the obstacles in shaping a spontaneous and authentic response to fulfill a moment of meeting is the anxiety experienced by the therapist during the now moment. The easiest and fastest way to reduce the anxiety is to fall back on, and hide behind standard technical moves. Both the anxiety and the sense of being disarmed are eliminated, but the therapy may have lost the opportunity to leap ahead.

It is essential to add that this moment of meeting in the previous example was never further discussed in the therapy until years later, when the patient said, in passing, that the "hello" was a nodal point in her therapy. It made her realize, at some level, that her analyist was "on her side" and "truly open to her." For her, it changed their relationship and reorganized the intersubjective field irreversibly. However, this moment was never verbalized at the time, nor was it ever interpreted during the treatment. It had worked its magic implicitly.

Several of my colleagues have asked why the therapist does not at some point verbally mark such a nodal happening—for instance by saying, "Something important just happened between us." The reason is this: The therapist and patient already know that something important has happened. They are still reeling under the force of the event. Such a response may cause many interesting things to emerge, but it has a major disadvantage. It makes the implicit explicit, which necessarily pulls the process away from the ongoing here and now to a different here and now in which the stance is more abstracted and removed. The flow gets cut. Instead, one should let the flow accomplish its work and find its own immediate destiny.

Take, for example, this exaggerated parallel from everyday life. Suppose a boy says to a girl, "I like you very, very much." What would be the effect of her responding, "I think it is very important that you said that to me." (If he is smart he would run away.) She has not allowed the event to play out. She has kicked it up to a different and more removed level. She has refused to encounter him where he is. She has redefined the nature of their immediate relationship. That is the risk of verbally marking the implicit. The process flow gets interrupted, the perspective shifts, and the immediate relationship is abandoned to go elsewhere.

It is probably true that interesting but different material would emerge if these moments of meeting were verbally marked rather than left to play out. The point is that we are generally less inclined to tolerate the increased tension of staying in the here and now. It becomes the path not taken, with all the lost opportunities that implies.

Another way to describe the moment of meeting is to speak of "fittedness" of intentions. (At times the Boston Group in its writings uses "fittedness of intentions," "recognition of fittedness," and "moments of meeting" almost interchangeably.) The term *fittedness* comes from Sander's work on the parent-infant interaction (Sander, 1995a, 1995b, 1997, 2002; Lyons-Ruth, 2000; Seligman, 2002), where he speaks of the "recognition of fittedness" and "specificity of fittedness." Initially he was concerned with the regulation of physiological states, especially sleep. The intentions (enacted) by the two partners may start to flow together. They begin to share the same intention—for example, for the baby to pass from fussiness / drowsiness in to sleep. And at a certain moment their intentions become fitted together. At that point the baby can change his physiological state.

In one beautiful case, which I micro-analyzed with Sander using a special movie editor, a father was standing and cradling his infant son in his arms. The baby was fussy and drowsy but couldn't break through the barrier and fall into sleep. The father was interacting with others at that moment but at the same time gently bouncing the baby in his arms. At one moment, he looked at the baby and the baby looked at him. Just after that, the baby slowly extended his arm to the side and up and opened his hand. The father, almost at the exact instant, slowly brought his hand up to meet the baby's. (The father was only partly attending to his own act.) The two hands met. The baby circled his fingers around the father's pinkie. And the father's hand closed gently around the baby's hand, now resting in his palm. At that instant, the baby pierced the physiological barrier and fell asleep. The last tumbler in the lock fell into place (fittedness), and the door to sleep opened. For Sander, that moment was the "recognition of intentional fittedness" (for a social-physiological system).

Here, Sander's basic idea is retained but applies to shifts in intersubjective states rather than in physiological ones. We look for shared intentions, fitted intentions, and something like "recognition of fittedness." The word *recognition* carries the implication of being consciously aware of the fittedness. I intend something less explicit—a *sense of fittedness*.

The moment of meeting is one of the key events in bringing about change. A moment of meeting creates an experience with another that is personally undergone or actually lived through in the present. I want to clarify what I mean by "actually lived through," when it is done by two (or more) people. I will call this process a *shared feeling voyage*. This term keeps the temporal aspect in the forefront and feeling at the center. It is a kind of journey, lasting seconds, taken by two people, roughly together through time and space.

During a shared feeling voyage (which is the moment of meeting), two people traverse together a feeling-landscape as it unfolds in real time. Recall that the present moment can be a rich, emotional lived story. During this several-second journey, the participants ride the crest of the present instant as it crosses the span of the present moment, from its horizon of the past to its horizon of the future. As they move, they pass through an emotional narrative landscape with its hills and valleys of vitality affects, along its river of intentionality (which runs throughout), and over its peak of dramatic crisis. It is a voyage taken as the present unfolds. A passing subjective landscape is created and makes up a world in a grain of sand.

Because this voyage is participated in with someone, during an act of affective intersubjectivity, the two people have taken the voyage together. Although this shared voyage lasts only for the seconds of a moment of meeting, that is enough. It has been lived-through-together. The participants have created a shared private world. And having entered that world, they find that when they leave it, their relationship is changed. There has been a discontinuous leap. The border between order and chaos has been redrawn. Coherence and complexity have been enlarged. They have created an expanded intersubjective field that opens up new possibilities of ways-of-being-with-one-another. They are changed and they are linked differently for having changed one another.

Why is a shared feeling voyage so different from just listening to a friend or patient narrate episodes of their life story? There too, one gets immersed in the other's experiences through empathic understanding. The difference is this. In a shared feeling voyage, the experience is shared as it originally unfolds. There is no remove in time. It is direct—not transmitted and reformulated by words. It is cocreated by both partners and lived originally by both.

Shared feeling voyages are so simple and natural yet very hard to explain or even talk about. We need another language that does not exist (outside poetry)—a language that is steeped in temporal dynamics. This is paradoxical because these experiences provide the nodal moments in our life. Shared feeling voyages are one of life's most startling yet normal events, capable of altering our world step by step or in one leap.

One major difficulty in grasping the concept is that explicit content must be momentarily put aside and out of mind. Another is to stay focused on the temporal unfolding of feelings. Finally, it is difficult is to think of two people cocreating their joint experience in an intersubjective matrix. Another nonclinical example that picks up pieces from previous chapters may be useful here.

A young man and woman go out together for the first time one winter evening. They barely know each other. They happen to pass a lighted ice-skating rink. On the spur of the moment they decide to go ice-skating. Neither of them is very good at it. They rent skates and stumble onto the ice. They trace a clumsy dance. She almost falls backwards. He reaches out and steadies her. He looses his balance and tilts to the right. She throws out a hand and he grabs it. (Note that each is also participating neurologically and experientially in the bodily feeling centered in the other. And each of them knows, at moments, that the other knows what it feels like to be him or her.) For stretches they manage to move forward together, holding hands with a variety of sudden muscular contractions sent from one hand and arm to the other's to keep them together, steady, and moving. There is much laughing and gasping and falling. There is no space in which to really talk.

At the end of a half hour, tired, they stop and have a hot drink at the side of the rink. But now their relationship is in a different place. They have each directly experienced something of the other's experience. They have vicariously been inside the other's body and mind, through a series of shared feeling voyages. They have created an implicit intersubjective field that endures as part of their short history together. When they now have the physical ease and freedom to look at each other across the table, what will happen? There may be an initial social disorientation between them. They do not yet know each other officially, explicitly. But they have started to implicitly. They are in a no-man's land. And what will they see? Different people with a different past and different potential futures than before they skated. One could attempt to explain the altered relationship on the grounds of the symbolic and associative meanings attached to their touching and acting on each other. I find this explanation weak and round about even though it could add additional meaning.

What will our ice-skaters say? They will talk across the table and share meanings. And while they talk, the explicit domain of their relationship will start to expand. Whatever is said will be against the background of the implicit relationship that was expanded before, through the shared feeling voyages they had on the ice. Once they start talking, they will also act along with the words—small movements of face, hands, head, posture. These accompany, follow, or precede the words. The explicit then becomes the background for the implicit, momentarily. The expansion of the implicit and explicit domains play leapfrog with each other, building a shared history—a relationship.

If their implicit and explicit shared intersubjective field has altered enough that they mutually feel that they like one another, enough to want to go further in exploring the relationship, what might happen? They will engage in a sequence of intention movements. Kendon (1990) described intention movements exchanged between people to test the waters of their motivation toward each other. They consist of split-second, incomplete, very partial fullness of display, abbreviated movements that belong to the behavioral sequence leading to the consummation of an intention or motivation. (They are the physical-behavioral analogs of intersubjective orienting.)

Our skaters will now engage in a series of intention movements. Short head movement foward, stopped after several centimeters, slight mouth openings, looks at the other's lips and then their eyes, back and forth, leaning forward, and so on, will take place. This choreography of intention movements passes outside of consciousness but is clearly captured as "vibes." These vibes are short-circuited shared feeling voyages and deliver a sense of what is happening. An evolving pattern develops as the sequence of intensity, proximity, and fullness of display of their intention movements progresses. These relational moves are enacted out of consciousness, leading up to the moment of meeting—their hands move to meet.

Here, too, a notion of readiness is needed, because suddenly the full act is executed in a leap. The present moment surfaces quickly like a whale breaching the water's surface. There is not an incessant, agonizing progression up to the final act.

The above account can make only limited sense if we remain blind to temporal dynamics and fail to see them as the tissue of lived experience.

In summary, moments of meeting provide some of the most nodal experiences for change in psychotherapy. They are very often the moments most remembered, years later, that changed the course of therapy. What we are talking about is basically as simple as "doing something together," be it mental, affective, or physical. A moment of meeting is a special case of "doing something together." However, it is not so simple after all. Some things we do together occur under the special conditions that are found in a moment of meeting, such as: when the two minds doing something together are partially permeable, promoting intersubjectivity; when the experience of other-centered-participation results from that intersubjectivity; when the present moment of doing something together is charged with greater affect, and a stronger *kairos*, so as to get elevated as a sort of peak amidst the other surrounding moves and present moments; when the something that gets done together involves a time voyage of riding vitality affects accross the span of a present moment. When all these conditions are met, a nodal event occurs that can change a life.

Missed Opportunities

Moving along can result in failed or missed opportunities for change with negative therapeutic consequences. Moments of meeting follow now moments. It very often occurs that the therapist simply misses that a now moment is being experienced by the patient. Or the therapist realize that a now moment has been entered, but it makes him too anxious and he runs away to hide behind technical moves. Or therapists enter and stay in the now moment but cannot find an authentic, spontaneous response that is fitted to the immediate situation. In most of these failed situations, the consequences are not disastrous. A similar now moment will probably reappear. There are usually several chances. However, sometimes a therapy can be seriously wounded or even brought to termination by these failures. For example:

An adolescent boy was in a psychodynamic therapy. As a child he had suffered a severe burn on much of his chest and abdomen that left an impressive discolored scar. Much therapeutic time had been spent talking about it, in particular the extent to which the scar disgusted or put off girls. It was summertime and social life was on the beach. One day in session, without planning to do so, he said, "After all this talking, you should see what it looks like." And he immediately began to pull his shirt up. (A now moment.) The therapist very rapidly said, "No," with much emphasis and hurry. "You don't need to show it to me—only to tell me how it is for you." The boy stopped in his tracks and expressed his nonunderstanding of why the therapist did not want to see the scar. They argued about it for the rest of the session and the next session as well. (There may have been several cogent reasons for the therapist's refusal. Perhaps he saw it as exibitionistic, homosexual, or some other form of acting in. Although any of these reasons might have been true, the therapist acted with an excessive speed that prevented much reflection, and the boy picked up on that.) Finally, at the next session, the therapist said, "I have been thinking about what happened and feel that I disappointed myself in not looking at the scar." The boy answered, "I don't care if you disappointed yourself, you disappointed me." And they began another disagreement. The issue was never completely resolved to the patient's satisfaction. The scar was never viewed. And the therapy was seriously wounded even though it continued. But a significant part of the patient's world was cut off from further intersubjective sharing. The therapeutic world shrunk rather than expanding.

Even worse, sometimes a failed moment of meeting brings a fairly sudden termination to the treatment. In such cases patients feel (rightly or wrongly) that the therapist is incapable of understanding them.

Progressive Changes

Moving along can result in progressive implicit changes in the therapeutic relationship that favor desired changes. In the first publications of the Boston CPSG (Stern et al., 1998; Tronick, 1998) the emphasis was on now moments and moments of meeting that were affectively charged—lit up in flashing neon, so to speak. Yet we knew that now moments / moments of meeting are fairly rare occurrances. Many sessions can pass without one. Still progress and change take place during the quieter, less charged moments that made up the daily moving along process. Similarly, we recognized that moving along did not have the sole purpose of preparing people for these charged present moments, but effected change in its own right. That realization forced us to shift our focus onto the moving along process to see how it worked. Our next two publications concentrated on this issue (Boston CPSG, Report No. 3, 2003; Boston CPSG, Report No. 4, in press).

The clinical anecdote presented in the beginning of this chapter is a good example. It starts with the patient saying, "I don't feel entirely here today," and ends nine relational moves later when she says, "Yeah . . . I didn't like it when you said . . ." In this example, the patient and therapist are getting experience in: how to-be-together when the patient is reluctant to bring something up that is charged and is about the two of them; how to accept the reluctance and still gently encourage but without applying too much pressure; and how to deal with and tolerate silences in this situation and what durations of silence are acceptable for this task. The patient is acquiring trust that these difficult situations can be successfully surmounted. The therapist is learning to trust the patient's way of getting there (with some help). They both are learning (implicitly) that together they can work this kind of situation out. They are cocreating ways-of-being-with-one another. In short, they are implicitly learning ways of regulating their intersubjective field. This delicate choreography goes on mostly outside of consciousness.

Such implicit knowing can be generalized to similar situations as they arise between the patient and therapist. It may also get generalized beyond the therapy to similar situations in other relationships. Suppose this kind of negotiating and regulating is something new for the patient. In her prior relationships, the patient may have had bad experiences in just this kind of situation, where she is not "entirely there" because there is something she wants to say but has to work against a reluctance to bring it up. It may have led to impatience and dismissal from her interlocutor, or anger and rejection, distain and belittlement, or an aggressive response that made her feel that telling was no longer possible. With the therapist, she experiences a new way of being-with "when not entirely there."

Some might consider this interaction as a sort of "microcorrective emotional experience." I see it more as a new experience that does not repair the past by filling in a deficit, but rather creates a new experience that can be carried foward and built upon in the future.

This view is not based on a deficit model, but one of creating contexts in which new emergent properties are permitted and encouraged to arise. These new emergent properties then establish the next context where something else can arise. This model is largely based on dynamic systems theory (Freeman 1999a, 1999b; Prigogine, 1997; Prigogine & Stengers, 1984) and its application to development (Thelen & Smith, 1994).

The question of how the patient and therapist may be-together in different situations is larger than the question of technique. The acceptable techniques provide rough guide-lines. Within these, the therapist and patient must fashion their mutual style of regulating the field of intersubjectivity and thus negotiating the course of therapy. Their style will have its own rituals, canons, rhythm, and flexibility.

Where and how does a sequence of moves and moments come to a close? It cannot go on leaning forward forever. End-points must somehow close out the process (even if temporar-ily). Something must happen that signals "we got there, now we can go somewhere else" or "we didn't get there, lets drop it and go elsewhere." The signal is the sense of fittedness of intentions or, stated differently, a sufficient degree of intersub-jectivity. This is where the emotional impact of intersubjectiv-ity comes in. At such moments an affective state of completion is felt. Sander (1995b) called it "vitalization," a sort of emo-tional affirmation in the sense of intersubjective sufficiency. Nevertheless, such endpoints are also objectively observable. When the moving along reaches one of these points, the pro-gression is bought to an intersubjective closure. In the previous clincal example, these end points were:

Now moment: *Something happened last session that bothered me . . . [pause] . . . but I'm not sure I want to talk about it.*

Attempt at a moment of meeting: *I see . . . so is the other place where you are now our last session?*

Relational move 9: *Yeah. . . . I didn't like it when you said. . . ."*

A series of eight relational moves have led up to this point where the next relational move became a present moment and the intersubjective environment could shift. A clear closure occurred because they could drop the negotiation of her hesitancy to be "there" and she could start to tell what was on her mind. They radically changed directions and goals. The sequence of relational moves accomplished its job; a piece of the intersubjective field was shared and claimed. They can now continue to move along but in a different area of the intersubjective field, as well as with a new explicit content until the next closure is cocreated.

How are we to view these closures? Dynamic systems theory provides a description. In complex systems with multiple, independent and interdependent variables (like the weather or pyschotherapy) change occurs in a nonlinear fashion, where one cannot predict the exact moment of change or the specific form it will take. These discontinuous leaps occur when the variables interact such that an "emergent property" appears. It represents a new element created by the auto-organization of the system and can throw the system into a new state.

How do you know you've gotten there? So much of the moving along process consists of repetitions and variations of relational moves. These recurrences have the advantage of keeping a relational move in working memory, which is constantly reactivated by rehearsal, in this case by repeats. Keeping a sequence of relational moves in working memory permits progressions from one move to the next to be noticed. In this way a sense of flow or directionality can be captured and the point of closure more readily identified.

The process of moving along leads to intersubjective closures (state shifts). These accumulate to alter the therapeutic relationship as implicitly known. This process is gradual, continual, and usually verbally silent. It works its mutative effects almost without notice. The accumulation of such changes is what we mean by therapeutically changing a patient implicitly. Nothing less is at stake. Most of the newly emergent intersubjective states that arise at these moments of closure need not be irreversible.

Is the process that we are calling *progressive implicit change* different from the process we have labeled *sudden dramatic change*? There is a clear difference in magnitude of change. There are also two other differences. The first concerns irreversibility. The dramatic shifts seem to be irreversible, while the progressive shifts may need to be reapplied. This issue requires more observation. A second qualitative difference is that the dramatic shifts result from moments of meeting. These intersubjective meetings bring the new implicit knowing into a state of "intersubjective consciousness." This coming into consciousness may be one of the reasons for the irreversibility. Nonetheless, one is always working "at the edge of order and chaos" (Waldrop, 1992), or in our terms, at the boundary between sloppiness and coherence. This applies to the dramatic irreversible as well as the undramatic reversible shifts in the intersubjective field.

New Explorations

Moving along can prepare the way for new explorations of explicit material. A shift in the intersubjective field can have the effect of creating a new context so that explicit material can emerge. Recall that the implicit agenda contextualizes the explicit agenda. A case reported by Harrison (2003), a child psychiatrist/ psychoanalyist demonstrates this. The sessions were video- and sound-recorded.

A very short portion of one session is presented here.[*] The therapist had cancelled her last session with the child. Although both explicitly knew this fact it was not being talked about. The transcript begins in mid-session. (The dialogue was performed in a very sing-song and rhythmic fashion.)

---

[*] For a full description of the case and the therapeutic dialogue, see Harrison (2003).

Mariah: *I think I'm going to make vegetable soup.*

Therapist: *Yes, that's right! Because I like vegetable soup!*

Mariah: *I know you do.*

Therapist: *You're a good . . . you're a good . . . ummm, mother.*

Mariah: *I'm not your mother.*

Therapist: *You're a good cooker.*

Mariah: *I'm not a cooker, I'm in a restaurant. And I'm making [mumble].*

Therapist: *Oh, that's much better! You're a good restauranteer!*

Mariah: *Nnnnn . . . a cook.*

Therapist: *A restaurant cook.*

Mariah: *I'm a girl.*

Therapist: *A restaurant girl—very good! This is our restaurant and. . . .*

The dialogue continued in this manner until the child suddenly asked, "Where were you on Thursday?" (the missed session).

Harrison (2003) commented that she tried "to set up a repetitive sequence of small turns that will allow for a lot of negotiation between them, while still keeping Mariah in the driver's seat. Clearly the pattern they are making together is more important than the verbal content. The rhythmic, repetitive turn-taking has the quality of a nursery rhyme or children's song." This permitted the therapist and child not only to stay in contact, but also to build up the momentum of experiencing something together. The intersubjective field was growing in spite of the lack of linear progression at the explicit level. An important part of the accumulating of implicit experience was that the child was given free rein to assert her agency with acceptance from the therapist and without fear of reprisal or rejection. This moving along reached a point where the intersubjective field was positioned so that it was possible for Mariah to suddenly ask, "Where were you on Thursday?" (the missed session). Without the preliminary testing of the inter-subjective field, and the assurance it gave, it is unlikely this child would have broached the missed session. See Harrison (2003) for exactly how they got there and the psychodynamic issues in play.

As this case illustrates, moving along often paves the way for the emergence of a new explicit topic. This also happened in the first clinical anecdote of the chapter ("I don't feel entirely here today"). The sequence of relational moves led to new con-tent material—namely what had happened in the last session that "bothered" the patient. The change to a new topic did not occur in a linear fashion. The patient and therapist were not following a logical line. Rather, the intersubjective field was altered (implicitly) during the sequence of relational moves, just enough to create a context favorable for the emergence of explicit material. The process agenda acted in the service of the content agenda. This is what I mean by the implicit agenda contextualizing the explicit.

Interpretations

Moving along can prepare the way for interpretations. It is extremely frequent in dynamic therapies where interpretation is a major tool that they are prepared for in the moving along process. Now moments indicate the "readiness" and propitious timing for an interpretation, as well as for a moment of meet-ing. The situation is resolved explicitly rather than implicitly. I will discuss this in greater detail in the next chapter. Here, I am concerned with implicit changes. The situation, in reality, is not so clear-cut, because when looked at closely, interpre-tation involves both a change in explicit knowledge and implicit knowing.

THE CENTRAL ROLE OF INTERSUBJECTIVE REGULATION

Almost since its beginning, psychotherapy has struggled with the therapeutic encounter of two subjectivities. Historically, in psychoanalysis, this took the initial form of transference bumping up against countertransference. The current focus on intersubjectivity in other therapies as well as psychoanalysis is a logical step in the evolution of this concept. At present, "intersubjectivity has emerged as the leading concept among psychoanalytic approaches to interaction" (Beebe & Lachmann, 2002, p. 2). This concept, however, has been applied in different ways. Beebe and Lachmann (2002), Knoblauch (2000), Mitchell (2000), and Aron (1996) have reviewed and compared the various uses of the concept of intersubjectivity in psychoanalysis by its main proponents (Benjamin, 1995, Ehrenberg, 1982, 1992; Jacobs, 1991; Lichtenberg, 1989; Mitchell, 1997; Ogden, 1994; Stolorow & Atwood, 1992; Stolorow, Atwood, & Bandschaft, 1994).

The approach taken here differs from most of the aforementioned intersubjective approaches in the following respects. First, I view the intersubjective exchange within the dyad as going on all the time, every minute, not as appearing periodically. Second, I see it as a basic condition of mind and of relationships (Stolorow & Atwood [1992] share this view). Third, I see it as a basic motivation and not only as a tool, method, or source of information for the treatment. Fourth, I see intersubjective exchanges as occurring largely in the implicit domain and not requiring verbalization to have their therapeutic effect. Fifth, I view intersubjectivity at the "local level" of the small, micro-acts that underlie it, not in broader clinical brushstrokes. Finally, because I see therapy taking place in the intersubjective matrix, I do not stress any of the various "forms of intersubjectivity" that Beebe and Lachmann

(2002) have delineated. For instance, for Benjamin (1995) the most important vector is the patient's recognition of the therapist's subjectivity. For Stolorow and colleagues (1994) the main vector is the analyst's experience of the patient's subjectivity. There is generally great asymmetry in the intersubjective vectors that are clinically stressed. In my view, the process is always dyadic, with frequently changing degrees of asymmetry in both directions.

The importance of the *here and now* is largely assumed and not underlined in most of these approaches. Ehrenberg (1992) and Knoblauch (2000) are partial exceptions, they grounded their work in the present, in the "heat and intensity" of the here and now, as Ehrenberg put it. This is closest to my approach, which views the presentness of the intersubjective work as an absolutely essential element. These views are largely in accord with the Boston CPSG's position.

In this chapter I have tried to bring the crucial change events in psychotherapy into the same micro-time scale and on to the same local level made of present moments that we have been discussing throughout the book. It is this perspective that forms the picture described here.

Chapter 11

INTERWEAVING THE IMPLICIT AND EXPLICIT IN THE CLINICAL SITUATION

MOST PSYCHODYNAMIC and cognitive therapies use interpretation (in one form or another) and narrativizing a life story as essential techniques. To do this the implicit must be made explicit and the unconscious, conscious. The relationship between the implicit and explicit has been less studied than that between the unconscious and conscious. It poses problems and fascinating questions. The implicit and explicit intermingle at many points. In narratives, there is a two-way traffic between the implicit and explicit. Images, feelings, intuitions in the implicit domain must get rendered into the verbal explicit domain by the speaker. And in the opposite direction, words must get rendered into images, feelings, and intuitions by the listener. The implicit (the intersubjective field) also has a role in creating the "right" context to permit explicit material to emerge. And telling and listening, as acts in themselves, combine elements of both the implicit and explicit.

Where do present moments fit in here? From a phenomenological point of view, an interpretation or narrative also creates present moments in the teller and listener. So we are still working with the same subjective process units.

187

INTERPRETATION AND MOMENTS OF MEETING

The moving along process leads not only to moments of meeting, but also to moments that are propitious for interpretive work, or work of verbal clarification. The same "good timing" and "readiness" that apply to present moments of meeting may equally apply to present moments when an interpretation is called for. When certain conditions flow together, the moment is ripe for an interpretation or a moment of meeting. These are: when the therapeutic relationship, in the form of transference, comes to the surface; when there has been a progression of events leading to a high point or crisis that requires some kind of action (a moment of *kairos*); and where this urgency calls both partners fully into the here and now.

Even when an interpretation rather than a moment of meeting is chosen as the therapeutic route to take, implicit processes are still called into play. In fact, they facilitate the effect of the interpretation. The implicit and explicit are deeply interwoven.

Suppose that an interpretation is given. Suppose further that it is an excellent interpretation offered at an ideal moment in the session and in the treatment. The patient will have a strong affective reaction. The emotional impact of the interpretation on the patient is an expected part of the clinical process when it is working well. The patient may have an "ah-ha" reaction, as in "Now I see!" But more frequently, the reaction is more affective than cognitive. The whole body and mind is gathered up in the reappraisal, which can feel something like, "Yes, I really have been like that." "That is really who they are and how they treated me." "I feel like I have to start over from scratch." "Where the hell was I all that time?" "I've been so handicapped." And then a silence follows as the patient takes it in. This silence is a charged moment. The patient is going through an important reorganization in the presence of the therapist—a reorganization that has been catalyzed by the remarks of the therapist. The patient's reaction is thus an interpersonal and intersubjective event because both the patient and therapist know, more or less, what the patient is experiencing. This silence, immediately after the interpretation, is a kind of now moment. What usually happens is this: The therapist feels called upon to say something to let the patient know he or she has understood the affective impact of the interpretation. The therapist may say something very minimal, like "yes," something indistinct like "hmm," or something more elaborate like "Yes, sometimes life feels like that." But the therapist says it in a special way with a special tone of voice that has overtones of empathic understanding, of dipping into their own world experience and expressing that, of standing alongside the patient in this moment of usually painful reappraisal. (Often, the therapists vocalization is elongated, falls more at the terminal pitch, and is lower in volume.) In other words, the therapist creates a moment of meeting about the reaction to the interpretation. Sometimes this takes the form of an affect attunement.

Most experienced therapists do this without thinking much about it. When it is pointed out many colleagues say, "Well, of course I do it; it's a natural part of the interpretive process." Yet, it is worth thinking about, because if this moment of meeting was not added to the affective events set in motion by the interpretation, the interpretation could be experienced as a technical maneuver from a neutral professional. It could have come from anywhere. It would then be sterile and only minimally interpersonal and intersubjective. It might have altered the patient's explicit understanding of herself, but not the intersubjective field between her and the therapist.

If, on the other hand, the therapist creates a moment of meeting around the impact of the interpretation, the sharing of the impact expands their intersubjective field. A moment of meeting around the interpretation locks in the interpretation and its impact as a joint experience. The patient can then proceed in new directions on the basis of both an altered implicit knowing and explicit knowledge of herself and the theraputic relationship.

It is true that most experienced psychoanalysts and psychotherapists create these moments of meeting around impactive interpretations. But it is not considered a formal part of the interpretation. Some say that it is a part of the larger category of "interpretive activity," but that blurs things too much and too easily. The examination of these intersubjective moments is bypassed and they are taken for granted when mentioned at all. Nevertheless, they play an important role and require a different descriptive terminology and explanatory model than that which applies to the interpretation standing alone.

Often, this response to the impact of the interpretation is overlooked, as it falls in the turbulent aftermath of the verbal interpretation. But it occurs anyway and accomplishes its work. An example provided by Margherita Spagnuolo-Lobb (personal communication, January 22, 2000) serves best. She was in treatment with Isadore From, a well-known Gestalt therapist. He was ill with cancer and did not have a long life expectancy. This was publicly known in the therapeutic community of which Spagnuolo-Lobb was also a member. However, she and her therapist had never brought it up, though each had to have known that the other knew. One day, she had a telephone session with him after a disturbing dream in which she saw a poster typical of those printed to announce a death and pasted on the walls in Sicily. It had fallen from the wall and was lying in the road and had her name on it. Cars were running over it. After she recounted the dream, her therapist said, "It should have had my name on it." The subject of his imminent death thus sprung up with some force. It had never been mentioned before. His interpretation deeply moved her. She mentioned this to me as an example of the power of an interpretation.

I agreed, but asked what happened right after he said that. She said, "Well, after a moment or so we hung up." Being curious if there had been a moment of meeting about this powerful intervention, I questioned her using a shorthand version of the micro-analytic interview technique. I asked her what exactly happened to her when he had made the statement. She said that she took a very big breath in and held it, then let it out in progressive heavy exhales. There was a silence over the phone. I asked if she had been crying. She said "no." I suggested that she was breathing as if she were crying. She said, "Yes, that was true." I then asked what he did to break the silence. She described that he said something not very unusual or memorable. In fact, she did not remember what it was. But she remembered his tone of voice. It was unusually soft, not a voice that she had heard from him before. It felt like a caress carried to her across the telephone. That was a moment of meeting. They had accomplished an implicit contact beyond words. And this implicit contact became joined to his verbal intervention to make a whole experience.

Just as an interpretation can give rise to a moment of meeting, a moment of meeting can give rise to an interpretation. But it doesn't have to. For example, recall the anecdote where the therapist responded to the patient who sat up from the couch to look at her by saying "hello." No interpretation followed this but one can readily imagine one. I suggested earlier that an attempt to make this moment of meeting explicit, especially immediately after it occurred, could undo some of its effect. But other times an interpretation can be helpful. It is a question of clinical judgement, but one must be aware of both the advantages and disadvantages. If the therapist had asked the patient after she laid back down how she felt about what just happened and the patient responded by saying that for the first time she felt that the therapist was open to her and on her side, it might have been an excellent opening for a broader interpretation on the part of the therapist. She might have suggested that the patient felt that her parents were not on her side or open to her, how she had come to expect that of others, how she had missed several life opportunities because of what had become a defensive stance, how that had happened at the office last week, and how she had viewed her therapist in that light and had thus put some limitation on the therapeutic work. Such an interpretation may have advanced the therapeutic work, but it also could have slowed it. Apparently it was not necessary in this case.

The point is that verbal interpretations and implicit expansions of the intersubjective field are complementary acts. In practice they serve one another. However, they require different explanatory models.

NARRATIVE-MAKING, NARRATIVE-TELLING, AND LISTENING TO NARRATIVES

Language is the vehicle for putting experience into a told narrative. This is mostly true even in therapies that are referred to as "beyond talk" therapies (Wiener, 1999). What is "beyond talk" is the means to coax and pull the implicit experiences into the explicit open. But once they are there, the problem of putting them into some kind of form that is meaningful remains a linguistic task of narrative-making. But there, too, the implicit and explicit keep close company.

Narrative-telling is the main, common, final path for data in both talking therapies and those that use other techniques to create explicit experiences. But making narratives involves not only words, but also direct experiences that are in the implicit domain. It is these direct implicit experiences that interest us.

Three parallel present moments are involved: (1) the present moment of getting the original experience into verbal narrative form; (2) the present moment created in the teller during the telling it to someone; and (3) the present moment evoked in the listener during the telling. First, the patient must (re)live (now) the experience to be verbalized and forge it into a narrative form. This is not automatic. Thinking at this stage is largely in the form of visual, sensorimotor, visceral images, and feelings—not language. There is an effortful matching of the verbal account to the experience. This process creates its own present moments with its own intentions, vitality affects, and so on. The listener (the therapist) observes the mental and physical acts of transposition in the teller. This is a performance. Ease, difficulty, groping, hesitating, blocking, frustration, effort, changes in flow, speed, volume, and force, and a sense of relief, surprise, or inevitability make up the performance. Each of these implicit experiences, in itself, could be a productive focus for a therapeutic intervention. In addition to the words that come out, and even the paralinguistics, there is the entire performance, which, like any other performance, evokes in the teller and listener a constant stream of implicit experiences, including other-centered participation about the act of transposition. In brief, there is an implicit intersubjective sharing about the experience of transposing the implicit material into an explicit narrative form. Even while we are heavily focused on the words that come out and their meaning as it forms, we remain exquisitely sensitive to the implicit (partially shared) experience of transposition as it is occuring.

And finally the narrative must be fashioned for an audience, real or imagined. Telling a narrative is a constant task of intersubjective searching, testing, and adjusting to the listener. There are many implicit goings-on during this aspect of the performance. Ultimately, the performance of arriving at a narrative and telling it is a special kind of enactment, where the content is made explicit but the process remains implicit. These constitute the several parallel present moments.

In psychotherapy, narratives are told or enacted, not read, so the performance as performance is paramount. A told narrative in psychotherapy is not just a coherent story but also an expressed emotional experience. Both the story and its expression are valuable clinical material.

Ricoeur (1984–88) has commented on the time of telling a narrative, in contrast to the time of, or in, the story. By thinking of the acts of narrative-making and telling in terms of present moments, I am adding an internal temporal dynamic as part of the telling—and listening.

The central point is that even in considering therapeutic narratives, we have not escaped beyond the world of present moments. Of course the narrative, once constructed, can be viewed objectively and be deconstructed. But not while it is being told and heard. And even after it is told, when it is laid out and viewed objectively, its wholeness, including its central meaning, will be grasped in yet another present moment of capture.

The phenomenology of telling and listening to narratives requires far more attention than it has received or that can be given here.

INTERMINGLING THE IMPLICIT AND EXPLICIT

A sentence with a clear explicit meaning also makes up a present moment while the sentence is unfolding. When the sentence is considered from the point of view of the listener, recall that an average spoken phrase takes 3–4 seconds to say (the duration of the present moment). Also recall that the meaning of the spoken phrase is constructed as it is heard over time. Its whole meaning only falls into place when the last word is said. This construction in time is not simply a matter of progressively understanding the syntax. It is also a matter of tracing the course of the syntax falling into its cognitive and affective place. As an illustration, consider a simple phrase such as "Would you like to go to the movies tonight?" As the listener rides the crest of the sentence as it unfolds, he first hears, "Would you." It is immediately clear that something is about to be asked of him. There is a rise in his interest and alertness. The next subgrouping he hears is "like to go." This maintains and perhaps raises his interest and alertness as things begin to become more specific. Then comes "to the movies." Depending on the context and history, this could add pleasure to the feeling mix or it could make what went before fall flat, with an attendant loss of interest and surge of negative feelings as in "That is all you ever want to do." Finally, the "tonight" arrives. It was probably understood implicitly by the context and adds little. Yet it steadies the emotional tone before the response and thus the next present moment must begin.

In this phrase, then, there is a syntactic journey, a journey of explicit meaning making, and a journey of contoured affective experience. When the phrase is over one forgets the syntactic journey that took place outside awareness. One remembers primarily the gestalt of the meaning journey and, importantly, how it has been colored by the affective journey.

Here is another example provided by Patel (2003). He suggests that there is a surprising overlap, neuroanatomically, between the processes of chunking and organizing sequential elements in both language and music. They are not as separate as previously conceived. The sentence is "The girl who kissed the boy opened the door." Once again, we will follow the affective journey. "The girl," the first subgroup encountered, creates its own affective charge. Then comes "who kissed the boy." With this, interest, curiosity, and affective charge rise rapidly. Then comes "opened the door." There is a fall off in affective charge that is replaced by an arousal due to a potential cognitive problem. Who opened the door? It says "the boy opened the door," but we know, following the syntax, that the girl did it. This is a curious journey. Now, using the same words, suppose the phrase had read "The girl who opened the door kissed the boy." We would have been lead along a quite different micro-affective journey. The order and timing of the arrival of meaning also determines the implicitly felt affective experience. (We need not enter further into questions of style.)

In brief, the intricate interdependence of explicit meaning and implicit affective experience is clear at the local level of the present moment.

Still there is an important difference between the two parsings (meaning and affect) within the present moment. The difference is their respective time frames. The affective journey and the spoken journey have the same duration, a few seconds. However, the event to which the words refer took much longer. There is a discrepancy in timing, level of abstraction, and, necessarily, in closeness to the original experience. Feeling the affective contouring, hearing the words and having their meaning fall into place are direct, original experiences. What the words refer to is an indirect experience, once removed. We will return to this important difference in Chapter 13.

Chapter 12

THE PAST AND THE PRESENT MOMENT

THE PAST MUST be able to influence the experience of the present. Said differently, the past must somehow get folded into the present experience. Without that, the past can not play any role in current life, and there can be no psychic determinism, and no psychodynamics. On the other hand, present experience must be able to alter the past, by diminishing its influence, by reselecting which past elements will play the major influencing role, or simply by changing the past. If the present cannot do that there can be no therapeutic change. But because we only live in the present, subjectively, the action of the past on the present and the action of the present on the past must be played out in the present moment. The present moment is the meeting ground between the past and the present.

THE ACTION OF THE PRESENT ON THE PAST

The concept of a *present remembering context* helps explain one way the present moment can act upon the past. The functional past, the one that influences the present, can be rearranged at the meeting ground of the present moment. The example of memory serves well in clarifying this concept. The notion of the *present remembering context* is widely accepted in thinking about memory (e.g., Damasio, 1999, 2000; Edelman, 1990). In brief, memory is not viewed as a library of experiences where the first editions are kept in their original form and one of them can be called up and pulled into the present as a memory to be relived faithfully. Instead, memory is viewed as a collection of fragments of experiences. These get turned into a whole remembered experience in the following way. Events and experiences going on at the present time act as a context (a present remembering context) that selects, assembles, and organizes the fragments into a memory. The present remembering context is whatever is happening now on the mental stage in this present moment. This can include a smell, a sound, a melody, a word, a face, the quality of light, internal feeling states, bodily feelings, a thought, and so on. It can also include experiences that are less fleeting and more ongoing, such as a mood, a preoccupying thought or feeling, a lingering dream, a conflict, a desire for revenge, a pain, or a loss. The present remembering context is not only just one of these ongoing experiences, it is the totality of what is going on now. It is the complete amalgam of perpeptions, sensations, cognitions, affects, feelings, and actions that are currently acting upon us, consciously and unconsciously, implicitly and explicitly. In this sense, past traumas, conflicts, and other basic elements of traditional psychoanalysis that remain partially activated can be a foreground or background part of the present remembering context.

These presently ongoing experiences act as triggers to select and assemble fragments from the past that, when integrated, help us to recognize what is happening now in the present and deal with it, for better or for worse. It is in this sense that Edelman spoke of "remembering the present" (Edelman, 1990). We do not remember a fixed historical past, we can only "remember" the present. In this view, memories are more present-centered than past-centered. Their function is to make life as we are currently meeting it more familiar and easier to adapt to. One corollary of this is that each memory, even of the "same thing" is different because it is selected and assembled under different present remembering contexts, which almost never repeat in their entirety. For each remembering context a slightly different set of fragments is selected, or they are assembled differently. This may sound radical and counterintuitive, but only because some memories have been repeatedly rehearsed, locked into narrative form, and seem not to vary across rememberings. The place of traumatic memories is less clear here (Siegel, 1995, 1996, 1999).

A present moment is a *present remembering context* par excellence. During the unfolding of the present moment, as it passes from the horizon of the past-of-the-present to the horizon of the future-of-the-present, there are analogic or categorical changes along its course. Each change can act as a separate remembering context. This allows the past to be constantly folded in, not in the form of discrete whole memories but rather in the form of influences out of awareness.

But can this meeting happen in a time as short as a present moment? Recent neuroscience studies on decision making suggest that when a new stimulus is presented, the neurophysiological effect of a related but past stimulation can be recorded within a few hundred milliseconds of the onset of the new stimulation (Romo, Hernandez, Zainos, Lemus, & Brody, 2002)—in other words, the past is brought into or alongside the present present almost instantly and many times during the evolution of a present moment. In this way many different past influences could be folded into the present moment at many points along its passage.

How does the present remembering context "select," nonconsciously, what pieces of the past to activate and reassemble into a new memory? In other words, what is the nature and process of creating links and associations between experiences with different time dates, addresses, and natures? There are some useful hints from descriptions at the mental and phenomenological levels in discussions of dreams, free association, the workings of the primary process, and dissociation. Freud from the very beginning was acutely aware of the possible mechanisms for the complex linking or unlinking of the past and present. The Gestalt theorists added other linking processes that govern perception and association, such as proximity or common fate. Currently, metaphor is an interesting candidate for this crucial role. Modell (2003) suggested that metaphor is a major form of linkage between unconscious autobiographical memory and conscious experience. Supporting Modell's ideas, cognitive linguists such as Lakoff and Johnson (1980, 1999), Turner (1991), and Gibbs (1994) proposed that metaphor is not just a figure of speech but a primary form of cognition (prior to symbol formation and language) that links different domains of experience, including past and present. Language can later use theses linkages and turn them into linguistic metaphors, but it does not start with language except in the mind of the one listening to a spoken metaphor. To this must be added all the clinical experience about metaphor that is tapped in body and drama therapies, (Landy, 1990, 1993). Bucci (1997) suggested that all experience is multiply coded (Multiple Code Theory) and is linked through a referential process. The problems of linking and dissociating the past and present remain at many levels of clinical inquiry (see Siegel, 1999).

A second more radical way to view the action of the present on the past is to imagine that as each new present moment takes form, it rewires the actual neural recording of the past and rewrites the possible memories of the past. The originals are changed and no longer exist in the way they were initially laid down. This is partially the experience one has while listening to music. As one hears the presently unfolding phrase, the experience of the preceding phrase is altered—a form of *après coup*.

There is neuoranatomical evidence supporting such a view (Freeman, 1999a). Freeman has shown that when young rabbits are first exposed to a new smell (e.g., carrots) a pattern of neural activation is established. Later, when they are exposed to a second smell (e.g., turnips) a different pattern of activation is established for that smell. However, the establishment of the second pattern changes the activation pattern for the first smell. And later when another new pattern is established for a third smell, the two previous patterns will be altered. In other words, the past is always being permanently revised, both as a neural pattern and as an experience of recall. Or to put it more strongly, the present can change the past. Of course it does not change it from a historical perspective, but it is changed functionally and experientially, and that is where we live.

Can a moment of meeting or an interpretation change the past in this fashion? Yes. But only in small pieces at a time. And this does not mean that one cannot also retain a memory of the past before it was changed. Two memories for the same experience is not only possible but common. The neurosciences will have to figure out the neural circuitry for such parallel pasts and discover how one knows which one is the updated past.

The clinical fact of inflexible patterns that appear resistant to change from new present experiences runs counter to the idea that the present can easily, naturally, and rapidly change the past. This stuckness supports the idea of the "repetition compulsion." There are conditions (conflicts, traumas, first-shot learning) that render some past experiences relatively immune to the influence of the present. Nonetheless, the general principle holds that the present constantly rewrites the past. The exceptions require a separate inquiry, not a questioning of the basic concept.

A third way the present can change the functional past is to alter the selection process of the present remembering context so that different pieces of the past are activated and brought to bear on the present.

Phenomenologically the process of the present altering the past occurs out of awareness. We usually only become aware when we are faced with the final product, and not necessarily even then.

THE ACTION OF THE PAST ON THE PRESENT

I will now take up the influence from the other direction, the effect of the past on the present. There are several different pasts. The nature of their influence and its felt presence takes different forms. I will take a phenomenological stance, again, to explore the different kinds of pasts that interest us clinically.

The "Silent Past" As a Fractal

This kind of past is acting upon the felt present but is not, itself, felt. It is silent and only recognizable by taking an objective stance. It consists mainly of the repressed unconscious and the implicit nonconscious. In psychoanalysis this would include all repressed past influences (e.g., conflicts, phantasies, traumas) that have been rendered unconscious and thus not experienced as acting in the felt present. It would also include character traits that are traditionally viewed as nonconscious through becoming automatic.

It also includes the nonconscious past of the memories, representations, and response patterns that belong to implicit knowing. These, too, are acting in the present, unfelt. Examples of this "past" are what Fogel (2003) called "regulatory implicit memories" of how to negotiate social space, interpersonal interactions, and the intersubjective field. Things we begin learning in infancy. Such regulatory patterns have accumulated, have taken shape over a lifetime, and are ongoing influences on the present. Much of our past is ongoing and updated all the time. This "updated ongoing past" is highly active, though silent. The idea of a phenomenologically silent but active past has always been intriguing.

How can we explain that present experience can be largely determined by the silent past? We usually think in terms of past events influencing attentional processes, perceptions, feelings, and cognitions, such that each present moment becomes just another instantiation of past patterns. A similar question has been asked of processes in physical nature. Why does each chamber of a snail's shell have the exact same form but only at a different scale? The question brings to mind a comparison between a present moment and a fractal as described in dynamic systems theory. A fractal is a pattern that has the same general form regardless of its size or scale, like a crystal or a sea snail's shell (Fivaz, 1989; Gleick, 1987). They can have some variations depending on the initial and local conditions of their formation. These fractals have been identified in the physical world as an important aspect of auto-organization. Is there an analogy in the temporally dynamic world of human experience? For instance, recall the graduate student from the breakfast interview in Chapter 1 who tested the limits of how far he could go while swinging open the refrigerator door and filling his glass with orange juice. The essence of these small acts of limit testing is identical to his struggles of the night before, when he was seeing how far he could push the conclusions of his thesis research. The size is different. The importance is different. But is the basic form truly different, except in variations dictated by altered local conditions? The opening of the refrigerator door or the filling the glass become a world in a grain of sand. Psychic determinism works at the level of the present moment.

Another example from a "breakfast interview": A subject described how, during breakfast, she watched the last drops of coffee drip into the cup from her old-fashioned, well-loved espresso machine. There was a buildup of expectation and impatience in her as each drop formed, grew, and took about 4 seconds to fall. When it finally fell into the cup, the satisfaction was short-lived and the expectation for the next drop to fall began to crescendo again, almost right away. When the interview was over, she reflected that she often felt she lived too much in the future, that she permitted herself to be in the present too infrequently, and for spurts that were too short. Again, is the mental / affective activity of watching the coffee drop fractal-like?

Where does the overriding pattern for the fractal come from? It does not come from the crystal's past. It does not pre-exist in a latent form waiting to be expressed or instantiated. In physical nature it comes from the internal and external constraints / degrees of freedom as they operate on a dynamic system that self-organizes in changing local conditions. How do we translate that into a human system with a history, habits, and so on, where the constraints can be modified by life experience or therapy?

Psychodynamically, we have assumed that the present moment is an instantiation of a preexisting more general pattern that (especially when it is unconscious or nonconscious) finds its exact form of expression as it is put into action in a particular setting. Its influence is expressed in all activities regardless of their size. This view is surprisingly close to the notion of fractals. One can substitute representations / original phantasies / conflicts / traumatic memories / defenses / coping strategies or "regulatory implicit memories" as conceived in psychologies, for intrinsic constraints and degrees of freedom as defined in a self-organizing dynamic physical system.

Still, important differences remain between fractals and psychodynamic instantiations or implicit enactments. The one that interests us most is that a fractal is not assumed to contain a preestablished design or blueprint. In other words, it has no active past. It has no past in the sense that the past is a product of human subjectivity. A fractal only has intrinsic tendencies that always operate. The pattern emerges from a dynamic dialogue of intrinsic tendencies with local conditions. In contrast, for the psychodynamic past and implicit knowing there is the clear assumption of active, preformed past patterns that seek expression and thus determine behavior. In this view, each successive present moment in life is a different instantiation of the past acting in the present. Variability comes only from the constraints and affordances of the immediate local conditions. If this were not true we would be psychodynamically incoherent or discontinuous, and only the narrative stringing together of events would hold us and the psychically fragmented time together. On the other hand, if this were completely true, one moment would contain all and we could not change.

In short, as far as the "silent past" is concerned, the difference between fractals and psychodynamic instantiations is only theoretical and not phenomenological. A personal past that acts silently to make someone repeat patterns at any and all scales and in any and all conditions can only feel like an intrinsic constraint reducing the degrees of freedom in the present.

The past is phenomenologically silent rather than nonexistent. But it can be made to speak and reveal itself under the right conditions. It then becomes an "alive past." When the silent past is acting there is often a background sense of familiarity, of being there before, or of being where you are meant

205

to be. The unique freshness has been taken from novelty. Phenomenological silence can be felt as a faint shadow falling on the experience of the present moment.

The Nonexistent Past

There are past events that radically influence the present, not by actively shaping it in an ongoing fashion, but rather by imposing initial constraints and degrees of freedom on what are possible experiences. These constraints include neurophysiological alterations that were irreversibly fixed early in development due to sensitive / critical periods, trauma, conflict (Schore, 1996, 1997, 1998, Siegel, 1996, 1999; Solomon & Siegel, 2003). The consequences of early, massive, socioaffective deprivation as seen in some orphanages (Gunnar, 2001) or the later developmental consequences of early attachment patterns (Sroufe, 1999) are examples.

This past is no longer an active influence. It is a past only in the historical sense or the narrative sense, when viewed from the outside. Phenomenologically it does not exist and never will exist.

The Alive Past

The third phenomenological combination of past and present is where the past is felt to be acting now, although it is still recognized as a past. A simple memory provides a good example. During the memory, experiences from the past are brought foward into the felt present. The sense of having a memory, of its belonging to a personal past but happening now, is the result of two times being brought together and superimposed: the remembered past and the existential present. If the existential presentness of the present moment (captured through background bodily feelings, ambiant light, space, and other contextual impingements) were not acting as the felt time-space in which the past event is now (re)happening (being remembered), one could never know that the past moment is a memory and not a reality or a hallucination. So we have a felt present in which a felt past is acting. This is the past that is alive and felt in the present.

This alive past results from a *multitemporal presentation* in which two events, the reconstituted past and the existential present, enter into dialogue, even though each carries a different time stamp. It is only through such a dialogue that we can "remember the present."

The alive past is of extreme importance in understanding the process of a session or a sequence of sessions at the local level, a relatively near-past. We, as therapists, spend much time and effort trying to discern patterns over time, within and across sessions. This past consists of what has been happening prior to the current present moment and where is it likely to go. The past becomes a pattern of change revealed in sequences. Here the past is not a single event, but rather the differences and similarities between successive events that trace a pattern and direction of movement. It is a past made up of in-betweens. And the present moment that grasps this evolving pattern is like the final chord in a succession of chords. There are many kinds of such pasts in psychotherapy. Following are some general examples.

"Expansion of the present moment." Expansion is a familiar concept in the arts, but less so in clinical psychology. It is essential for understanding one important influence of near-past patterns on the present. Once again, an example from music is helpful. Minsky (1981, p. 15) concluded his description of Beethoven's *Fifth Symphony* by asking, "What is the subject of Beethoven's *Fifth Symphony*? Is it just those first four notes? Does it include the twin, transposed companion, too [the next four notes]? What of the other variations, augmentations, and

inversions? Do they all stem from a single prototype? In this case, yes. Or do they?"

The first four notes may have been a prototype for Beethoven or for those familiar with the music, but for a first-time listener they simply fill a present moment. (Most of life, unlike art, does not faithfully repeat.) For the first-time listener, there are, of course, cultural guidelines about Western music, but for this particular piece there is as yet no specific representation. Each subsequent present moment (phrase) builds toward what? a generalization? a representation? a prototype? Again, the answer is yes and no. Yes, because a representation is indeed forming. No, because other things, as important, are also happening.

Previous phrases build to a deeper understanding of the phrase now being played. And subsequent phrases will build to a deeper understanding of what was already heard, such as Beethoven's first four-note phrase. The implications and richness of both are expanded. After the whole movement is heard, we end up with a richer, deeper appreciation of something, but again, what? This is not a deepening or enriching of a meaning, but of an experience. This distinction cannot be neglected because the enriching of experience is among the most powerful and precious aspects of human life. The same enrichment takes place through human interactions, not just through art.

Expansion of the moment stands in contrast to generalization in the following sense. Generalization is the process of extending from particular, specific cases to general, more abstract conclusions. *Expansion* is the process of staying with or within each specific moment as it comes along, treating it more fully and endowing it with more import and deeper appreciation.

During expansions, the past is actively felt as a background against which the present events are being played out and take form. Expansion is well-suited to a phenomenological approach because it does not require a side-step out of the first-person stance into the objective mode. It is a process, par excellence, of the subjective stance, which entails encountering new experience that lays down a layered world as it is lived—all in a matter of seconds.

Relational progressions. Relational progressions are another example of patterns that accumulate in the near-past and are felt in the present. They abound in therapy. They are "relational" in the sense that it is the therapeutic relationship that is tracing a pattern of change. Subjectively, as a therapy session proceeds, the therapist and patient have to construct what is happening to the relationship as it happens, taking into account, somehow, where it has just come from and where it seems to be going. One single present moment is clearly not sufficient for this task. Nonetheless, you cannot wait until the session is over, or for the next session or two, to see these patterns repeat again and again. (Of course, one does that, too.) We need a subjective process unit that is intermediary in size, larger than a single present moment and shorter than a whole session—a process unit that lumps sequences into larger, coherent, subjective experiences that are, so to speak, the stanzas or movements of the session. Several occur within a session. I call these sequences "relational progressions" because they carry a sense of movement toward relational endpoints or resting places within a session. (Many therapists find it useful to also think of the whole session as a felt gestalt—e.g., Spanuolo-Lobb [2001]. That would be yet a larger and probably different unit.)

How does the present moment fold into itself a relational progression that is a patterned sequence of past happenings? And how is this experienced phenomenologically? Let us go to a clinical example to frame the question. The following material (abbreviated by the author) comes from a member of

209

the Boston CPSG.* The patient is talking about a dream she had the night before.

Theme

Patient: *It was like [in the dream] I was feeling accepted the way I am, and there is something about that that makes me afraid.* (She establishes the theme "acceptance leads to fear." At the same time, she creates an experience with the therapist in the telling. She also establishes the context for whatever will follow. The time context [referent] for this theme is far from the here and now; it is not even in waking reality. It occurs in the past, in a dream, and in recounting the theme she says it was "like." The therapist pauses and then makes some background noise to indicate that she continue.)

Variation 1

Patient: *I start to be afraid of being hurt when I notice I'm letting my guard down.* (The same theme is restated, but with slight variations that make little difference. The trigger for her fear is stated with more precision. Most importantly, she makes it a more general statement applicable beyond the dream. It is no longer outside of reality. She has altered the context for the emergence of what may follow. The therapist again pauses and makes background noise to suggest that she go on.)

Variation 2

Patient: *And you know, one of the things that's disturbing me is that I'll wake up with the feeling of being accepted.* (The same theme is varied again, slightly. But there are two new elements introduced very peripherally and without much emphasis. The therapist is introduced explicitly when she says, "and

---

* For a more extensive exposition of this clinical example, see Boston CPSG, Report No. 4 (in press).

you know." She also is still moving from the dream to reality; "I'll wake up with the feeling. . . .")

Variation 3

Patient: *And then as soon as I'm conscious that it's a dream, I start to feel afraid of the feeling.* (The original theme is now recontextualized by positioning it in reality and closer to the present, as if the theme were beginning to shift into another key, that of the here and now.)

Variation 4

Patient: *It's like I really don't want to feel that with you.* (The elements that have been building have come to the fore and the same theme is now in an altered key—namely, the context of here-and-now-with-the-therapist. She mitigates the fullness of the new key by saying that "it is like." But it is clearly out there to be seen by both of them.)

The progression is not in the development of the theme itself. It hardly develops at all. It was clearly stated in the beginning. The progression is in the context, including the stance of the speaker—in other words, in the directional readjustments of the intersubjective field. There are two progressions in this example. The first is from the patient's standing far away, in a past event, and not quite in reality, to moving closer to the here-and-now and the real. The second shift is the replacing of the theme squarely within the therapist-patient relationship.

The last variation brings the double progression to something that feels like a temporary closure, a resting place. The therapist clearly feels that some point of arrival has been achieved, because he now intervenes.

Therapist: *Huh! Something's scary.* (As if to say, "Okay, I got it. It's on the table now where we both see it and can deal with it.")

Joint Action

The patient responds, *Yeah,* and the therapist immediately joins in, *Yeah.*

They have shared a short journey of incremental movements that makes up the relational progression. Their agreement is mutully ratified with the "Yeah," "Yeah."

We now have seven relational moves in sequence (one original theme, four variations by the patient, one statement by the therapist, and a joint ratification of their mutual acceptance). The experience of each of the relational moves must enter awareness. But each of the moments leading up to variation 4 ("It's like I really don't want to feel that with you") do not require much consciousness, no more than needed to get them into words. (Remember you need not be aware that you are conscious of something.) The patient and therapist are struggling together to let or make something emerge. And what emerges is a sort of minor now moment, "I don't want to feel that with you," which the therapist keeps at center stage, in the here and now, by saying, "Huh! Something's scary." This then leads into and becomes part of a small moment of meeting—the "Yeah," "Yeah." This mutually confirms the whole progression of bringing this sequential pattern forward. Remember, there are large *Moments of Meeting*, with capital letters, and small moments of meeting.

There is no reason to imagine that each step of the progression (i.e., each individual relational move) needs to become a present moment, with its requirement of some kind of consciousness, and be remembered for itself. The progression resides not in any one move but in the sequential changes.

How can we capture the sense of a progression that comes from many moves already past and squeeze it into a single present moment? How do we do that while still insisting that subjective experience happens only in the present? The same problem arises when listening to music. You can only listen to the part of the music that is being played now. The phrases that preceded it have slipped into the past yet continue to act.

How does a string of events, while they are happening, get brought together to make a larger unit? It is the "while they are happening" that is the hard part. The notion of multitemporal presentations is helpful here. The first moment in the sequence (which has just passed) and the second moment (occurring now) form a multitemporal presentation when brought together. We assume that the first (previous) moment is reactivated and brought forward from working memory because of its similarity (repeats and variations of) and adjacency to the second moment. The presently occurring moment acts as the remembering context to evoke the moment that just passed. This is inevitable, because if the present is to be evaluated for its novelty, it must be compared to what is familiar, which lies in the past.

With each successive present moment the multitemporal presentation changes. The presentation made up of moments #1 and #2 gets added to moment #3, making a multitemporal presentation combining all three moments (experiences). And so on. With each addition to the sequence, the evolving multitemporal presentation advances like a run of chords in music in which the entire progression is brought to rest and felt in the last chord, which contains the history of its own evolution. In this fashion, the last present moment of the sequence encompasses the sense of the progression, and the near-past made up of changing patterns is brought into the present moment.

This kind of run-up to a final event that encompasses the sequential process is similar to the model of affect appraisal proposed by Scherer (2001). In this model an event that produces an affect goes through a rapid succession of evaluations or checks, each lasting split seconds (and each being performed in a fixed sequential order: first, a novelty check (is the event novel?); second, an action check (is it to be approached or withdrawn from?); third, a hedonic check (is it pleasurable or unpleasurable?); forth, a cognitive / perceptual check (what is it?); fifth, a coping check (can it be dealt with?); and sixth, a moral check (is the coping mechanism morally acceptable?). The quality and type of affect that finally emerges, and that is felt, is the result of all of these evaluations taken together, which give it its particular essence. It is like a run of multitemporal presentations being superimposed, where only the last one enters awareness—like the last chord in the run, like the last present moment in the progression series. Relational progressions are very well created in dance, music, movement therapies, where the implicit agenda is so often in the forefront.

Why or how do relational progressions end or come to a rest, making a unit? This is a key clinical point. The awareness of a relational progression pops into consciousness as an emergent property. It comes about something like this: The differences or directionality inherent in the progression of multitemporal presentations stays in the background. These differences (wherein the progression resides) are being worked on, out of awareness, until the relational progression is "ready" to emerge into consciousness. At that point it is assembled and surfaces in a fresh present moment, and the progressing pattern is grasped. Most of the groundwork has already been done.

At the same moment that the progression reaches a point of sufficient completeness, both the patient and therapist become aware of it, as well as aware that the other is also aware. The moment becomes shared and enters intersubjective consciousness. In this way the last three moments of the previous example (variation 4, the therapists' response, and the joint "Yeah," "Yeah") enter intersubjectively consciousness. This makes these moments more therapeutically useful. A larger unit with a felt past has been locked in. The requirement that all subjective experience occurs only now, in the present, is preserved, while accounting for the impression of building up over past time.

Working memory is a needed mechanism for this kind of evolution of multitemporal presentations. The separate moments that make up the sequence have passed out of the felt present when the next moment in the sequence arrives. They are no longer part of the "comet's tail." They have slipped into the discontinuous past. Working memory serves to hold these past moments in a state of activation so that they can be evoked and experienced as superimposed or alongside the present moment. Here, the enormous number of repetitions and variations that make up a therapy session acquire a function. Working memory is kept activated by rehearsal. If it is rehearsed, something can be held in short-term memory well beyond its usual limit of many seconds. A kind of rehearsal (in the form of variations) is exactly what we see in the sequences of moments that make up a therapy session. Because moments are of relatively short duration, lasting seconds, most often with pauses in between, a repetition or new variation appears well within the limit of working memory and constantly primes the memory to keep it activated. In this way the essential (varied) bits of the sequence can be held in memory and ultimately made contemporaneous with present happenings, thus permitting the multitemporal presentations in which the progression is felt.

It should be noted that multitemporal presentations are largely treated in the implicit domain. They involve nonlinear and noncausal processes and have a closer relationship to metaphor as a fundamental mode of cognition.

There are many different types of relational progressions, each describing a different felt past. I will mention only a couple other examples in addition to those I have already given to fill out the general idea.

Emotional momentum is another progression in which the past is the pattern of a sequence felt in the present. It is a well-known way-to-be-with-someone, a technique of rhetoric, a tactic of emotional diplomacy, and a way to convince oneself of something.

Dr. Seuss, writer of children's books, provided an excellent example. Sam-I-Am is the main character of *Green Eggs and Ham* (1960). He is repeatedly asked if he will eat green eggs and ham. The question and his negative answers get sillier, more delightful, and convincing because of the shear weight of their repetition and the progressive accumulation of new ways of saying "No!" Sam-I-Am answers the question of whether he likes green eggs and ham by replying, "I do not like them / in a house. / I do not like them / with a mouse. / I do not like them / here or there. / I do not like them anywhere. / I do not like green eggs and ham. / I do not like them, Sam-I-Am." He is then asked if he would eat them in a box or with a fox. He replies, "Not in a box. / Not with a fox. / Not in a house. / Not with a mouse. / I would not eat them here or there. / I would not eat them anywhere. / Sam-I-Am." And so on, with amusing variations and repeats. What is progressing here? Besides delight and pleasure, the emotional conviction of Sam-I-Am is growing and gaining momentum. This is augmented by his adding after each string of negatives, "Sam-I-Am," as if his identity is closely tied to this refusal to eat green eggs and ham. This gives growing momentum to his reaffirmations. (In the end he eats and loves them.)

This is another example of a kind of accumulating pattern getting carried along in successive present moments. We have already seen this pattern in the dialogue of Mariah and her therapist (Chapter 9), where the main action is in the fluctuation of the affective tone. Mariah, also, finally "eats the green eggs and ham."

A sense of exploding possibilities is another example of a relational progression that holds yet a different felt past in the present. A musical invention is an uncomplicated example. It is usually defined as a short composition developing a single theme (usually in two-part counterpoint as in Bach's piano inventions). A more complicated example might be Jerome Robbins's ballet *Dances at a Gathering*, where there is no particular story line but many variations of the ways people can move and be together in twos, or threes, or fours, or eight, performing what seems like unlimited variations that continue to amaze. Each successive moment carries a feeling of the past moments. But what is the theme in such works? One is astounded by each variation. And when it is over one is left pleased and satisfied. The sequence of variations creates the experience of expanding multiple possibilities. And the opening of each one creates a sense of surprise and wonder. The flow of variations constantly reanimates our interest in the infinite possibilities that exist in the world. Is that a theme or a meaning? We leave the performance feeling bigger, more opened up, more aware of the possibilities in our own lives.

This can also happen in psychotherapy in short stretches, for example, when the patient grasps that he or she can say anything they think or want to say. All paths of exploration suddenly open up as potential trails to follow. This is an affectively loaded present moment. The particular content of each possible path is not as important as the sense of as-yet-unthought-of possibilities to explore. An attitude has been captured—one that is extremely valuable in psychotherapy. Patients keep rediscovering it in the course of a therapy.

Beyond therapy, being with certain people can give this impression of exploding possibilities. There is a sense that one could talk about anything with them, that topics change inexplicably and are inexhaustible. This situation is a powerful way-of-being-together, especially when there is a mutual recognition of this dyadic state of affairs.

The Temporally Unanchored Past

The emergence of certain dissociated traumatic memories may represent a fourth phenomenal combination of past and present. When these memories burst on the scene, they are not experienced as a felt past or even as coming from the past. Nor, do they occur in a felt ambient present inhabited by a self who is existentially situated in the present. The relevant aspects of self are in abeyance. These experiences "just are." They are temporally unanchored. Normally memories emerging from working memory seem to walk into the room of the present and sit down in their designated chair. Recalled episodic memories or unrepressed memories can burst into the room of the present in full disorientation and bang about the place before they settle down. In both cases, however, there is a felt past inhabiting a separately felt present. That is not the case for some recalled traumatic memories. They annihilate both the felt present and felt past. This is an extreme situation of being temporally unanchored.

In summary, I have tried to show that the present moment can hold the past within its small grasp and that the past is only "alive" when on the stage of the present moment. The past plays a constant role in influencing what we experience from second to second. And the present moment constantly reorders our memory of the past. The present moment and the past are each the parent and child of one another. This is true regardless of whether the past is unconscious nonconscious or conscious. In the dialogue between the past and present, psychodynamics need not be abandoned. However, the traditional stranglehold of the past over the present is mitigated. Past and present become equal partners. Perhaps what is most important therapeutically is that one begins to see how the experience of the present moment can rewrite the past.

Chapter 13

THERAPEUTIC CHANGE: A Summary and Some General Clinical Implications

WE NOW HAVE all the pieces in place. We have a process unit of subjective experience: the present moment. It has a duration and a temporal architecture that permits it to chunk and make sense of experience while it is happening. This results in the experience of being in a lived story as it evolves. The lived story has a beginning, end, affective highpoints, a primitive plot, implied intentions, and, most importantly, a duration with a temporal contour along which the experience forms during its unfolding. This is its temporal dynamic. In short, the present moment is directly lived through in real time. It is undergone in reality as it is happening. It is a direct, temporal experience. It is not an experience once-removed by language or twice-removed by abstraction, explanation, or narrativization. Its formation in real time is crucial.

A therapy session (or any intimate dialogue) is made up of a series of present moments that are driven forward by the desire for intersubjective contact and an enlargement of the shared intersubjective field. Intersubjectivity is a primary motive in this movement. As the dyad moves along, linking together present moments, a new way of-being-with-the-other may arise at any step along the way. These new experiences enter into awareness but need not enter consciousness all the time. They add to the domain of implicit knowing. This kind of change occurs at the local level. These moments, each lasting only several seconds, accumulate and probably account for the majority of incremental therapeutic change that is slow, progressive, and silent.

Less often, more sensationally and less silently, these relational moves can prepare the ground for the emergence of a special present moment, the *now moment*. This is an emergent property of the moving along process, a process that is unpredictable, sloppy, dynamic, and cocreated—an ideal milieu for the irruption of emergent properties. These special present moments, when they suddenly arise, threaten the status quo of the relationship and challenge the intersubjective field as it has been mutually accepted up until then. These are moments of *kairos*. They test the therapist and the therapy. They set the stage for a crisis that needs some kind of resolution.

The resolution occurs in a different special present moment called a *moment of meeting*. When successful, the moment of meeting is an authentic and well-fitted response to the crisis created by the now moment. It is a moment that implicitly reorganizes the intersubjective field so that it becomes more coherent, and the two people sense an opening up of the relationship, which permits them to explore new areas together implicitly or explicitly. The moment of meeting need not be verbalized to effectuate change. A now moment followed by a moment of meeting is the nodal event that can dramatically change a relationship or the course of a therapy.

Because of their affective charge and import for the immediate future, the now moment and the moment of meeting, focus the participants on the presentness of the moment they are now living. They are both experiencing the unfolding of a piece of reality. They read in the behavior of the other a reflection of their own experience. This provides a form of reentry via another's mind so that the experience becomes *intersubjectively conscious*. This opens the door for the experience to be verbalized and narrated and to become a landmark reference point in the narrative history of the treatment.

The question of the mechanism of change now comes up. The reason I put the emphasis on experience and not meaning is as follows. It is my basic assumption that original experiences are laid down (inscribed in memory and in the neural circuitry) in a form that retains the real-time flow of their unfolding. They are a temporal record as well. I assume that these formative memories must be as temporally based as life is when subjectively lived. This is why temporal dynamics have been stressed throughout the book.

If past experiences are to be changed, they must be rewritten or replaced by a new temporal experience occurring in the same time framework. The rewriting must also be lived through with its own temporal dynamics. In contrast, the content of language and narrative is an abstracted experience. It is once-removed from direct experience and shortcircuits its temporal flow. It has different temporal dynamics from direct experience. But it can only rewrite the explicit past, not the implicit experienced past.

One cannot change without altering the functional past—in other words, the past that is activated and now influencing present behavior. The present moment is a "present remembering context" that selects which pieces of the past will be activated and brought into the present, as well as how they will be assembled to best deal with the present situation and influence it.

The present moment changes the functional past (not the historical past as seen from the outside by a third-person) in two ways. First, to the extent that the current present moment is a new experience that arises in the moving along process, it will act as a novel *present remembering context*. As such it will select and assemble never-before-seen or less-used pieces of the past to create a new functional past to bear on the present. The old functional past is not reassembled and not brought forward. It is bypassed, and the new functional past is ready to act on the future. This process must be repeated over and over to strengthen the selection of the particular new functional past and its neural basis. That is why this mode of change is slow, progressive, and silent. The past is, so to speak, replaced by being reassembled differently.

The second way the present moment changes the functional past is by rewriting it and erasing the old record in the course of one experience. Here, I reemphasize that present moments are real experiences lived in real time. Recall the evidence (e.g., the rabbits' repertoire of odors) that a new experience can rewrite the neural circuitry and phenomenal expression of a previously written and remembered experience. The key notion, again, is a real happening in real time with a temporal dynamic—a lived story that is being rewritten by writing over the old.

It is important to remember that the experience contained in present moments is occurring in parallel with the exchange of language during a session. The two support and influence each other in turns. I am not trying to lessen the importance of language and the explicit in favor of implicit experience. I am trying to call attention to direct and implicit experience because it has been relatively neglected.

With an emphasis on implicit experience rather than explicit content, therapeutic aims shift more to the deepening and enriching of experience and less to the understanding its meaning.

SOME GENERAL CLINICAL IMPLICATIONS

The aim of this book has not been to develop a new clinical approach but rather to suggest a different vision of the clinical process when seen at the momentary, local level. Nonetheless, there are some implications for theory and practice. Where they will eventually lead remains to be seen. My experience and that of the clinicians in the Boston CPSG has been that our clinical sensibilities have been altered by this view in ways that are hard to pin down. Nonetheless, here are some of them.

When we focus at the local level made up of present moments, a different clinical sensibility arises. One becomes more aware of small events, especially nonverbal and implicit events. These also occur in the form of speech acts. They surround and accompany what is being talked about. They make up the parallel implicit agenda. The observer / listener must be attentive to the explicit verbal content and the implicit experience simultaneously. But it is difficult to follow both equally if one does not believe that they both may have equal value in the treatment. And many approaches do not believe that. However, when the two are given equal weight, it becomes just as reasonable and fruitful to intervene about a small implicit behavior as about a verbalization. And the intervention can be in the implicit domain as well as in the explicit. This greatly increases the spectrum of therapeutic opportunities.

When the flow of a session is thought to be driven by the desire to regulate and enlarge the intersubjective field, some events fall more into the background, particularly the search for explicit meaning (at least for a while). Other hitherto less attended events jump to the foreground, such as the direction in which the intersubjective field is being led. Strategically, it is often initially more important to follow the movement of the intersubjective field toward a place that can permit the explicit agenda to open up than it is to focus on the production of explicit material en route. The emphasis shifts temporarily from intrapsychic content to intersubjective regulation. Recall the case of Mariah and the amount of time needed to set up the appropriate intersubjective field before any explicit content could even appear. One could easily have focused on her negativity and aggressiveness while moving along, rather than on her working toward an acceptable intersubjective jumping-off place to talk about what was uppermost on her mind.

The same applies to progressions of present moments. The clinical action is likely to be in the sequential shaping of the intersubjective field, as well as, or even more than, in the development of explicit content.

In a similar light, the transference-countertransference moves are subordinate to the more overarching regulation of the therapeutic relationship, particularly its intersubjective aspects. Not all acts to define or alter the nature of the therapeutic relationship are primarily transferential, or defensive.

This brings up a larger issue. The point of view developed here suggests the advisibility of holding theory at a further distance during the session so that the immediate relationship can be lived more fully. When should interpretations be made or held off in order to stay inside the cocreated dyadic process and wait until it has run a fuller course? This is a question of good timing, which is accounted for in traditional techniques. In practice, however, an interpretation is usually conceived and used as an hypothesis to be tested by the patient and therapist for its truth and heuristic value. That is all very well, but it adds a powerful directional influence on the flow of the moving along process, an influence that comes largely from outside the immediate dyadic process and arises from theory and metapsychology residing only in the therapist's mind. The interpretation-as-hypothesis pulls the therapeutic process into a more assymetrical relationship with regard to cocreation. It also sets a direction that was not necessarily what was happening at that moment in the process. During and right after the interpretation, the therapist is standing on a very different ground than the patient. They must renegotiate the distance between them while they negotiate the value of the interpretation-as-hypothesis. Yet interpretations must be made when deemed appropriate. The only way around this dilemma is to treat interpretations as potential sloppiness as much as a reasoned (possibly true) hypotheses.

I have the impression that in certain therapeutic schools, very early and frequent interpretations are given. These appear to force the direction of the dyadic process along theoretical lines, leaving unexplored the unique lines intrinsic to the patient.

Attention to the implicit flow of the session has implications for viewing and dealing with the sloppy nature of the therapeutic process, its unpredictability, and its spontaneity. If one accepts that sloppiness is not only necessary but potentially creative, and not necessarily psychodynamically determined but inherent in the moving along process, one treats it differently. First, it does not have to be treated as the breakthrough of unconscious material, like a slip of the tongue or a defensive mishearing or misunderstanding, at least not right away. The clinical question becomes not why that misunderstanding occurred, but where may it lead us, now, that is interesting. Second, the therapist can always double back later and pick up the psychodynamic aspects if they then still seem salient. They usually don't. Stated otherwise, defense analysis comes second. But this will only happen when there is a full recognition of the scope and potential creativity of sloppiness and unpredictablity.

Another implication concerns now moments. Now moments carry a double danger. If not responded to and redirected toward another purpose, they can quickly lead to greater and more disruptive acting in. Additionally, they may provoke anxiety in the therapist, who responds by hiding behind technique which prevents the now moment from bearing much fruit. The acceptance of the now moment as not only a normal event in therapy, but also as a rare creative opportunity, changes the therapists' threshold for this kind of anxiety. This permits him or her to tolerate the situation with enough ease to be more authentic and find a response that is both well fitted to the specific situation and carries the therapists' personal signature. All members of the Boston CPSG have noticed this change within themselves.

Finally, I have emphasized at several points that the approach taken here focuses on experience rather than cognitive meaning. I again fall back on the experience of music, (it could be any of the arts) to explore this distinction further. One can listen to and deconstruct music, rendering an explicit understanding of how it is constructed. This takes some training. More often we do not do that. Rather, with repeated listenings, we come to experience it more deeply. It becomes enriched. Different aspects interest, surprise, and delight us at subsequent hearings. One "knows" it better, in the sense that the experience is enriched. When a patient and therapist work together, something similar happens. The distinction between the cognitive understanding of experience and the enriching of experience is vital.

Of course there must be a search for meaning so that a psychodynamic understanding can be constructed, and a life narrative created. For this, a verbal explicit account of the patient's experience is paramount. But there must also be a process of appreciating the experience of the patient more deeply, of feeling his experience and sharing it with him so that there is an enriching of who he is, what it is like to be him, and what it is like to be-with-him. For this enriching of the experience of an other to occur, the flow of moving along in the session, the intersubjectively shared present moments, and the implicit knowings are paramount.

The distinctions between implicit / explicit, nonverbal / verbal, appreciating / understanding, and experience / meaning can be summarized in terms of their role in therapeutic change. In talking therapies the work to interpret, to make meaning, and to narrativize can be seen as an almost nonspecific, convenient vehicle by which the patient and therapist "do something together." It is the doing-together that enriches experience and brings about change in ways-of-being-with-others through the implicit processes discussed. Complementary to this, verbal meaning making and narrativizing as forms of explicating can be viewed as also bringing about therapeutic change. Here the implicit doing-together and altered implicit knowing frames the flow of explicit understanding and locks it home.

Both are needed. But each demands a different descriptive and explanatory model. I have concentrated on the implicit and experiential because it is a less charted territory. To do this has required looking at the therapeutic process through the lens of the present moment.

Appendix

THE MICRO-ANALYTIC INTERVIEW

INTRODUCTION: WHAT IS BEING STUDIED?

It is important to be clear about what aspect of consciousness is being studied. Even though the major focus of the book has been on experience as it is lived, the exploration of the micro-analytic interview is a pilot experiment that concerns the after-the-fact telling about what was consciously lived. The subject of study, then, is a special kind of narrative about conscious experience. However, it is a special narrative. It is derived from an interview technique that constructs the narrative account from multiple tellings of the same material, where each telling can "correct," add to, subtract from, or enrich the previous tellings; where the events recounted are of short duration, rarely more than a minute; where the interview is *micro-analytic* in the sense that the smallest remembered happening, feeling, thought, or action is explored until it is exhausted of remembered content; where the telling is coconstructed by the experimenter with the subject; where all the narrated elements are graphed along the dimensions of time (estimated) and intensity (subjectively judged).

The result is a single account a layered, micro-analytically focused, coconstructed narrative. I will tentatively call it a *composite narrative*. This composite narrative is not the lived experience, nor is it a normally constructed narrative, which is sketched rapidly in the mind more or less as it is being told and is usually recounted only once or periodically. Although a normal narrative account is derived from an original conscious experience, it is, in itself, also a fundamental datum in the sense that it is the way we commonly "mindsize," or think and tell about our experiences. The composite narrative probably lies somewhere between lived experience and a normal narrative. It is a more artificial, experimental product.

Why, then, is this level of analysis justified and possibly interesting? It is an attempt to move closer to an objectification of the lived subjective experience. Consciousness studies are at a stage where a dialogue between different levels of description is needed. The present account is an attempt to develop another level of description to join the dialogue. The necessity of such dialogue has been amply suggested by many others (cited elsewhere in this book).

The idea behind the micro-analytic interview came from experience with the micro-analysis of parent-infant interactions using film and videotape as a microscope to understand more deeply how they worked. The descriptions at the split-second micro level that emerged were fascinating and very useful in conceptualizing and treating the parent-infant relationship (see citations elsewhere in this book). However, their phenomenal reality was unexplored.

I assume that the composite narrative, which is analogous to the micro-analysis of behavior, will get us closer to lived experience and thereby yield new insights and ideas. It is with this in mind that the method and results are presented.

METHODOLOGY

The Population

The interview has been tried on students, colleagues, and friends. Initially, beginning a decade ago, twelve interviews were conducted. I used these to establish the method. The results from these interviews are not be included here, as they were not quantified in a standard manner.

With the aid of several of my research assistants at the University of Geneva (Philip Santos, Janine de Haller, and Pierre Scheidegger), I interviewed a second group of six subjects. The method and quantitative results from this second subject group, summarized here, are described and discussed in detail by Santos (2000). One subject was dropped because she could not maintain the distinction between what one is aware of and what one is fully conscious of. A third group of five subjects was collected by me after the second experiment was over. The purpose of this third group was to clarify and refine aspects of the interview. The total number of separate cases reported on quantitatively with the same methods is eight.

The insightfulness or narrative facility of the subjects was not evaluated. Suffice it to say that even though all subjects were of roughly equivalent educational and intelligence status, there was wide variation in insightfulness and narrative facility. I have no data on variations across different cultures, ages, sexes, or types of psychopathogy, much as that would be interesting.

The Subject Matter of the Interviews

All of the reported interviews had only one general subject: what was consciously experienced that morning at breakfast (thus the original name "the breakfast interview"). Breakfast was chosen because we could count on its occurance on the morning just before the interview. In other words, it had a constant recency, it was sufficiently automated (meaning that the mind was freer to wander), and it usually did not contain emotional events that would require much censoring. This last reason proved to be less true than anticipated. The subjects chose which segment of the breakfast period to explore. The basis of the choice was not known. This left the door open for selection on the basis of psychodynamic factors, narrative facility, emotional charge, and so on.

I have also conducted this interview where the subject matter was the most affectively charged experience the subject had during the past week. A slightly different picture emerges. However, this will not be commented upon here.

The Procedure

General Directions

Volunteers who knew nothing of our study were invited to our laboratory at 10 A.M. They were only told that we were conducting a study about the experience of consciousness and that we would explain it further at the end of the study. They were then asked, "Tell me about what you consciously experienced this morning during breakfast." I went over the difference between what they logically knew must have happened (which is usually quite automatic and nonconscious) and what they were clearly conscious of. They were also asked to notify me about any pieces of the experience they did not wish to tell us about, so I knew if there were holes in the account.

It is important to ask about what they *experienced*—not about what *happened* (which leads to recounting actions or events), what they *thought*, what they *felt*, or about anything that leads them to favor any modality or type of experience. These modality-specific questions come later.

Choosing a Segment and its Boundaries

The first task is to establish the segment of the breakfast experience to be explored. The segment cannot be too much longer than 30 to 90 seconds because of the time constraints of an intensive examination. The segment should be continuous, in real time, even if it is composed of several separate pieces of consciousness.

The segment is chosen as follows. First the subject tells the narrative of the whole breakfast experience. This is invariably a brief summary without great interest. He or she is then asked to pick out any part of the whole that has a clear beginning and ending. The subject then chooses which clearly defined (in his or her mind) happenings will serve as boundaries.

Parsing the Segment

The subject breaks the segment into pieces (see example from Chapter 1). The first parsing occurs at the level of the *episode of consciousness*. The episode is a stretch of continuous consciousness surrounded by periods of nonconsciousness, or *non-CS holes*. The second parsing breaks the continuous episodes of consciousness into present moments.*

Some episodes of consciousness contain only one present moment, in which case the main boundary markers for that present moment are also non-CS holes surrounding the present moment. More frequently, each episode of consciousness contains several present moments that are temporally adjacent to each other. In this case, the boundaries between adjacent present moments consist of noticable changes in the experience. These changes usually involve a shift in place, action, characters, time, stance of the teller relative to the experience,

---

* In the work of Santos (2000), what I am calling *episodes of consciousness* are called "present moments," and what I am calling *present moments* are called "takes."

or any combination of these. One ends up with a parsing that looks like this:

Segment Chosen to Be Narrated

hole——episode of csness——hole——episode of csness——hole

(present moment # 1) (present moment # 2) (etc.)

Repeated attention is given to the distinction between things that must have happened and those that clearly entered into consciousness. The question is posed to the subject over and over.

Graphing the Parsed Segment for the First Time

The subject is instructed how to graph their experience along the two dimensions: estimated time of duration (in seconds or fractions thereof), and subjective intensity (1 to 10). (See Figure 1.1, Chapter 1.) The graphed elements of the experience are drawn as lines, curves, or contours. The absissa of the graph is time and the ordinate is intensity of the experience. The first graph is very rough and approximative. It is a working sketch.

Multiple Passes Through the Experience to Compose the Composite Narrative

Any one of the elements of the experience within a present moment is then picked out for further exploration. For instance, if affects are the first element taken up, the subject is asked exactly what he or she felt and to draw its time-intensity-shape on the graph. That is the first pass. On the second pass, the subject's thoughts are added to the graph. On subsequent passes, actions, memories, postures or postural shifts, gestures, images, phantasies, feelings, and so on are separately added in sequence.

Each time a new pass is made and new elements are added,

it is usually necessary to make corrections in the previous passes, which may alter the whole graph, including its parsing or timing or the shape of previously placed curves. The order of questions asked about different elements (e.g., thoughts or affects) is variable and usually made on the basis of its apparent salience. One ends up with a graph that resembles a peculiar musical score for a symphony. This is then compressed into one composite graph.

A Final Check on Consciousness

After all the passes have been made and the progressive alterations added, the subject is asked to pick the exact moment that an element became conscious by thickening the line of its curve at that point. This is necessary because many physical and mental acts trace a long line that is vaguely in awareness but only jumps into or out of consciousness at certain points (see Figure 1.1).

Estimations of Durations

After an almost final graph is in place, the subject is asked to estimate in seconds how long each element, present moment, and episode of consciousness lasted in real time. Many of the experiences are described as momentary or flashes. They are given an arbitrary duration of ¼ second. The total time is estimated in three ways. *Total added time* is arrived at by adding up the separate durations given to each of the present moments. *Total global time* is the estimated duration of the entire narrated segment. The subject is also asked to enact the experience in the same time frame that it seemed to occur. The time needed for this enactment is the *total enacted time*.

When is the Interview Over?

After all the passes have been made, and some are made more than once, a point is reached when the subject feels that the interview has harvested all the information the experience contained. A final verisimilitude check is made. The subject is asked if the final graph is a faithful representation of what the experience was like. If it isn't, final adjustments are made.

Questions About the Phenomenological Status of Aspects of the Experience

Three questions are posed after the graph is finalized. The first examines the *existential status* of the experience during the present moment. Does it concern *objects of experience* that are real and present or objects that are absent or virtual?

The second question examinines the *placement in time* of the experience. Is it in the past, the present, or the future, or does it occupy an indeterminate time?

The third question examines the *stance* of the narrator relative to the experience narrated. Is the subject viewing the experience at a distance or is he or she fully present in it? Is the subject more a spectator or an actor in the experience? Is the subject loosely focused and distractable or highly focused on the experience?

Duration of the Interview

The entire interview takes about an hour and a half.

The Results

The Temporal Structure of Conscious Experience as Found in the Composite Narrative

The longest unit is *the segment of experience chosen to be narrated.* Using "total added time," the range was from 4.5 seconds to 367 seconds, with a mean of 91.7 seconds and a median of 28.5 seconds (see Table A.1). Although this range is large, it did not greatly influence the durations of the smaller, more basic units.

The next-shorter unit, the *episodes of consciousness*, were quite easy for the subjects to identify because they were surrounded by non-CS holes. These episodes had a duration with a mean

Table A.1. THE TEMPORAL STRUCTURE OF EPISODES OF CONSCIOUSNESS AND PRESENT MOMENTS (durations in seconds.)

A. *Episodes of Consciousness*

	SUBJECTS								
	1	2	3	4	5	A	B	C	mean
Number	11	3	7	4	6	3	4	1	4.9
Mean duration	2.6	8.7	52.4	52	4.5	15	20	4.5	20.2
Median duration	2	8	5	8.5	4	9	12	4.5	6.6

B.*Present Moments*

	SUBJECTS								
	1	2	3	4	5	A	B	C	mean
Number	29	10	19	14	22	10	16	1	16.4
Mean duration	8	2.6	19.3	15.4	1.2	7	16	4.5	9.3
Median duration	2.6	3.3	2.7	3.5	3.7	2.9	4.2	4.5	3.4

C. *Present Moments per Episode of Consciousness*

	SUBJECTS								
	1	2	3	4	5	A	B	C	mean
number	2.6	3.3	2.7	3.5	3.7	3.3	2.5	1	2.8

D. *Total Time of Segment Chosen to Narrate*

	SUBJECTS								
	1	2	3	4	5	A	B	C	mean
Added time	25	26	367	216	27	30	38	4.5	91.7
Global time	35	10	720	210	600	40	50	8	209.1

of 20.2 seconds and a median of 6.6 seconds (see Table A.1). This variability is to be expected because the number of present moments per episode is variable.

The shortest units, the *present moments*, were, at times, more difficult to separate and identify because the boundary criteria are more subtle. There were on average 2.8 present moments per episode of consciousness, with a range 1 to 3.7 present moments per episode of consciousness. Present moments had a mean duration of 9.3 seconds (with two out of eight being much higher than the others).

Table A.2. THE NATURE OF BOUNDARIES BETWEEN ADJACENT
PRESENT MOMENTS (expressed as percentage of total adjacencies)

	SUBJECTS								
	1	2	3	4	5	A	B	C	mean
Shift in stance	100	100	95	100	91	100	94	100	98
Shift in scene	100	100	100	100	100	100	100	100	100

The most striking finding, however, was that the median duration was rather constant: 3.4 seconds, with a range of 2.6 to 4.5 seconds (see Table A.1). This duration is what would have been predicted from the data presented in Chapter 3 on the duration of the present moment in different domains.

The Nature of Boundaries Between Adjacent Present Moments

Because there are no non-CS holes separating adjacent present moments, less obvious criteria are used. In between adjacent present moments there is a shift in the scene (place, time, characters, or action) in 100% of instances. There is a shift in the subject's stance relative to the action in 98% of instances (see Table A.2).

The Phenomenological Status of Experiences Within
a Present Moment (Selected Aspects)

Three aspects are identified: the existential status of the object of experience, the time placement of the object of experience, and the stance of the subject relative to the object of experience. The results are presented in Table A.3. Overall, they support the idea of a polyphonic, polytemporal present moment that changes dynamically as it unfolds.

DISCUSSION

A critical question concerns to what extent the duration of events in the composite narratives (as remembered, recounted, and coassembled as a composite) corresponds to the events as

Table A.3. PHENOMENOLOGICAL STATUS OF EXPERIENCE
WITHIN A PRESENT MOMENT

A. *Existential Status of Experience in a Present Moment (percent)*

	SUBJECTS								
	1	2	3	4	5	A	B	C	mean
Object is present	51.7	50	57.9	74.1	45.6	49.4	35	100	57.5
Object is absent	44.8	30		36.8	28.6	45.6	50.6	65	0	45.8
Object is both present and absent	6.9	20	21.1	42.8	0	0	10	0	12.6

B. *Placement of the Present Moment in Time (percent)*
   (There can be simultaneous placements)

	SUBJECTS								
	1	2	3	4	5	A	B	C	mean
Past	6.9	90	10.5	28.6	45.6	33	40	0	31.8
Present	79.3	10	84.2	78.5	77.3	80	60	100	71.2
Futur	24.1	20	26.3	35.7	50	10	15	0	24.5
Indeterminate	3.4	10	15.5	2.1	0	5	12.5	0	7.6

C. *Range of Stances Taken across Different Present Moments (range from 1-5)*

	SUBJECTS							
	1	2	3	4	5	A	B	C
At a distance (1) Fully present (5)	1-5	3-5	1-5	2-5	1-5	2-5	2-5	4
Spectator (1) Actor (5)	2-5	2-5	1-5	1-5	1-5	2-5	2-5	3
Open to distraction (1) Tightly focused (5)	1-5	2-5	2-5	2-5	1-5	2-5	1-5	4

originally experienced. Several authors have suggested that the duration of events as remembered or represented is fairly close to the actual time of the lived events. For example, concerning physical movement, Jeannerod (1999) suggested that the mind accurately represents the moving body in time and space. There may, however be domain-specific differences in the tightness of this matching, for example, for affects compared to thoughts, compared to actions, and so on.

A second critical question is: What kind of validity can be attached to these findings? The strongest case can be made for face validity. The composite narratives feel like it felt when it happened. The verisimilitude to life-as-lived is strong. This is a pervasive impression. Often when I talk about the results of the breakfast interview to the subjects, they laugh and say, "Yeah, that's what it was really like." The fact that we find the same mean duration and range for present moments from different domains of experience (see Chapter 3) lends convergent validity. In the last analysis, studies of brain recordings of neural activity will go far in establishing a form of correlational validity about the duration of events as remembered and as lived.

To date only one published study has raised the question of the utility of the micro-analytic interview in exploring clinical phenomena. Nachman's (2001) study of maternal identification with a child in real time used the technique. It revealed many rapid shifts in the strength and nature of the mother's identification with her child. These shifts were measured in seconds, depending on the changing contexts. Identification from this perspective is seen as a highly temporally dynamic process rather than a state that is long in duration or even static, as we sometimes think about it.

I anticipate that the composite narrative that results from the micro-analytic interview will help in further exploring phenomenological features of clinical and neuroscientific interest. I would anticipate that the quantitative profile of different features of the composite narrative would be different under different conditions, settings, psychological or other pathological states, and cultural contexts. Even the duration of the present moment, which appears to be the most constant element, may vary under different conditions. All such differences, however, would further our understanding.

In any event, the results attest to the richness of the micro-momentary world of present moments, and suggests that the notion of a present moment as "a world in a grain of sand" provides a tenable hypothesis.

GLOSSARY

Affect attunement (also **attunement**) is a special form of behavior in response to the communicative affective behavior of another. Just as imitation is a faithful rendering of the other's overt actions, affect attunement is a faithful rendering of what the other must have felt like when he or she expressed him- or herself with those actions. This requires that the attunement imitates only the temporal dynamics of the intensity, form, or rhythm of the other's behavior but in a different modality or at a different scale. In this way, the actual actions of the other do not become the referent of the attunement (as they would for imitation); rather, the feeling behind the actions becomes the referent. It is a way of imitating, from the inside, what an experience feels like, not how it was expressed in action.

Altero-centered participation (Braten, 1998b) is the innate capacity to experience, usually out of awareness, what another is experiencing. It is a nonvoluntary act of experiencing as if your center of orientation and perspective were centered in the other. It is not a form of knowledge about the other, but rather a participation in the other's experience. It is the basic inter-

The terms contained here are specific to the author's usage or that of the Boston Change Process Study Group (BCPSG).

subjective capacity that makes imitation, empathy, sympathy, emotional contagion, and identification possible. Although innate, the capacity enlarges and becomes refined with development.

Fuzzy intentionalizing is (1) the inexact nature of trying to express your felt intentions—in other words, of putting them into words; (2) the error-filled process of trying to infer another's intentions on the basis of their words, behaviors, and context; and (3) the approximations negotiated as two people try to share or understand the intentional state of one of the partners. This fuzziness is thought to be intrinsic to the process of "reading" one another. It is clearly seen during moving along at the local level during psychotherapy.

Implicit relational knowing is the domain of knowledge and representation that is nonverbal, nonsymbolized, unnarrated, and nonconscious. It consists of motor procedures, affect patterns, expectations, and even patterns of thinking. In this book, it is mainly concerned with knowing how to be with other people, a form of interpersonal and intersubjective knowing. Thus, the term *implicit relational knowing*. The participle *knowing* is used instead of *knowledge* because knowledge most often implies conscious knowledge. Implicit relational knowing is nonconscious; it is not unconscious in the sense of repressed. Rather, it has never, as yet, needed to be put into words and may never need to be. It is nonconscious in the sense of never becoming reflectively conscious. The vast majority of all we "know" about how to be with others (including the transference) resides in implicit relational knowing.

Intentional-feeling-flow is the subjective sense of an intention moving towards its goal. It includes the sense of leaning forward toward the goal and the sense of decreasing "distance" from the goal, as well as shifts in the intensity of anticipation and hedonics as the trajectory is traveled.

Intersubjective anxiety is the feeling that arises when the process of intersubjective orientation does not provide sufficiently clear coordinates about where one is in the intersubjective field. It is a form of anxiety not directly identified in psychological theories or in the Darwinian categories. Perhaps it is closer to an existential anxiety.

Intersubjective consciousness is a form of consciousness that arises when a reentry loop is established between the direct experience in one person's mind and the same person's experience of second person experiencing the first person's experience. This intersubjective recursive loop allows the double experience of the first person to emerge into consciousness—intersubjective consciousness. Intersubjective consciousness is socially based and not derived from reentry loops of experience originating solely within a single mind. It need not become reflectively conscious, nor be verbalized. But it enters into episodic memory.

Intersubjective field is the domain of feelings, thoughts, and knowledge that two (or more) people share about the nature of their current relationship. Not only is this intersubjective domain shared, but the sharing also is validated between them, implicitly or explicitly. This field can be reshaped. It can be entered or exited, enlarged or diminished, made clearer or less clear.

Intersubjective orientation is both the need to test and the act of testing the intersubjective field, knowing "where it stands" between two people, sensing "where the relationship is at" at this moment, knowing "where the two people are going with each other." It functions to orient one in the intersubjective field and to evaluate the nature of the field at the moment. It is an almost continuous process and at times has an imperative feel (when lost and intersubjective anxiety arises). It is akin to spatial orientation, but in an intersubjective space.

Lived story (or **micro-lived story**) refers to the structure of the experience that unfolds during a present moment. It consists of a narrativelike plot and a line of dramatic tension that rises and falls during the present moment. It is a lived, felt, or experienced story that is not verbalized or narrated. Later, real narratives can be forged out of these lived stories.

Local level is the interaction as viewed at a micro scale from moment to moment where the units are made up of the smallest behavioral gestalts for which an intention could be inferred. These units consist of relational moves and present moments that have durations measured in seconds. The local level is made up of the sequences of these units. It is the fundamental psychological level for the enactment of relatedness.

Moment of meeting is a present moment between two participants that potentially resolves the crisis created by a now moment. It thereby reshapes the intersubjective field and alters the relationship. It is called forth as an emergent property from the micro-context of the now moment and must be exquisitely sensitive to this context. It involves a response to the crisis that is well fitted to the specificity of that particular crisis. It cannot be a general technical response but must be a specific, authentic one that carries the therapist's personal signature, so to speak. This is necessary because there is an intersubjective sharing in this moment that alters the intersubjective field between the two. The affectively charged sharing expands the intersubjective field so that their relationship as mutually sensed is suddenly different from what it was before the moment of meeting. This change in the intersubjective field by virtue of the moment of meeting does not require verbalization or narration to be effective and lasting.

Moving along is the process of proceeding through the session at the local level. This process finds its way as it proceeds. Its path is not known in advance. It consists of the relational moves and present moments that strung together make up the session. It is characterized by attempts to achieve a greater and more coherent intersubjective field. This, however, involves much unpredictability about what will happen next because the process is extremely inexact, nonlinear, and sloppy. Because of the nature of the process, it gives rise to many emergent properties, such as now moments and moments of meeting.

Now moment is a present moment that suddenly arises in a session as an emergent property of the moving along process. It is an affectively charged moment because it puts the nature of the patient-therapist relationship into question. This usually involves bumping up against or threatening to break the habitual framework or "rules" of how they work together and are together. What is at stake is how they will be with each other. The level of anxiety in the patient and therapist rises. They are both pulled forcefully into the present. The therapist feels that a routine technical response will not suffice. This adds to his or her anxiety. A crisis that needs resolution has been created. The resolution can come in the form of a moment of meeting or an interpretation.

Present moment is the span of time in which psychological processes group together very small units of perception into the smallest global unit (a gestalt) that has a sense or meaning in the context of a relationship. Objectively, present moments last from 1 to 10 seconds with an average around 3 to 4 seconds. Subjectively, they are what we experience as an uninterrupted *now*. The present moment is structured as a micro-lived story with a minimal plot and a line of dramatic tension made up of vitality affects. It is thus temporally dynamic. It is a conscious phenomenon, but need not be reflectively conscious, verbalized, or narrated. It is viewed as the basic building block of relationship experiences. Abstractions such as generalizations, explanations, and interpretations, or higher-order phenomena such as narratives, are made up of these basic, primary, psychological experiences. It is only these that happen "now" and only these that are directly lived.

Relational moves are overt behaviors (including speech or silences) that are the smallest units for which an intention to alter or adjust the relationship can be attributed by an interactive partner or observer. They are present moments which

245

have not become conscious. With present moments, they make up the moving along process.

Shared feeling voyage refers to the joint experience of a moment of meeting. It emphasizes that the two people travel together during a present moment through a similar landscape of feelings where shifts in feeling serve as landmarks. It is thus a voyage of feelings. Further, there is a mutual recognition of making this voyage together—in other words, it is shared. It is an intersubjective phenomenon.

Sloppiness refers to disorderliness of the moving along process. It includes the following: unpredictability, fuzzy intentionalizing, redundancy, and frequent variations, all of which tend to make the moving along process less linear and more complex. At the same time sloppiness is viewed as adding potentially creative elements to the process. These creative elements are emergent properties that when used well can shift the nature of the intersubjective field in new directions.

Temporal contour is the temporal shape of stimulations that impinge on the nervous system, from within or from without. The temporal contour consists of the analogic shifts, split second by split second in real time, in the intensity, rhythm, or form of the stimulation. It is, in theory, an objectifiable entity.

Temporal dynamics are changes in time or over time, particularly shifts in the force, intensity, quality, form, or rhythm of an experience over time. As used in the book, it usually refers to what might best be called micro-temporal dynamics because the changes occur over seconds.

Vitality affects are subjective experiences. They consist of the temporal dynamics of changes in feelings consisting of analogic shifts, split second by split second in real time, of affects, thoughts, perceptions, or sensations. For instance, the felt acceleration and then explosion of anger. They generally occur in parallel with the temporal contours of stimulations. Vitality affects are subjective experiences. Temporal contours of stimulations, in contrast, are objectifiable events. There is incomplete isomorphism between temporal contours and vitality affects. Vitality affects are synonymous with temporal feeling shapes, feeling shapes, or temporal shapes.

REFERENCES

Ainsworth, M. D. S., Blehar, M. C., Waters, E., & Wall, S. (1978). *Patterns of attachment*. Hillsdale, NJ: Erlbaum.

Aron, L. (1996). *A meeting of minds: Mutuality in psychoanalysis*. Hillsdale, NJ: The Analytic Press.

Astington, J. W. (1993). *The child's discovery of the mind*. Cambridge, MA : Harvard University Press.

Augustine (1991). *Confessions* (H. Chadwick, Trans.). New York: Oxford University Press.

Bachmann, M. (1994). *Dalcroze today: An education through and into music*. London: Oxford University Press.

Baddeley, A. D. (1984). *Working memory*. London: Oxford University Press.

Baddeley, A. D. (1986). *Working memory*. Oxford: Clarendon Press.

Baddeley, A. D. (1989). The use of working memory. In P. R. Solomon, G. R. Goethals, C. M. Kelley, & B. R. Stephens (Eds.), *Memory: Interdisciplinary approaches* (pp. 107–123). New York: Springer Verlag.

Bailey, A. R. (1999). Beyond the fringe: William James on the transitional parts of the stream of consciousness. *Journal of Consciuosness Studies, 6*(2–3), 141–153.

Baldwin, J. M. (1895). *Mental development in the child and the race*. New York Macmillan.

Bänninger-Huber, E. (1992). Prototypical affective microsequences in psychotherapeutic interaction. *Psychotherapy Research*, *2*(4), 291–306.

Baricco, A. (2002). *Lands of glass* (A. Goldstein, Trans.). London: Penguin.

Baron-Cohen, S. (1995). *Mindblindness: An essay on autism and theory of mind.* Cambridge, MA: MIT Press.

Beebe, B., Jaffe, J., Feldstein, S., Mays, K., & Alson, D. (1985). Interpersonal timing: The application of an adult dialogue model to mother-infant vocal and kinesic interactions. In F. M. Field & N. Fox (Eds.), *Social perception in infants* (pp. 217–247). Norwood, NJ: Ablex.

Beebe, B., Knoblauch, S., Rustin, J., & Sorter, D. (2002). Forms of intersubjectivity in infant research and their implications for for adult treatment. *Psychoanaytic Dialogues*.

Beebe, B., & Lachman, F. (2002). *Infant research and adult treatment: Co-constructing interactions.* Hillsdale, NJ: Analytic Press.

Beebe, B., Stern, D., & Jaffe, J. (1979). The kinesic rhythm of mother-infant interactions. In A. W. Siegman & S. Feldstein (Eds.), *Of speech and time: Temporal speech patterns in interpersonal contexts* (pp. 23–34). Hillsdale, NJ: Erlbaum.

Beer, R. (1995). A dynamical systems perspective on agent-environment interaction. *Artificial Intelligence, 72,* 173–215.

Benhôte, H. (1972). *Welte-Mignon.* L'Auberson, Switzerland: Musée Band.

Benjamin, J. (1995). *Like subjects, love objects: Essays on recognition and sexual difference.* New Haven, CT: Yale University Press.

Bergson, H. (1988). *Matter and memory* (N. M. Paul & W. S. Palmerg, Trans.). New York: Zone Books. (Original work published 1896)

Blakemore, S. J. & Decety, J. (2001). From the perception of action to the understanding of intention. *Nature Reviews. Neuroscience, 2,* 561–576.

Block, N. (1995). On a confusion about a function of consciousness. In N. Block, O. Flanagen, & G. Guzzeldere (Eds.), *The nature of consciousness* (pp. 375–415). Cambridge, MA: MIT Press.

Block, N., Flanagan O., & Guzeldere, G. (Eds.) (1997). *The nature of consciousness*. Cambridge, MA: MIT Press.

Bollas, C. (1987). *The shadow of the object: Psychoanalysis of the unthought known*. London: Free Association Books.

Boston Change Process Study Group (2002). Explicating the implicit: The local level and the microprocesses of change in the analytic situation (Report No. 3). *International Journal of Psychoanalysis, 83*, 1051–1062.

Boston Change Process Study Group (in press). The "something more that interpretation": Sloppiness and co-construction in the psychoanalytic encounter (Report No. 4). *Journal of the American Psychoanalytic Association.*

Bowlby, J. (1969). *Attachment and loss. Vol. 1: Attachment*. New York: Basic Books.

Braten, S. (Ed.) (1998a). *Intersubjective communication and emotion in early ontogeny*. Cambridge, U.K.: Cambridge University Press.

Braten, S. (1998b). Infant learning by altero-centric participation: The reverse of egocentric observation in autism. In S. Braten (Ed.), *Intersubjective communication and emotion in early ontogeny* (pp. 105–124). Cambridge, U.K.: Cambridge University Press.

Brentano, F. (1973). *Psychology from an empirical standpoint*. London: Routledge & Kegan Paul. (Originally work published 1874)

Bruner, J. S. (1990). *Acts of meaning*. New York: Basic.

Bruner, J. S. (2002a). *Making stories: Law, literature, life*. New York: Farrar, Strauss, & Giroux.

Bruner, J. S. (2002b, October). *Narrative and culture*. Paper presented at the symposium "We Share Therefore We Are" in honor of Jerome Bruner, Crete, Greece.

Bruner, J. S., Olver, R. R., & Greenfield, P. M. (1966). *Studies in cognitive growth*. New York: Wiley.

Bucci, W. (1997). From subsymbolic to symbolic—and back: Therapeutic impact of the referential process. In R. Lasky (Ed.), *Symbolization and desymbolization: Essays in honor of Norbert Freedman*. (pp. 50–74) New York: Other Press, Karnap.

Bucci, W. (2001). Pathways of emotional communication. *Psycho-analytic Inquiry, 21*(1), 40–70.

Burke, K. (1945). *A grammar of motives.* New York: Prentice-Hall.

Byng-Hall, J. (1996). *Family scripts.* New York: Guilford.

Cabeza, R. (1999). Functional neuroimaging of episodic memory retrieval. In E. Tulving (Ed.), *Memory, consciousness and the brain: The Tallinn Conference* (pp. 76–90). Philadelphia: Psychology Press.

Cartier-Bresson, H. (1952). *The decisive moment.* New York: Simon & Schuster.

Chalmers, D. J. (1995). Facing up to the problem of consciousness. In J. Shear (Ed.), *Explaining consciousness: The hard problem* (pp. 379–422). Cambridge, MA: MIT Press.

Chalmers, D. J. (1996). *The conscious mind: In search of a fundamental theory.* New York: Oxford University Press.

Clark, A. (1997). *Being there: Putting brain, body, and world together again.* Cambridge, MA: MIT Press.

Clark, A. (1999). An embodied cognitive science. *Trends in Cognitive Sciences, 3,* 345–51.

Clarke, E. F. (1999). Rhythm and timing in music. In D. Deutsch (Ed.), *The psychology of music* (pp. 473–500). London: Academic Press.

Clynes, M. (1978). *Sentics: The touch of the emotions.* Garden City, New York: Anchor Books.

Cooley C. (1902). *Human nature and the social order.* New York: Scribner.

Cotterill, R. M. J. (2001). Evolution, cognition, and consciousness. *Journal of Consciousness Studies, 8*(2), 3–17.

Cowan, N. (1984). On short and long auditory stores. *Psychological Bulletin, 96,* 341–370.

Cowan, N. (1988). Evolving conceptions of memory storage, selective attention, and their mutual constraints within the human information processing system. *Psychological Bulletin, 104,* 163–191.

Crystal, D. (1975). *The English tone of voice.* London: Edward Arnold Publisher.

Csikszentmihalyi, M. (1990). *Flow: The psychology of optimal experience*. New York: Harper & Row.

Dalla Barba, G. (2001). Beyond the memory-trace paradox and the fallacy of the homunculus: A hypothesis concerning the relationship between memory, consciousness and temporality. *Journal of Consciousness Studies*, 8(3), 51–78.

Damasio, A. (1994). *Descartes' error: Emotion, reason, and the human brain*. New York: Putnam.

Damasio, A. (1999). *The feeling of what happens. Body and emotion in the making of consciousness*. New York: Harcourt.

Damasio, A. (2002). Remembering when. *Scientific American, 287*(3), 48–55.

Darbellay, E. (1996). "Measure" et démeasure du tempo dans le stile fantastico frescobaldien [Exploring tempo in the "fantastico" style of Fresco baldi]. In *Actes du Colloque de Metz : Le mouvement dans la musique autour du 1700* (pp. 198–200). Metz, France: Editions Jerpenoire.

Dennett, D. C. (1998). The Cartesian theater and "filling in" the stream of consciousness. In N. Block, O. Flanagan, & G. Guzzeldere (Eds.), *The nature of consciousness* (pp. 83–88). Cambridge, MA: MIT Press.

de Roten, Y., Fivaz-Depeursinge, E., Stern, D., Darwish, J., & Corboz-Warnery, A. (2000). Body and gaze formations and the communicational alliance in couple-therapist triads. *Psychotherapy Research, 10*(1), 30–46.

Deutsch, D. (Ed.) (1999a). *The psychology of music* (2nd ed.). London: Academic Press.

Deutsch, D. (1999b). Grouping mechanisms in music. In D. Deutsch (Ed.), *The psychology of music* (pp. 299–348). London: Academic Press.

Dilthey, W. (1976). *Selected writings* (H. P. Riokmen, Ed.). London: Cambridge University Press.

Dornes, M. (2002). *Psychanalyse et psychologie du premier âge* [Psychoanalysis and psychology of the first year of life.]. Paris: Presses Universitaires de France.

Dretske, F. (1998). Conscious experience. In N. Block, O. Flanagen, & G. Guzzeldere (Eds.), *The nature of consciousness* (pp. 773–788). Cambridge, MA: MIT Press.

Dunn, J. (1999). Making sense of the social world: Mind reading, emotion and relationships. In P. D. Zelazo, J. W. Astington, & D. R. Olson (Eds.), *Developing theories of intention.* Mahwah, NJ: Erlbaum.

Edelman, G. M. (1990). *The remembered present: A biological theory of consciousness.* New York: Basic Books.

Ehrenberg, D. B. (1982). Psychoanalytic engagement: The transaction as primary data. *Contemporary Psychoanalysis, 10,* 535–555.

Ehrenberg, D. B. (1992). *The intimate edge.* New York: Norton.

Emde, R. N., & Sorce, J. E. (1983). The rewards of infancy: Emotional availability and maternal referencing. In J. D. Call, E. Galenson, & R. Tyson (Eds.), *Frontiers of infant psychiatry* (Vol. 2, pp. 17–30). New York: Basic.

Favez, N. (2003). Patterns of maternal affect regulation during the co-construction of preschoolers' autobiographical narratives. In R. Emde, D. Wolf, & D. Oppenheim (Eds.), *Affective meaning making with narratives: Studies with young children.* Oxford, U.K.: Oxford University Press.

Feldman, C. F., & Kalmar, D. (1996). Autobiography and fiction as modes of thought. In D. Olson & N. Torrence (Eds.), *Modes of thought: Explorations in culture and cognition* (pp. 106–122). Cambridge, U.K.: Cambridge University Press.

Fischer, K., & Granott, N. (1995). Beyond one-dimensional change: Parallel, concurrent, socially distributed processes in learning and development. *Human Development, 38,* 302–314.

Fivaz, R. (1989). *L'ordre et la volupté* [Order and beauty]. Lausanne, Switzerland: Presses Polytechniques Romandes.

Fivaz-Depeursinge, E. (1991). Documenting a time-bound, circular view of hierarchies: A microanalysis of parent-infant dyadic interaction. *Family Process, 30*(1), 101–120.

Fivaz-Depeursinge, E. (2001). Corps et intersubjectivité [Body and intersubjectivity]. *Psychothérapies, 21*(2), 63–69.

Fivaz-Depeursinge, E., & Corboz-Warnery, A. (1998). *The primary triangle*. New York: Basic.

Fivaz-Depeursinge, E., Corboz-Warnery, A., & Frascarolo, F. (1998). *The triadic alliance between father, mother and infant: Its relations to the infant's handling of triangular relationships*. Paper presented at the International Society for the Study of Behavorial Development, Berne, Switzerland.

Fodor, J. (1992). A theory of the child's theory of mind. *Cognition, 44*, 283–296.

Fogel, A. (2001). *Infancy: Infant, family, and society* (4th ed.). Belmont, CA: Wadsworth.

Fogel, A. (2003). Remembering infancy: Accessing our earliest experiences. In G. Bremner & A. Slater (Eds.), *Theories of infant development*. Cambridge, U.K.: Blackwell.

Fonagy, P. (2001). *Attachment theory and psychoanalysis*. New York: Other Press.

Fraisse, P. (1964). *The psychology of time* (J. Leith, Trans.). London: Eyre & Spottiswoode.

Fraisse, P. (1978). Time and rhythm perception. In E. C. Carterette & M. P. Friedman (Eds.), *Handbook of perception* (Vol. 8, pp. 203–254). New York: Academic Press.

Freeman, W. J. (1999a). *How brains make up their minds*. London: Weidenfeld & Nicholson.

Freeman, W. J. (1999b). Consciousness, intentionality, and causality. *Journal of Consciousness Studies, 6*(11–12), 143–172.

French, R. M., & Cleeremans, A. (2002). *Implicit learning and consciousness*. New York: Psychology Press.

Frey, S., Hirsbrunner, H. P., Florin, A., Daw, W., & Crawford, R. (1983). A unified approach to the investigation of nonverbal and verbal behavior in communication research. In W. Doise & S. Moscovici (Eds.), *Current issues in European social psychology* (pp. 143–199). Cambridge, U.K.: Cambridge University Press.

Frey, S., Jorns, U., & Daw, W. (1980). A systematic description and analysis of nonverbal interaction between doctors and patients in a psychiatric interview. In S. Corson (Ed.), *Ethology and nonverbal communication in mental health* (pp. 231–258). New York: Pergamon.

Freud, S. (1959). Inhibitions, symptoms, and anxiety. In J. Strachey (Ed. & Trans.), *The standard edition of the complete psychological works of Sigmund Freud* (Vol. 20, pp. 77–172). London: Hogarth Press. (Original work published 1926)

Gallagher, S. (1997). Mutual enlightment: Recent phenomenology and cognitive science. *Journal of Consciousness Studies, 4*(3), 195–214.

Gallese, V. (2001). The "shared manifold" hypothesis: From mirror neurons to empathy. *Journal of Consciousness Studies, 8*(5–7), 33–50.

Gallese, V., & Goldman, A. (1998). Mirror neurons and the simulation theory of mind reading. *Trends in Cognitive Science, 2,* 493–501.

Gardiner, J. M. (2000). On the objectivity of subjective experience and autonoetic and noetic consciousness. In E. Tulving (Ed.), *Memory consciousness and the brain: The Tallinn conference* (pp. 159–172). Philadelphia: Psychology Press.

Gendlin, E. T. (1981). *Focusing.* New York: Bantum.

Gendlin, E.T. (1991). Thinking beyond patterns: Body, language and situations. In B. denOuden & M. Moen (Eds.), *The presence of feeling in thought* (pp. 21–151). New York: Peter Lang.

Gergely, G., Nadsasdy, Z., Csibra, G., & Biro, S. (1995). Taking the intentional stance at 12 months of age. *Cognition, 56,* 165–193.

Gergely, G., & Watson, J. S. (1999). Early social-emotional development: Contingency, perception, and the social biofeedback model. In P. Rochat (Ed.), *Early social cognition* (pp. 101–136). Hillsdale, NJ: Erlbaum.

Gibbs, R. (1994). *The poetics of mind.* Cambridge, U.K.: Cambridge University Press.

Gleick, J. (1987). *Chaos: Making a new science.* New York: Viking.

Goldman, A. (1992). In defense of the simulation theory. *Mind and Language, 7,* 104–119.

Grandin, T. (1995). *Thinking in pictures.* New York: Doubleday.

Green, A. (2000). *Le temps eclaté* [Fragmented time]. Paris: Les Editions de Minuit.

Gunnar, M. (2001). Effects of early deprivation: Findings from orphanage-reared infants and children. In C. A. Nelson & M. Luciana (Eds.) *Handbook of developmental cognitive neuroscience* (pp. 617–629). Cambridge, MA: MIT Press.

Happé, F. (1998). *Autism: An introduction to psychological theory.* Cambridge, MA: Harvard University Press.

Harris, P. (1989). *Children and emotion.* Oxford, U.K.: Blackwell Publishers.

Harrison, A. (2003). Change in psychoanalysis: Getting from A to B. *Journal of the American Psychoanalytic Association,* 51(1):221–257.

Heath, C. (1988). Embarrassment and interactional organization. In P. Drew & A. Wooton (Eds.), *Erving Goffman: Exploring the interaction order* (pp. 136–160). Cambridge, MA: Polity Press.

Heidegger, M. (1996). *Being and time* (J. Stambaugh, Trans.). New York: New York State University Press. (Original work published 1927)

Hobson, P. (1993). *Autism and the development of mind.* Hove / Hillside, NJ: Erlbaum.

Hobson, R. P. (2002). *The cradle of thought.* London: Pan Macmillan.

Hockney, D. (1986). *Photographs.* Washington, DC: International Exibitions Foundation.

Hofer, M. A. (1994). Hidden regulators in attachment, separation and loss. In N. A. Fox (Ed.), The development of emotion regulation: Biological and behavioral considerations. *Monographs of the Society for Research in Child Development,* 59(2–3, Serial No. 240), 192–207.

Husserl, E. (1960). *Cartesian meditations* (D. Cairns, Trans.). The Hague: Martinus Nijohff. (Original work published 1931)

Husserl, E. (1962). *Ideas pertaining to a pure phenomenology and to a phenomenological philosophy. First book: General introduction to pure phenomenology* (B. Gibson, Trans.). New York: Collier. (Original work published 1913)

Husserl, E. (1964). *The phenomenology of internal time-consciousness* (J. S. Churchill, Trans.). Bloomington: Indiana University Press.

Husserl, E. (1980). *Ideas pertaining to a pure phenomenology and to a phenomenological philosophy. Third book: Phenomenology and the foundation of the sciences* (T. E. Klein & W. E. Pohl, Trans.). The Hague: Martinus Nijoff. (Original work published 1930)

Husserl, E. (1989). *Ideas pertaining to a pure phenomenology and to a phenomenological philosophy. Second book: Studies in the phenomenology of constitution* (R. Rojcewicz & A. Schuwer, Trans.). Dordrecht, Netherlands: Kluwer Academic Publishers. (Original work published 1930)

Imber-Black, E., & Roberts, J. (1992). *Rituals for our times*. Northvale, NJ: Jason Aronson.

Jacobs, T. J. (1991). *The use of the self: Countertransference and communication in the analytic situation*. Madison, CT: International Universities Press.

Jaffe, J., Beebe, B., Feldstein, S., Crown, S., & Jasnow, M. (2001). Rhythms of dialogue in early infancy. *Monographs of the Society for Research in Child Development, 66*(2), Serial No. 264.

Jaffe, J., & Feldstein, S. (1970). *Rhythms of dialogue*. New York: Academic Press.

James, W. (1972). *Principles of psychology* (Vols. 1 & 2). New York: Dover. (Original work published 1890)

Jeannerod, M. (1999). To act or not to act: Perspectives on the representation of actions (The 25th Bartlett Lecture). *The Quarterly Journal of Experimental Psychology, Section A. Human Experimental Psychology 52A,* 1, 1–29.

Jowitt, D. (1988). *Time and the dancing image*. Berkeley and Los Angeles: University of California Press.

Kelso, J. A. S., Holroyd, T., Hovarth, E., Raczaszek, E., Tuller, E., & Ding, M. (1994). Multistability and metastability in perceptual and brain dynamics. In M. Staedler & P. Kruse (Eds.), *Ambiguity in mind and nature: Multistable cognitive phenomena,* (pp. 159–184). Berlin: Springer.

Kendon, A. (1990). *Conducting interaction: Patterns of behavior in focused encounters*. Cambridge, U.K.: Cambridge University Press.

Kern, I. (1988). The structure of consciousness according to Xuan-zang. *Journal of the British Society for Phenomenology, 19*(3), 282–295.

Kestenberg, J. (1965a). The role of movement patterns in development: I Rhythms of movement. *Psychoanalytic Quarterly, 34,* 1–36.

Kestenberg, J. (1965b). The role of movement patterns in development: II Flow of tension and effort. *Psychoanalytic Quarterly, 34,* 517–563.

Kestenberg, J. (1967). The role of movement patterns in development: III The control of shape. *Psychoanalytic Quarterly, 36,* 356–409.

Klinnert, M. D., Campos, J. J., Sorce, J. F., Emde, R. N., & Svejda, M. (1983). Emotions as behavior regulators: Social referencing in infancy. In R. Plutchik & H. Kellerman (Eds.), *Emotion, theory, research, and experience* (pp. 57–86). New York: Academic Press.

Knoblauch, S. (2000). *The musical edge of theraputic dialogue*. Hillsdale, NJ: The Analytic Press.

Koffka, K. (1935). *Principals of Gestalt psychology*. New York: Harcourt.

Krause, R., Steimer-Krause, E., & Ullrich, B. (1992). The use of affect research in dynamic psychotherapy. In M. Leuzinger-Bohleber, H. Schneider, & R. Pfeifer (Eds.), *Two butterflies over my head: Psychoanalysis in the interdisciplinary scientific dialogue* (pp. 277–291). Heidelberg, Germany: Springer.

Kugiumutzakis, G. (1998). Neonatal imitation in the intersubjective companion space. In S. Braten (Ed.), *Intersubjective communication in early ontogeny* (pp. 63–88). Cambridge, U.K.: Cambridge University Press.

Kugiumutzakis, G. (1999). Genesis and development of early human mimesis to facial and vocal models. In J. Nadel & G. Butterworth (Eds.), *Imitation in infancy* (pp. 36–59). Cambridge, U.K.: Cambridge University Press.

Kugiumutzakis, G. (2002, October). *On human development, edu-*

cation and culture. Paper presented at the symposium "We Share, Therefore We Are" in honor of Jerome Bruner. Crete, Greece.

Laban, R. von (1967). *The mastery of movement.* London: Macdonald and Evans.

Labov, W. (1972). *Language in the inner city.* Philadelphia: University of Pennsylvania Press.

Labov, W., & Fanshel, D. (1977). *Therapeutic discourse.* New York: Academic Press.

Lakoff, G., & Johnson, M. (1980). *Metaphors we live by.* Chicago: University of Chicago Press.

Lakoff, G., & Johnson, M. (1999). *Philosophy in the flesh.* New York: Basic.

Lamb, W. (1979). *Body code: The meaning in movement.* London: Routledge and Kegan Paul.

Lancaster, B. L. (1997). On the stages of perception: Towards a synthesis of cognitive neuroscience and the Buddhist Abhidhamma tradition. *Journal of Consciousness Studies, 4*(2), 122–142.

Landy, R. (1990). The concept of role in psychotherapy. *The Arts in Psychotherapy, 17,* 223–230.

Landy, R. (1993). *Persona and performance: The meaning of role in drama, therapy, and everyday life.* New York: Guilford Press.

Langer, S. K. (1967). *Mind: An essay on human feeling* (Vol. 1). Baltimore: Johns Hopkins University Press.

Laplanche, J., & Pontalis, J. B. (1988). *The language of psychoanalysis* (D. Nicholson-Smith, Trans.). London: The Institute of Psychoanalysis and Karnac Books. (Original work published 1967)

Lee, D. N. (1998). Guiding movements by coupling taus. In *Ecological Psychology, 10*(3–4), 221–250.

LeDoux, J. (1996). *The emotional brain.* New York: Simon & Shuster.

Lichtenberg, J. D. (1989). *Psychoanalysis and motivation.* Hillsdale, NJ: The Analytic Press.

Lyons-Ruth, K. (1998). Implicit relational knowing: Its role in development and psychoanalytic treatment. *Infant Mental Health Journal, 19* (3), 282–289.

Lyons-Ruth, K. (1999). The two-person preconscious: Intersubjective dialogue, implicit relational knowing, and the articulation of meaning. *Psychoanalytic Inquiry, 19,* 567–617.

Lyons-Ruth, K. (2000). "I sense that you sense that I sense": Sander's recognition process and the specificity of relational moves in the psychotherapeutic setting. *Infant Mental Health Journal, 21*(1), 85–99.

Lyons-Ruth, K., Bruschweiler-Stern, N., Harrison, A. M., Morgan, A. C., Nahum, J. P., Sander, L., Stern, D. N., & Tronick, E. Z. (1998). Implicit relational knowing: Its role in development and psychoanalytic treatment. *Infant Mental Health Journal, 19*(3), 282–289.

Maestro, S., Muratori, F., Cavallaro, M. C., Pei, F., Stern, D. N., Golse, B., & Palacio-Espasa, F. (2002). Attentional skills during the first six months of age in autism spectrum disorder. *Journal of the American Academy of Child and Adolescent Psychiatry, 41,* 1239–1245.

Malloch, S. N. (1999 / 2000). Mothers and infants and communicative musicality. *Musicae Scientiae: Special Issue, Rhythm, Musical Narrative, and Origin of Human Communication,* 29–58.

Maratos, O. (1973). *The origin and development of imitation in the first six months of life.* Unpuplished doctoral dissertation, University of Geneva.

Marbach, E. (1988). How to study consciousness phenomenologically or quite a lot comes to mind. *Journal of the British Society for Phenomenology, 19*(3), 252–268.

Marbach, E. (1993). *Mental representation and consciousness: Towards a phenomenological theory of representation and reference.* Dordrecht, Netherlands: Kluwer Academic.

Marbach, E. (1999). Building materials for the explanatory bridge. *Journal of Consciousness Studies, 6*(2–3), 252–257.

Marcel. A. (1983). Conscious and unconscious perception: Experiments on visual masking and word recognotion. *Cognitive Psychology, 15,* 197–237.

McDonald, K. (1992). Warmth as a developmental construct: An evolutionary analysis. *Child Development, 63,* 753–773.

Mead, G. H. (1988). *Mind, self and society.* Chicago: University of Chicago Press. (Original work published 1934)

Melikian, S. (2002). Auction. *International Herald Tribune.* November 2–3, p. 9.

Meltzoff, A. N. (1981). Imitation, intermodal coordination and representation in early infancy. In G. Butterworth (Ed.), *Infancy and epistemology* (pp. 85–114). Brighton, U.K.: Harvester Press.

Meltzoff, A. N. (1995). Understanding the intentions of others: Re-enactment of intended acts by eighteen month-old children. *Developmental Psychology, 3,* 838–850.

Meltzoff, A. N., & Gopnik, A. (1993). The role of imitation in understanding persons and developing a theory of mind. In S. Baron-Cohen, H. Tager-Flusberg, & D. J. Cohen, (Eds.), *Understanding other minds: Perspectives from autism* (pp. 335–366). New York: Oxford University Press.

Meltzoff, A. N., & Moore, M. K. (1977). Imitation of facial and manual gestures by human neonates. *Science, 198,* 75–78.

Meltzoff, A. N., & Moore, M. K. (1999). Persons and representations: Why infant imitation is important for theories of human development. In J. Nadel & G. Butterworth (Eds.), *Imitation in infancy* (pp. 9–35). Cambridge, U.K.: Cambridge University Press.

Merleau-Ponty, M. (1962). *Phénoménologie de la perception* [Phenomenology of perception]. Paris: Librairie Gallimard. (Original work published 1945)

Michon, J. A. (1978). The making of the present: A tutorial review. In J. Requin (Ed.), *Attention and performance VII* (pp. 89–111). Hillsdale, NJ: Erlbaum.

Minsky, M. (1981). Music, mind, and meaning. *Computer Music Journal, 5*(3), 1–18.

Mitchell, S. (1997). *Influence and autonomy in psychoanalysis.* Hillsdale, NJ: The Analytic Press.

Mitchell, S. (2000). *Relationality: From attachment to intersubjectivity.* New York: Analytic Press.

Modell, A. H. (2003). *Imagination and the meaningful mind*. Cambridge, MA: MIT Press.

Moran, D. (2000). *Introduction to phenomenology*. London and New York: Routledge.

Nachman, P. (2001). Maternal identification: A description of the process in real time. *Journal of the American Psychoanalytic Association, 46*(1), 208–228.

Nadel, J. (1986). *Imitation et communication entre jeune enfants* [Imitation and communication among young infants]. Paris: Presses Universitaires de France.

Nadel, J., & Butterworth, G. (Eds.) (1999). *Imitation in infancy*. Cambridge, U.K.: Cambridge University Press.

Nadel, J., & Peze, A. (1993). What makes immediate imitation immediately communicative in toddlers and autistic children? In J. Nadel & L. Camaioni (Eds.), *New perspectives in early communicative development* (pp. 139–156). London and New York: Routledge.

Nagel, T. (1998). What is it like to be a bat? In N. Block, O. Flanagen, & G. Guzzeldere (Eds.), *The nature of consciousness* (pp. 514–528). Cambridge, MA: MIT Press.

Narmour, E. (1990). *The analysis and cognition of basic melodic structure: The implication-realization model*. Chicago: University of Chicago Press.

Narmour, E. (1999). Hierarchical expectation and musical style. In D. Deutsch (Ed.), *The psychology of music* (pp. 442–472). London: London Academic Press.

Naudin, J., Gros-Azorin, C., Mishara, A., Wiggins, O. P., Schwartz, M. A., & Azorin, J. M. (1999). The use of Husserlian reduction as a method of investigation in psychiatry. *Journal of Consciousness Studies, 6*(2–3), 155–171.

Nelson, K. (Ed.) (1989). *Narratives from the crib*. Cambridge, MA: Harvard University Press.

Ogden, T. (1994). *Subjects of analysis*. Northvale, NJ: Aronson.

Parnas, J., Bovet, P. & Zahavi, D. (2002). Schizophrenic autism: Clinical phenomenology and pathogenic implications. *World Psychiatry, 1*(3), 131–136.

Patel, A. D. (2003). Language, music, syntax, and the brain. *Nature Neuroscience, 6*(7), 674–681.

Pearson, D., Rouse, H., Doswell, S., Ainsworth, C., Dawson, O., Simms, K., Edwards, L., & Faulconbridge, J. (2001). Prevalence of imaginary companions in a normal child population. *Child Health Care and Development, 27*(1), 13–22.

Person, E. S. (1988). *Dreams of love and fateful encounters: The power of romantic passions.* New York: Norton.

Peterson, C. & McCabe, A. (1983). *Developmental psycholinguistics: Three ways of looking at a child's narrative.* New York: Plenum.

Port, R., & van Gelder, T. (Eds) (1995). *Mind as motion: Explorations in the dynamics of cognition.* Cambridge, MA: MIT press.

Prigogine, I. (1997). *The end of certainty.* New York: Free Press.

Prigogine, I., & Stengers, I. (1984). *Order out of chaos: Man's new dialogue with nature.* New York: Bantum.

Reddy, V. (1991). Playing with other's expectations: Teasing and mucking about in the first year. In A. Whiten (Ed.), *Natural theories of mind: Evolution, development, and simulation of everyday mindreading* (pp. 143–158). Oxford, U.K.: Blackwell.

Reddy, V., Williams, F., & Vaughn, A. (2002). Sharing humour and laughter in autism and Down's syndrome. *British Journal of Psychology, 93,* 219–242.

Reiss, D. (1981). *The family's construction of reality.* Cambridge, MA: Harvard University Press.

Reiss, D. (1989). The represented and practicing family: Contrasting visions of family continuity. In A. Sameroff & R. N. Emde (Eds.), *Relationship disturbances* (pp. 191–214). New York: Basic.

Renik, O. (1993). Analytic interaction: Conceptualizing technique in the light of the analyst's irreducible subjectivity. *Psychoanalytic Quarterly, 62,* 553–571.

Ricoeur, P. (1984–1988). *Time and narrative* (Vols. I, II, III) (K. Blamey, Trans.). Chicago: University of Chicago Press.

Rizzolatti, G., & Arbib, M. A. (1998). Language within our grasp. *Trends in Neuroscience, 21,* 188–194.

Rizzolatti, G., Fadiga, L., Fogassi, L., & Gallese, V. (1996). Premotor cortex and the recognition of motor actions. *Cognitive Brain Research, 3,* 131–141.

Rizzolatti, G., Fogassi, L., & Gallese, V. (2001). Neurophysiological mechanisms underlying the understanding and imitation of action. *Nature Reviews. Neuroscience, 2*(9), 661–670.

Rochat, P. (1995). Early objectification of the self. In P. Rochat (Ed.), *The self in early infancy: Theory and research* (pp. 53–72). Amsterdam, Netherlands: Elsevier Science.

Rochat, P. (Ed.) (1999). *Early social cognition.* Mahwah, NJ: Erlbaum.

Rochat, P., & Morgan, R. (1995). The function and determinants of early self-exploration. In P. Rochat (Ed.). *The self in infancy: Theory and research, advances in psychology* (vol. 112, pp. 395–415). Amsterdam: North Holland / Elsevier Science Publishers.

Romo, R., Hernandez, A., Zainos, A., Lemus, L., & Brody, C. D. (2002). Neuronal correlates of a decision-making process in the secondary somatosensory cortex. *Nature Neuroscience, 5*(11), 1217–1225.

Rorty, R. (1982). Comments on Dennett. *Synthese, 59,* 181–187.

Rubin, N. (2001). Figure and ground in the brain. *Nature Neuroscience, 4*(9), 857–858.

Sacks, O. (1995). Introduction. In T. Grandin, *Thinking in pictures.* New York : Doubleday.

Sander, L. W. (1975). Infant and caretaking environment: Investigation and conceptualization of adaptive behavior in a system of increasing complexity. In E. J. Anthony (Ed.), *Explorations in child psychiatry* (pp. 29–166). New York: Plenum.

Sander, L. W. (1977). The regulation of exchange in the infant-caretaker system and some aspects of the context-content relationship. In M. Lewis & L. A. Rosenblum (Eds.), *Interaction, conversation and the development of language* (pp. 133–155). New York: Wiley.

Sander, L. (1995a). *Thinking about developmental process: Wholeness, specificity, and the organization of conscious experiencing.* Invited address, annual meeting of the Division of Psychoanalysis, American Psychological Association, Santa Monica, CA.

Sander, L. (1995b). Identity and the experience of specificity in a process of recognition. *Psychoanalytic Dialogues, 5,* 579–593.

Sander L. W. (1997). Paradox and resolution: From the beginning. In J. D. Noshpitz, *Handbook of child and adolescent psychiatry* (pp. 153–160). New York: Wiley.

Sander, L. W. (2002). Thinking differently: Principles of process in living systems and the specificity of being known. *Psychoanalytic Dialogues, 12*(1), 11–42.

Santos, P. (2000). *Approache phénoménologique de la conscience* [A phenomenological approach to conscience]. Master's thesis, Faculty of Psychology and Educational Sciences, University of Geneva.

Schacter, D. L. (1994). Priming and multiple memory systems: Perceptual mechanisms of implicit memory. In D. L. Schacter & E. Tulving (Eds.), *Memory systems.* Cambridge, MA: Bradford Books / MIT Press.

Schacter, D. L. (1996). *Searching for memory: The brain, the mind, and the past.* New York: Basic.

Schafer, R. (1981). Narration in the psychoanalytic dialogue. In W.J.T. Mitchell (Ed.), *On narrative* (pp. 25–49). Chicago: University of Chicago Press.

Scheflen, A. E. (1973). *Communicational structure: Analysis of a psychotherapy transaction.* Bloomington: Indiana University Press.

Schenellenberg, E. G. (1996). Expectancy in melody: Tests of the implication-realization model. *Cognition, 58,* 75–125.

Scherer, K. R. (1992). Vocal affect expression as symptom, symbol, and appeal. In H. Papousek, U. Jürgens, & M. Papousek (Eds.), *Nonverbal vocal communication: Comparative and developmental approaches* (pp. 43–60). Cambridge, U.K., & Paris: Cambridge University Press.

Scherer, K. R. (2001). Appraisal considered as a process of multilevel sequential checking. In K. R. Scherer, A. Schorr, & T. Johnstone (Eds.), *Appraisal processes in emotion: Theory, methods, research* (pp. 92–120). New York & Oxford: Oxford University Press.

Schore, A. N. (1994). *Affect regulation and the origin of the self: The neurobiology of emotional development*. Hillsdale, NJ: Erlbaum.

Schore, A. N. (1996). The experience-dependent maturation of a regulatory system in the orbital prefrontal cortex and the origin of developmental psychopathology. *Development and Psychopathology, 8*, 59–87.

Schore, A. N. (1997). Early organization of the nonlinear right brain and development of a predisposition to psychiatric disorder. *Development and Psychopathology, 9*, 595–631.

Schore, A. N. (1998). The experience-dependent maturation of an evaluative system in the cortex. In K. H. Pribram & J. King (Eds.), *Brain and values: Is a biological science of values possible?* (pp. 337–358). Mahwah, NJ: Erlbaum.

Seligman, S. (Ed.). (2002). Symposium on Louis Sander's integration of early development, biological systems, and therapeutic process [Special issue]. *Psychoanalytic Dialogues, 12*(1).

Seuss, Dr. (1960). *Green eggs and ham*. New York: Random House.

Shapiro, T., Sherman, M., Calamari, G., & Koch, D. (1987). Attachment in autism and other developmental disorders. *Journal of the American Academy of Child and Adolescent Psychiatry, 26*(4), 480–484.

Shear, J., & Jevning, R. (1999). Pure consciousness: Scientific exploration of meditation techniques. *Journal of Consciousness Studies, 6*(2–3), 189–209.

Sheets-Johnstone, M. (1984). *The roots of thinking*. Philadelphia: Temple University Press.

Sheets-Johnstone, M. (1999). *The primacy of movement*. Amsterdam / Philadelphia: John Benjamins.

Siegel, D. J. (1995). Memory, trauma, and psychopathology: A cognitive science view. *Journal of Psychotherapy Practice and Research, 4*, 93–122.

Siegel. D. J. (1996). Cognition, memories and dissociation. *Child and Adolescent Psychiatric Clinics of North America, 5*, 509–536.

Siegel, D. J. (1999). *The developing mind: Toward a neurobiology of interpersonal experience*. New York: Guilford Press.

Sigman, M., & Capps, L. (1997). *Children with autism*. Cambridge, MA: Harvard University Press.

Silbersweig, D. A., & Stern, E. (1998). Towards a functional neuroanatomy of conscious perception and its modulation by volition: Implications of human auditory neuroimaging studies. *Philosophical Transactions of the Royal Society of London B., 353*, 1883–1888.

Solomon, M. F., & Siegel, D. J. (Eds.) (2003). *Healing trauma: Attachment, mind, body, brain*. New York: Norton.

Spagnuolo-Lobb, M. (Ed.) (2001) *Psicotherapia della Gestalt* [Gestalt psychotherapy]. Milan, Italy: Franco Angeli.

Spense, D. P. (1976). Clinical interpretation: Some comments on the nature of the evidence. *Psychoanalysis and Contempory Science, 5*, 367–388.

Sroufe, A. (1999). Implications of attachment theory for developmental psychopathology. *Development and Psychopathology, 11*, 1–13.

Steimer-Krause, E., Krause, R., & Wagner, G. (1990). Interaction regulations used by schizophrenic and psychosomatic patients: Studies on facial behavior in dyadic interactions. *Psychiatry, 53*, 209–228.

Stern, D. J., Fivaz-Depeursinge, E., de Roten, Y., Corboz-Warnery, A., & Darwish, J. (1996). Transitions and the sharing of interactional affective events. *Swiss Journal of Psychology, 55*(4), 204–212.

Stern, D. N. (1971). A micro-analysis of mother-infant interaction: Behaviors regulating social contact between a mother and her three-and-a-half month-old twins. *Journal of American Academy of Child Psychiatry 10*, 501–517.

Stern, D. N. (1974). The goal and structure of mother-infant play. *Journal of the American Academy of Child Psychiatry, 13*, 402–421.

Stern, D. N. (1977). *The first relationship: Infant and mother*. Cambridge, MA: Harvard University Press.

Stern, D. N. (1985). *The interpersonal world of the infant: A view from psychoanalysis and developmental psychology.* New York: Basic Books.

Stern D. N. (1990). *The diary of a baby.* New York: Basic.

Stern, D. N. (1992). Acting versus remembering: In transference-love and in infantile-love. In J. Sandler, E. Spector Person, & P. Fonagy (Eds.), *Freud's observations on transference-love* (pp. 172–185). New Haven, CT: Yale University Press.

Stern, D. N. (1994). One way to build a clinically relevent baby. *Infant Mental Health Journal, 15*(1), 9–25.

Stern, D. N. (1995). *The motherhood constellation.* New York: Basic.

Stern, D. N. (2000). *The interpersonal world of the infant: A view from psychoanalysis and developmental psychology.* New York: Basic.

Stern, D. N., Beebe, B., Jaffe, J., & Bennett, S. L. (1987). The infant's stimulus world during social interaction: A study of caregivers behavior with particular reference to repetition and timing. In H. R. Schaffer (Ed.), *Studies in mother-infant interaction* (pp. 177–202). London: Academic Press.

Stern, D. N., & Gibbon, J. (1978). Temporal expectancies of social behavior in mother-infant play. In E.B. Thoman (Ed.), *Origins of the infant's social responsiveness.* Hillsdale, NJ: Erlbaum.

Stern, D. N., Hofer, L., Haft, W., & Dore, J. (1984). Affect attunement: The sharing of feeling states between mother and infant by means of intermodal fluency. In T. Field & N. Fox (Eds.), *Social perception in infants* (pp. 249–268). Norwood NJ: Ablex.

Stern, D. N., Sander, L. W., Nahum, J. P., Harrison, A. M., Lyons-Ruth, K., Morgan, A. C., Bruschweiler-Stern, N., & Tronick, E. Z. (1998). Non-interpretive mechanisms in psychoanalytic therapy. The "something more" than interpretation (The Boston Change Process Study Group, Report No. 1). *International Journal of Psychoanalysis, 79,* 903–921.

Stern, W. (1930). William Stern. In C. Murchison (Ed.), *A history of psychology in autobiography* (Vol. 1, pp. 335–388). Worcester, MA : Clark University Press.

Stolorow, R. D., & Atwood, G. E. (1992). *Contexts of being: The intersubjective foundations of psychological life.* Hillsdale, NJ: The Analytic Press.

Stolorow, R. D., Atwood, G. E., & Brandchaft, B. (Eds.) (1994). The intersubjective perspective. Northvale, NJ: Jason Aronson.

Thelen, E., & Smith, L. (1994). *A dynamic systems approach to the development of cognition and action.* Cambridge, MA.: MIT Press.

Thompson, E. (2001). Empathy and consciousness. *Journal of Consciousness Studies, 8*(5–7), 1–32.

Tomkins, S. S. (1962). *Affect, imagery and consciousness. Vol. 1, The positive affects.* New York: Springer.

Torras, C. (1985). *Temporal-pattern learning in neural models.* Amsterdam: Springer Verlag.

Trevarthen, C. (1974). Conversations with a two-month-old. *New Scientist, 2*, 230–235.

Trevarthen, C. (1979). Communication and cooperation in early infancy: A description of primary intersubjectivity. In M. M. Bullowa (Ed.), *Before speech: The beginning of interpersonal communication* (pp. 231–347). New York: Cambridge University Press.

Trevarthen, C. (1980). The foundation of intersubjectivity: Development of interpersonal and cooperative understanding in infants. In D. Olson (Ed.), *The social foundation of language and thought* (pp. 316–342). New York: Norton.

Trevarthen, C. (1988). Universal cooperative motives: How infants begin to know the language and skills of the culture of their parents. In C. Jahoda & I. M. Lewis (Eds.), *Acquiring culture* (pp. 37–90). London: Croom Helm.

Trevarthen, C. (1993). The self born in intersubjectivity: An infant communicating. In U. Neisser (Ed.), *The perceived self* (pp. 121–173). New York: Cambridge University Press.

Trevarthen, C. (1999 / 2000). Musicality and the intrinsic motive pulse: Evidence from human psychobiology and infant communication. *Musicae Scientiae: Special Issue, Rhythm, Musical Narrative, and Origin of Human Communication,* 155–211.

Trevarthen, C., & Hubley, P. (1978). Secondary intersubjectivity: Confidence, confiders and acts of meaning in the first year. In A. Lock (Ed.), *Action, gesture, and symbol* (pp. 183–229). New York: Academic Press.

Tronick, E. Z. (1986). Interactive mismatch and repair challenges to the coping infant. *Zero To Three, 6,* 1–6.

Tronick, E. Z. (1989). Emotions and emotional communication in infants. *American Psychologist, 44,* 112–119.

Tronick, E. Z. (1998). Dyadically expanded states of consciousness and the process of therapeutic change. *Infant Mental Health Journal, 19*(3), 290–299.

Tronick, E. Z., Als, H., & Adamson, L. (1979). Structure of early face-to-face communicative interactions. In M. Bullowa (Ed.), *Before speech: The beginning of interpersonal communication* (pp. 349–370). New York: Cambridge University Press.

Tronick, E. Z., Als, H., & Brazelton, T. B. (1977). The infant's capacity to regulate mutuality in face-to-face interactions. *Journal of Communication, 27,* 74–80.

Tronick, E. Z., Bruschweiler-Stern, N., Harrison, A. M., Lyons-Ruth, K., Morgan, A. C., Nahum, J. P., Sander, L. W., & Stern, D. N. (1998). Dyadically expanded states of consciousness and the process of theraputic change. *Infant Mental Health Journal, 19*(3), 290–299.

Turner, M. (1991). *Reading minds.* Princeton, NJ: Princeton University Press.

Turner, F., & Pöppel, E. (1988). Metered poetry, the brain, and time. In I. Rentschler, B. Herzberger, & D. Epstein (Eds.), *Beauty and the brain: Biological aspects of aesthetics* (pp. 71–90). Basel, Switzerland: Birkhauser.

Turow, S. (1987). *Presumed innocent.* New York: Farrar, Straus, & Giroux.

Tustin, F. (1990). *The protective shell in children and adults.* London: Karnac Books.

Varela, F., Lachaux, J. P., Rodriguez, E., & Martinerie, J. (2001). The brainweb: Phase synchronization and large scale integration. *Nature Reviews. Neuroscience, 2*(4), 229–239.

Varela, F. J. (1996). Neurophenomenology. *Journal of Consciousness Studies, 3*(4), 230–349.

Varela, F. J. (1999). Present-time consciousness. *Journal of Consciousness Studies, 6*(2–3), 111–140.

Varela, F. J. & Shear, J. (1999). First person methodologies: What, why, how? *Journal of Consciousness Studies, 6*(2–3), 1–14.

Varela, F. J., Thompson, E., & Rosch, E. (1993). *The embodied mind: Cognitive science and human experience.* Cambridge, MA: MIT Press.

Vygotsky, L. S. (1962). *Thought and language* (E. Hanfmann & G. Vakar, Trans.). Cambridge, MA: MIT Press. (Original work published in 1934)

Waldrop, M. M. (1992). *Complexity: The emerging science at the edge of order and chaos.* New York: Simon & Schuster.

Wallace, B. A. (1999). The Buddhist tradition of Samatha: Methods for refining and examining consciousness. *Journal of Consciousness Studies, 6*(2–3), 175–187.

Watson, J. S. (1979). Perception of contingency as a determinant of social responsiveness. In E. Thoman (Ed.), *The origin of social responsiveness* (pp. 33–64). Hillsdale, NJ: Erlbaum.

Watson, J. S. (1994). Detection of self: The perfect algorithm. In S. Parker, R. Mitchell, & M. Boccia (Eds.), *Self-awareness in animals and humans: Developmental perspectives* (pp. 131–149). Cambridge, U.K.: Cambridge University Press.

Weinberg, K. M., & Tronick, E. Z. (1994). Beyond the face: An empirical study of infant affective configurations of facial, vocal, gestural and regulatory behaviors. *Child Development, 65,* 1503–1515.

Whitehead, C. (2001). Social mirrors and shared experiential worlds. *Journal of Consciousness Studies, 8*(4), 3–36.

Whiten, A. (1991). *Natural theories of mind: Evolution, development, and simulation of everyday mindreading.* Oxford, U.K.: Blackwell.

Whittman, M., & Poppel, E. (1999 / 2000). Temporal mechanisms of the brain as fundamentals of communication—with special reference to music perception and performance. *Musicae Scien-*

tiae: Special Issue: Rhythm, Musical Narrative, and Origins of Human Communication, 13–28.

Widlocher, D. (1996). *Les Nouvelles Cartes de la Psychanalyse* [New psychoanalytic cards]. Paris: Odile Jacob.

Wiener, D. J. (Ed.) (1999). *Beyond talk therapy: Using movement and expressive techniques in clinical practice*. Washington, DC: American Psychological Association.

Wingfield, A., & Nolan, K. (1980). Spontaneous segmentation in normal and in time-compressed speech. *Perception & Psychophysics, 28*, 97–102.

Woolf, V. (1977). *The diary of Virginia Woolf, 1920–1924*. New York: Harcourt Brace Jovanovich.

Zacks, J. M., Braver, T. S., Sheridan, M. A., Donaldson, D. I., Snyder, A. Z., Ollinger, J. M., Buckner, R. L., & Raichle, M. E. (2001). Human brain activity time-locked to perceptual event boundaries. *Nature Neuroscience, 4*(6), 651–55.

Zahavi, D. (1996). Husserl's intersubjective transformation of transcendental philosophy. *Journal of the British Society for Phenomenology, 27*, 228–245.

Zahavi, D. (1999). *Self-awareness and alterity: A phenomenological investigation*. Evanston, IL: Northwestern University Press.

Zahavi, D. (2001). Beyond empathy: Phenomenological approaches to intersubjectivity. *Journal of Consciousness Studies, 8*, 151–167.

Zahavi, D. (2002). First person thoughts and embodied self-awareness: Some reflections on the relation between recent analytical philosophy and phenomenology. *Phenomenology and the Cognitive Sciences, 1*, 7–26.

Zelazo, P. D. (1996). Towards a characterization of minimal consciousness. *New Ideas in Psychology, 14*, 63–80.

Zelazo, P. D. (1999). Language, levels of consciousness, and the development of intentional action. In P. D. Zelazo, J. W. Astington, & D. R. Olson (Eds.), *Developing theories of intention: Social understanding and self-control* (pp. 95–117). Mahwah, NJ: Erlbaum.

Index